WITH THE 10TH ESSEX
IN FRANCE.

"ONCE MORE UNTO THE BREACH."
Essex moving forward under cover of dusk.

WITH THE 10TH ESSEX IN FRANCE

BY

LT.-COL. T. M. BANKS, D.S.O., M.C.

AND

CAPT. R. A. CHELL, D.S.O., M.C.

Illustrated by NORMAN HOWARD

Second Edition

1924.
GAY & HANCOCK, LTD.,
LONDON.

We take this opportunity of expressing our thanks to the ESSEX CHRONICLE, *in whose columns a large part of the matter of this book has already been published.*

First Edition - May, 1921
Second Edition, October, 1924

Dedicated
TO THE MEMORY OF COMRADES OF ALL RANKS WHO WERE KILLED WHILE WITH THE 10th ESSEX IN FRANCE

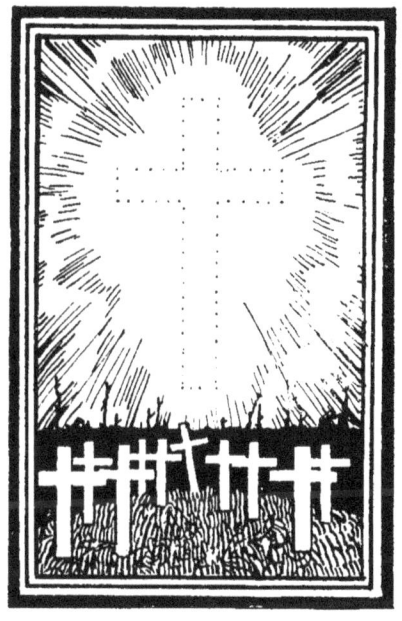

THEY SLEEP MORE THAN A THOUSAND STRONG IN THE TUMBLED SOIL ACROSS THE CHANNEL, BUT THEY LIVE IN THE HEARTS OF COMRADES AND FRIENDS FOR WHOM, IN THE WEALTH OF COMRADESHIP, THEY LAID DOWN THEIR LIVES

✠

"TO LIVE IN HEARTS WE LEAVE BEHIND IS NOT TO DIE"

PREFACE.

This is a belated story. The Tenth Essex, one of the best fighting units that ever marched, exists no longer. The War, which called it into a meteoric existence, has receded into the distance, and public interest in deeds of battle has cooled from red-heat into a pale unconcern. But to those who in its ranks saw the reality which is war, these glinting recollections will perhaps serve to recall some of the ideals and the wonder of the times when duty beckoned unmistakably and death was very near. And to those whose dear ones paid the full toll of sacrifice it is hoped that this little narrative of the doings of the unit which owed so much to them may bring some ray of comfort.

It is only a partial picture, seen through the eyes of a few, and the scattering to civil life has precluded the attempt at anything more complete. And so for lapses and omissions we crave pardon. Many an individual deed of gallantry has gone unchronicled for one reason or another, and the mention of some individuals and deeds to the exclusion of others is not intended to stamp them with greater worth. For if the War has brought home any one lesson it is that of the value of the ordinary man, of the wealth of nobility of character which lies unperceived in all ranks of our great Nation until the furnace of a great testing-time burns off the trappings of everyday life and the true gold shines out from underneath.

PREFACE—*continued*.

And if the Colonel is mentioned more than the Private, the Major than the Lance-Corporal, it is by the chance of circumstance. To the heroic part played by the man in the ranks his leaders are more than proud to pay unstinted tribute.

We are specially indebted to David Randell, to J. C. Parke, to Norman Howard and to Mr. A. H. Archibald for their help in compiling this book.

Chapters 1-22 are by Chell, the essence of Chapters 28-31 by David Randell, and the remainder by Banks.

PREFACE TO SECOND EDITION.

It is something noteworthy to publish a second edition of the history of a Service battalion of the Great War. And that in itself is a commentary on things as they were and as they are. When the first edition was published they were things of a very real and present memory. And now, as they are, other things are apt to efface the memory of what once seemed ineffaceable.

Is it well to revive those dormant reminiscences which we are so loth to release even when we encounter those who have them in common with us? Is it not best perhaps that Time's eraser should cancel them out? These were questions which framed themselves when a second edition came to be considered. But an insistent demand for copies of this book from those who failed to obtain it before the first edition was exhausted has outbalanced such questionings and impelled again into the printing press. There may perhaps be other considerations—considerations which it is hoped are not based on motives of boasting or vainglory.

Nineteen twenty-four. A battalion of the Guards was marching along a London street where, unobtrusively, a home for war-incurables is situated. A tall, broad-shouldered man hunched on his crutches was at the door, and as familiar khaki fours came up he pulled himself pathetically into a semblance of "attention." The leading officer, a boy without a ribbon on his breast, caught sight of him, hesitated, then gravely returned the salute. And all down the column the young commanders without exception followed suit.

PREFACE TO SECOND EDITION—*continued.*

Ten years. The younger generation are filling up the ranks. And if we, recapitulating memories of past sacrifice and past achievement, straighten our shoulders just a little, it may be that they, the joint inheritors, may find some inspiration and return the gesture.

CONTENTS.

			PAGE
INTRODUCTION	... ...	TRAINING TIMES IN ENGLAND ...	13
CHAPTER I.	... ...	THE JOURNEY ACROSS AND EARLY DAYS IN FRANCE	31
CHAPTER II.	... ...	INSTRUCTION IN TRENCH WARFARE	40
CHAPTER III.	... ...	THE LINE BEFORE MAMETZ	47
CHAPTER IV.	... ...	INSPECTION BY KITCHENER AND THE LINE AT LA BOISSELLE	57
CHAPTER V.	... ...	ALBERT AND FURTHER TOURS AT LA BOISSELLE	63
CHAPTER VI.	... ...	XMAS, 1915	74
CHAPTER VII.	... ...	FURTHER ADVENTURES NEAR LA BOISSELLE	84
CHAPTER VIII.	... ...	FRANVILLERS AND THE LINE AT MARICOURT	92
CHAPTER IX.	... ...	TRAINING AND PREPARATION FOR THE SOMME OFFENSIVE	102
CHAPTER X.	... ...	JUNE, 1916	109
CHAPTER XI.	... ...	JULY THE FIRST, 1916	116
CHAPTER XII.	... ...	JULY 8TH—JULY 18TH, 1916	125
CHAPTER XIII.	... ...	DELVILLE WOOD	131
CHAPTER XIV.	... ...	A HOLIDAY IN THE NORTH	138
CHAPTER XV.	... ...	PREPARING FOR THIEPVAL	144
CHAPTER XVI.	... ...	THE STORMING OF THIEPVAL ...	152
CHAPTER XVII.	... ...	OCTOBER, 1916	159
CHAPTER XVIII.	... ...	NOVEMBER AND DECEMBER, 1916 ...	166
CHAPTER XIX.	... ...	JANUARY AND FEBRUARY, 1917 ...	174
CHAPTER XX.	... ...	THE CAPTURE OF IRLES	179

CONTENTS—continued.

		PAGE
CHAPTER XXI.	A TALE OF MANY JOURNEYS	186
CHAPTER XXII.	ROUND ABOUT ARRAS. MAY AND JUNE, 1917	191
CHAPTER XXIII.	PREPARATIONS FOR PASSCHENDAELE	197
CHAPTER XXIV.	YPRES III.	203
CHAPTER XXV.	STRENUOUSNESS AT STIRLING CASTLE AND REST AT RUBROUCK	208
CHAPTER XXVI.	THE EPIC OF POELCAPELLE	218
CHAPTER XXVII.	A MONTH'S HARD LABOUR AT HOUTHULST FOREST	230
CHAPTER XXVIII.	XMAS, 1917	240
CHAPTER XXIX.	EMILE CAMP, ROUSBRUGGE AND SOUTHWARDS TO THE OISE	245
CHAPTER XXX	WAITING HOURS, MARCH, 1918	251
CHAPTER XXXI.	THE FLOOD-GATES OPEN	257
CHAPTER XXXII.	THE VILLERS-BRETONNEUX FIGHTING	267
CHAPTER XXXIII.	BACKS TO THE WALL, MAY-JULY, 1918	277
CHAPTER XXXIV.	HITTING BACK, AUGUST 8TH, 1918	284
CHAPTER XXXV.	THE " MARCH TO BERLIN " BEGUN	293
CHAPTER XXXVI.	CRACKING THE HINDENBURG LINE	302
CHAPTER XXXVII.	AT LONG LAST!	309
L'ENVOI	THE LAST DAYS OF THE " OLD GUARD "	318

INTRODUCTION.

Training Times in England.

Heppel and the Hungry Hundreds—An Early Episode.

"What the 'ell did we join the Army for, Bill? Fust of all they tells us that hevery man is wanted, and then they gets us dahn 'ere and tries to blinkin' well starve us to death."

"I'm wiv yer 'Arry. And wot's more we ain't goin' to stand it. We'll just go and see the Boss, and hif 'e don't turn out something to heat in arf a shake of a flipper, we'll blanketty well show 'im oos oo."

So an indignant Bill and his trusty mate of the Crown and Anchor Saloon Bar, somewhere east of the Commercial Road, proceeded across the parade ground at the head of what was perhaps the prettiest lot of ruffians that London was able to produce at a moment's notice. And in a crescendo of wrath, nothing lessened by the heat of the sun beating on the Shorncliffe Downs, they presented themselves at the mouth of a bell tent which bore the chalk inscription: "ORDERLY ROOM. 10TH ESSEX."

"Horderly Room be blowed!" soliloquised Bill, "never see'd such adjectival disorder since the Coldstreams fought the battle of Sidney Street," and without more ado he accosted the youthful Captain within, who now controlled the destinies of a thousand men, but who, if the truth were known, but a short week before was the junior sub. in his regiment.

"Look 'ere, Mister. We didn't come down 'ere to be blinkin' well starved. We came to fight the Germans."

Captain Heppel explained patiently, as he had already done a hundred times before, that the War Office had sent a thousand men down to where none were expected, and that he was doing his level best to get them food at the very earliest moment possible. But the crowd couldn't understand. They wanted a meal, and if they didn't jolly well get it there was going to be trouble.

"Well, boys," said the Captain, "if you don't believe that I'm doing my damndest, I'm ready to fight each one of you in turn until you do."

There was silence for a brief moment, and Harry looked at Bill and Bill looked at Harry, until someone at the back of the crowd started a laugh. For Heppel was looking woefully disappointed that no-one accepted the challenge. And the laugh burst into a cheer for the Captain, and the first and last mutiny of the Tenth Essex was over.

The grievances, indeed, were legitimate enough,

for these ardent patriots, inspired, and perhaps a little terrorised by the menace of Kitchener's accusing finger pursuing them from hoarding to hoarding, had poured into the recruiting stations in numbers which upset all calculations. Trains were plentiful enough, and the sole object of the overworked recruiting staffs was to get the eager thousands somewhere outside London—it mattered little where.

And so a mixed and muddled mass of humanity found itself on the downs of Shorncliffe provided with numberless bell tents and rejoicing in the name of many strange units, but with no other assets than the garments in which they stood

No one knows exactly how order was eventually evolved out of chaos or comprehends the miracle of organisation which was performed by a microscopic handful of regular officers and n.c.o.'s But early in the game the maltreated masses began to understand that here was an experience entirely new, which could only be met by a patience and a mutual forbearance unknown to the civilian. Gradually each man began to subordinate himself to the good of the many, and the seeds of an instinctive discipline were sown.

Heppel's reign was a short one, for hardly had he seen the new Israel into their tents when he was transferred to the formation of the next Battalion— the sister 11th—and Major Scott and Captain Meares inherited the weighty cares of the new-born 10th Essex. Scott, imperturbable and of ferocious mien, but eke with the kindest of hearts, Meares, indefatigable and with no personal need or trouble too trifling for his courteous attention, worked veritable marvels. A few regular n.c.o.'s had been sent to them, and such of them who were Lance-Corporals were raised to the proud and dizzy rank of C.S.M.

upon the spot. Men who knew the difference between "Form Fours" and a "Four by Two" were seized upon feverishly, and their arms blossomed immediately into the glory of three stripes. But even this scanty military knowledge was possessed by few, and a straw hat or a bowler determined the choice of the Lance-Corporal, while a really clean white collar in addition to a decent hat was the sure passport to the rank of corporal.

Meanwhile a few brand-new officers, timid in the newness of wonderfully fresh khaki, began to appear. Their knowledge of the soldiers' art was not extensive, but the bookstalls were full of books on "How to be a Field-Marshal in Five Minutes," and, armed with a confidence snatched from these pages between Victoria and Folkestone, they confronted the herculean tasks before them undismayed.

"Carry on, Sergeant-Major," has won many a parade-ground victory during the stirring years of war, and it never was a more blessed discovery for the luckless subaltern than it was in these early days.

A passable organisation had been evolved and parades had lost a little of their resemblance to a football crowd when the Battalion was ordered to Colchester in October, 1914.

The move was not conducted in strict accordance with Field Service Regulations. Someone indeed, at one of the stations, suggested to a blue-eyed officer that his class was getting a bit old for the Sunday School.

And the knowledge that "the boys" were passing through Liverpool Street spread like wild-fire through the wild and woolly East, so that the departure platform was thronged by wives, parents and children eagerly besieging anyone with the least apparent vestige of authority for authentic details of how our 'Erbert was getting on, and how long it would be before he got at them there (somewhat dubiously qualified) Germans.

In the mêlée a proportion of our budding warriors got inextricably entangled with their demonstrative families and were left behind on the platform. But the expedient of detailing a rear party of officers to rope in the victims of this excess of filial emotion succeeded in bringing the stray sheep safely on to Colchester, and the Battalion ultimately reassembled in its new residence at Hyderabad Barracks, where all ranks settled in with no small contentment.

In Colchester the 10th Essex found its true spiritual home. It was not merely that the ancient town was a friendly home country for the regiment, nor that the place was full of memories and traditions of the famous regular units in whose steps we were seeking to follow. But in its benign atmosphere the conglomeration of human flotsam which emergency had thrown together, first gained that corporate spirit that soldiers know as "esprit de corps." It arrived a rabble mob, it marched out as fine and as promising a Battalion as any of the great Captains of History could have wished to number in their armies.

It is true that the spirit of unity and fellowship was not an immediate growth. In the ranks there were many prejudices to be overcome. The East-Ender, hailing from Walthamstow, Stratford, Canning Town, Leytonstone and Bethnal Green, rubbed shoulders with men of the soil from Essex and Suffolk and men of the sea from Norfolk, and civil life does not teach the art of making allowances for the other fellow as does the Army. In the Officers' Mess, too, a spirit of aloofness was abroad. The seniority question there was acute and burning.

Fierce and bitter controversy raged and fulminated round the dating of War Office letters of appointment, and an entrant of a month's juniority had something of the leper about him. The truth was that captain and subaltern, private and sergeant, all were attempting to size the other man up. And that could not be done until each one had faced the furnace and made good in ordeal by battle—the test of real men and true pals.

"Gawd bless my soul!" ejaculated Regimental-Sergeant-Major Cooper, an incarnation of the standardised British version of the great god Mars, as he surveyed his flock of lambs on the parade ground behind the barracks. "Don't know what the Army is coming to now-a-days. Look at that little lot of adjectival sewers. How's a mortal man ever going to turn *them* into soldiers. Well, I 'spose you've got to take it or leave it."

And the prospect was indeed enough to cause the most pussyfooted of n.c.o.'s to retire for solace into the Sergeants' Mess.

By this time Kitchener's Army was arrayed in a heart-breaking uniform of blue and crowned with caps which had the homely stamp of Dartmoor upon them. We admit that one subaltern declared that he had discovered three professional burglars in the course of an investigation into the occupations of his platoon, but this percentage of light-fingered gentry was hardly sufficient to warrant the whole Battalion being labelled convicts. However, Kitchener had bidden, and so it was, for weal or woe—mostly woe in those early days.

The British working man, whatever his virtues (and those that have served with him in the fighting line will doff their hats to him every time) does not possess an instinctive pride in his appearance. Put him in uniform and he has something to live up to—put him in the atrocity they served out to Kitchener's cut-throats, and it needs a pair of sheer-legs and hydraulic power to raise the smallest modicum of pride.

Hence the R.S.M.'s despair.

But though the blue seats of the trousers fell out, and the seams of the coats split within a few days, and rifle grease lavishly besprinkled the soldier's facade, the men treated the whole affair with humour. Only when they wanted to visit home on week-end leave did any minor discontent ensue. But a ready expedient sprang up and a section would club together to buy a suit of khaki and each man took his turn to wear it as his time for leave came round.

By Christmas, 1914, the composition of the Battalion was virtually complete. The command had by this time been vested in Colonel E. R. Scott, a wise and paternal C.O., under whose fostering care the Battalion began to grow together into an all-essential unity.

Major Scott had now assumed the position of 2nd i/c, and was immersed in undetected duties and a large car.

Meares was the Battalion Adjutant, and the Orderly Room beneath his wizardry produced prodigies of "Loose Leaf" and other systems.

In the Stores a Regular Quartermaster resuscitated from the palæolithic ages dispensed instruction to Hawkins, an eager proselyte, and the nucleus of a Transport Section was growing up under Pinder-Davis, occasionally reviewed by Captain Gerrard in between a multiplicity of odd duties such as painting landscape targets and manipulating the machine-guns which no one possessed.

The Companies had taken on their own individual and distinctive characters under their respective commanders. They each inhabited separate blocks of the barracks, and were commonly considered to take precedence according to their distance from the Officers' Mess. Anyhow, Major Wheatley had assured himself of a short walk to his parade ground in the morning by assuming command of "*A*" Company, and had collected around him a select lot of young men of the highest respectability. "*A*" Company's Orderly Room was the Mayfair of Hyderabad Barracks, with C.S.M. Gaster as the spruce and debonair hallporter.

Next came "*B*" under Captain Stewart, the kindliest of Company Commanders, but with a liking for white boots with a khaki uniform which somewhat detracted from his martial appearance. Tween was already figuring large in its destinies, and, in harness with the inimitable "Bertie," sought to raise their Company to the social prestige of its neighbours of "*A*," as Forest Gate aspires to the ultra-respectability of Brentwood. But some admixture of sheep in the fold, and a dear old set of ruffians in the ranks were a sore handicap.

"*C*," under Lewis, was frankly brutal, as the essential passport to military efficiency. Riddles and Archie could not be easily converted to the stentorian tactics, but C.S.M. Lawrence struck terror into the heart of anything below a captain's rank, and it was inevitable that the Company should be dubbed "The Prussian Guard."

"*D*" Company, the pariah, for the late and luckless subaltern had to face the publicity of all the others before he could reach his own company parade, started out beneath the glare of Captain Wyeth's monocle to be a veritable lion, and came in as a lamb. Little Tommy's bark at the head of 13 Platoon and Willie Hunt's Highland dourness carried out the impression of ferocity. But the milder mannerisms of Western and Hawkins, the distraction of John Howitt's Bohemianism, and the urbanity of its efficient little C.S.M. Palmer, imparted a fraternal spirit into the atmosphere which, at later periods under the commands of Banks and Byerley (and eke of Wells), became its predominant characteristic.

The Battalion passed through varied phases of training. At one time the keys to a soldierly perfection lay in the ability to construct a trestle bridge, at other times it was essential to salvation to be able to knot and lash, then came the era of landscape targets and an enthusiasm, of short duration, for early morning runs across the Abbey Fields. From such fads and fancies we graduated to musketry training over the ranges of Middlewick and trench digging in the fields of Donyland until we were ambitious enough to attempt field operations on the familiar ground of Abberton and Wivenhoe. Then came the greater moments when the Battalion got together, the anxious flutterings of Company Commanders before the C.O. rode round, and the still greater agitation when on the line of march he happened to turn his head to see if the files were straight. "Cover off from front to rear," "Dress by the right each section of fours," ad nauseam, while the old piping fife and drum band made brave squeakings with the "Farmer's Boy"; and there was always some buffoon in your platoon who was habitually out of step. Goldberg, one remembers, was the consistent trial of "D" Company, and all the Companies had their own little mascots.

As the parade ground gave way to field training,

so we began to see more of our great man, General Maxse, and his personality commenced to infuse itself visibly into the corporate consciousness of what we were beginning to know as the 18th Division. " Good mawning, that young officer," to a subaltern who, seeking to escape recognition, had failed to salute him, was a constant password in the Division from Colchester days. And one remembers with marvelling the feat he used to perform when he would pass the Battalion, Brigade and later the Division in review on the line of march, and greet by name every subaltern that passed. It went right home, for you felt you were working for a chief who knew you, and not merely for an abstraction in a brass hat.

About this time, Colonel E. R. Scott gave place to Colonel Fyffe, and the Battalion found itself somewhat roughly shaken from a placid existence into a ruder insistence on efficiency. It did us good and it was remarkable to see the quiver which went through the parade when the C.O. lifted up his voice in reproof. As we came to learn, the bark did not always betoken a bite, and Colonel Fyffe had the interests of the 10th Essex keenly and deeply at heart.

Then came the crowning event in the Colchester training—the Brigade march into Suffolk. Starting out early one morning in full marching order—the Battalion had now been arrayed in khaki for some time—we footed the 18 miles to Ipswich in good style but with a weary sinking in the stomach and a pack steadily enlarging to nightmare proportions as the last few miles crawled slowly by. There was no longer the possibility of a friendly air-cushion to give the seeming proportions to the knapsack, for we were out for a week, and our hotels were on our backs. And the mildly dishonest subaltern who had indulged in such subterfuges now began to wish that he had accustomed himself before the day of trial.

At Ipswich we fell into the very lap of hospitality. Almost every man and officer made some acquaintance there with the friendly Ipswichians which still lingers in a pleasurable corner of his memory. Major Wheatley, and his good-looking myrmidons, made havoc with certain hearts in the Norwich Road, Captain Wyeth and Captain Western were hospitably entertained by Dr. Robbins, and there was keen rivalry for the gracious home from home offered by Mrs. Hull-Ryde. Unfortunately an early start next morning cut short the happiness of our Ipswich homes, though we were able to renew acquaintanceships on the return march. Next day found us at Woodbridge, where "*D*" Company were billeted in the somewhat inappropriate precincts of a Wesleyan chapel. So far as is known there were no conversions to the faith, although the congregation found a near way to Tommy's heart by providing him with a Sunday school tea and entertainment afterwards. There were some nervous moments when our own humorists performed, but the allusions were not always transparent to the old ladies in the audience, and, where they were particularly dubious, simultaneous attacks of throat trouble amongst the officers carried us through.

From Woodbridge we marched to Hollesley Bay, fighting battles on the way, and many unaccustomed feet were raw and bleeding by this time. For the first time the men were being given the chance to prove what they were made of. New boots, imperfectly seasoned, were making their mark on heel and toe, and the daily foot inspection was a pitiful sight. But not a man fell out.

We had some strenuous times at Hollesley Bay. One day's operations occupied all the morning and extended into the afternoon. And the same evening we were out again for night ops., and had our first experience of standing-to at dawn. We did not get back till late that morning, and officers and men were composing themselves peacefully to slumber when a diabolical order came round for church parade a mile away.

The air was blue with terse expression, and when the somnabulating battalion reached the scene of the outrage scarcely a voice joined in the hymns. It took a long time for the 10th Essex to recover from this experience of religious exuberance, and for long enough the mere sight of a sky-pilot set their backs bristling. David Randell, when he came to us in 1916, still found us prickly, and he can surely count it the greater achievement to have won the hearts of everyone as he did.

From Hollesley Bay we retraced our steps to Woodbridge and Ipswich. At the latter town someone in authority decided on a night alarm, but half the Battalion had moved quarters from their allotted billets to the houses of the friends they had made and the rendezvous was like a roll-call after the battle, with the Colonel's fulminations to add terrors to the dawn. For hours afterwards along the road to Colchester small shamefaced parties would attempt to steal up unnoticed from behind into their places in the ranks, and we had only just completed our complement when we met the 54th Brigade on their way out to do their week of hard labour. Hard labour it was indeed. We had covered 100 miles in 7 days, and suffered more blisters than we cared to count. But it was the finest thing in the world for us. Under General Maxse's skilful training we were graduating from barrack-room soldiers into something like campaigners.

Maxse took the salute on the Colchester road while the 53rd and 54th Brigades were passing each other, so that the order for one was "eyes right," and for the other "eyes left." This is probably a unique experience.

In May, 1915, the 10th Essex marched out down the Lexden Road to the brave strains of what, under the efforts of Pitt and through the access of the instruments of the Wivenhoe Town Band (recruited, so it was maliciously said, outside a pub on a Saturday night), had now become a brass band. And Colchester knew us no more. But to that town more than any other the memory flies when the early days of the Battalion are recalled. Rollicks in the billiard-room, with Beard or Byerley at the piano and Peevor perhaps circumnavigating the table on a bicycle to the nasal notes of Bertie's "I've got a yacht that sails upon the ocean "—or Burton holding the new C.O. in hour by hour converse on Canada or exchanging a predilection for stewed fruit—or else a concerted rag upon the beds and the Lares et Penates of certain officers in which the Plaskitts and the Boogerat usually figured unfortunately—excursions to the Hippodrome and the Red Lion—conversations with the fascinating Mrs. L in the tobacconist's parlour or with the little lady in the chocolate shop—a hundred and one happy memories mingled with the pathos of associations with the fellows that have gone.

To Colchester we hoped to return when our fighting days were finished. But it was not so decreed. And instead the Battalion saw the final moments of its attenuated existence on Salisbury Plain, not far from the scenes of the last stage of its English training.

Codford-St.-Mary, to which our course was now set, is a quiet little Wiltshire village on the Western borders of the Plain. It lies picturesquely in the Wylye valley, and for centuries it has slumbered beneath its thatched roofs under the shelter of the steep slopes above it.

Then, as the books say, came the War. And an army of Sir John Jackson's workmen descended upon it; and like the mushroom cities of Western America so there sprang up in the twinkling of an eye row after row and camp after camp of corrugated iron huts, sufficient to accommodate the whole of the 18th Division, men, horses, and guns (the latter so far, but for a wooden howitzer, a minus quantity).

Marching from Colchester we billeted for the night successively at Braintree, Bishop Stortford, and Hertford. There was a spell of warmer weather now and the marches were long ones and exhausting. At Hertford some magnificent billets awaited the weary officer, and the champagne of Dr. Odell, after the heat and dust of the highway, is still a joyous recollection to some.

Before dawn we were out of bed again and entraining for Salisbury Plain, and the early afternoon saw us marching into our tin houses on the Salisbury Road, South of Codford. John Jackson's mansions were not palatial, nor the pleasantest abodes when a full summer's sun beat down upon their oven-like roofs and sides. But we were gradually learning the soldierly art of making the best of things, and there were compensations in the shape of shower-baths and a running stream at the bottom of the garden which helped towards contentment.

On the whole, however, Codford saw a period of serious business with comparatively scanty time for extraneous occupations. Boots, boots, boots, went slogging up and down day in day out over Wiltshire until the 18th Division could really lay claim to be able to walk a little bit. Then there was trench-digging at Yarnboro' Castle, and manœuvres over

JOHN JACKSON'S MANSIONS.

Stony Hill, bomb-throwing with Heath-Robinson jam-pot contrivances and gas-mask drill with cotton-waste and black crape, Lewis-gun classes in the nullah behind the camp and range-finding on the hills above, early morning runs up precipitous slopes, which nearly killed Sergeant Sage and other antediluvian members of our cosmopolitan unit, and night-marching lectures conducted by an officer eager to sell his own book on the subject.

And all the time Maxse was hovering over us with the solicitude of a tribal chieftain, telling us what he "wahnted," and jolly well seeing that he got it.

True, there were interludes of lighter moments. Several people invested in motor-bikes which facilitated a run into Salisbury or further afield, and frequently stranded them at midnight on a lonely road or broke their collar-bones when they weren't looking. Others invested in the still more fluctuating stock of matrimony or sported with Amaryllis of Sarum along the shades of the Salisbury Road. Major Wheatley found consolation for his soul in the piscatorial art, and would set off for his fishing haunts in the back of a tradesman's cart in the early hours of a Sunday morning. The inclinations of his subalterns drew them to fish in deeper and more perilous waters further afield.

In July the Division was reviewed by H.M. the King near Stonehenge, and made a brave show as it marched past with bayonets glinting and fixed determination in every heart.

We all felt the pregnancy of that moment, and I suppose that many of us had the greeting of the gladiator in our minds. "Hail to thee, Emperor. Those who are about to die salute thee."

Before we sailed the King sent to the Division a message of farewell :—

"OFFICERS, NON-COMMISSIONED OFFICERS AND MEN.

> You are about to join your comrades at the Front in bringing to a successful end this relentless war of nearly twelve months' duration.

> Your prompt patriotic answer to the Nation's Call to Arms will never be forgotten. The keen exertion of all ranks during the period of training have brought you to a state of efficiency not unworthy of my Regular Army.

I am confident that in the field you will nobly uphold the traditions of the fine regiments whose names you bear.

Ever since your enrolment I have closely watched the growth and steady progress of all units. I shall continue to follow with interest the fortunes of your Division.

In bidding you farewell, I pray that God may bless you in all your undertakings."

To which General Maxse replied:

"I beg you will convey to His Majesty our unalterable devotion to His Person and to His Throne and our fixed determination to uphold the best traditions of the British Army in War."

How the 10th Essex vindicated that promise is told in these subsequent chapters.

"Ave Cæsar Morituri te Salutant."
The King's Farewell.

CHAPTER I.

THE JOURNEY ACROSS AND EARLY DAYS IN FRANCE.

Packing-up days came at last. We had hoped when we moved to Codford during the first week in May that we should be "out" and "in it" by mid-June at the latest. But a wise authority decreed some eleven weeks' intensive training on the Plain for us, and we were well on in July before our marching orders came. Our camp, which was much ornamented with chalk from the hillside, had many visitors that last week. Relations and friends were to be seen strolling round with their respective heroes at all times of the day. The band put up a good entertainment in the evenings. Great excitement prevailed in the Officers' Quarters as to what kit should be taken, and what sent home, for everyone during those nine months of training had accumulated kit far in excess of the 35lbs. allowed for active service. The enthusiasts had many packings and unpackings; the more dour just threw the few things they were sure they would want into one corner, and stored the rest away. Hudson was a tremendous "kit-wallah," and had his valise and pack half filled with the latest active service inventions. Among these was an excellent oilskin bivouac. Three weeks later he used it with great success in an orchard at Bouzincourt, while I, covered for the most part by my valise, received the night's rain on my face.

Sunday, the 25th July, 1915, was the day of our departure—a fine hot day, and worthy of the occasion. Two trains starting from Wylye bore us away during the afternoon. Our transport had departed two days before, as its route was *via* Southampton and Le Havre. There was a very tense feeling in all of us when at 4 p.m. we paraded in full kit, and carrying three days' rations. It just flashed in on us that this was the very last time the ceremonial of falling in, inspecting, and proving the Company would take place in the old country. We, who had paraded together at home for nine months, would next parade for *real* duty in France. Quite a number of villagers in their Sunday best watched our march to the station and there were many mutual cheers as the train pulled out. We had a through run to Folkestone. As we passed through various towns our train was heartily cheered by the inhabitants—the war had not yet become an established institution.

Our boat trip was as well managed as our train one had been. We walked straight on to the boat from the train, and in a very few minutes it was "full steam ahead."

Perhaps at this stage the "order of battle" as we left England may well be recorded—(I write from memory, so any slip or omission must be pardoned).

H.Q. COMPANY: Lt.-Col. B. O. Fyffe (Gloucestershire Regiment); Second-in-Command, Major H. L. Scott; Adjutant, Capt. G. K. Meares; Transport Officer, Lieut. E. B. P. Davis; Lewis Gun Officer, Lieut. W. C. Neild; Quartermaster, Lieut. D. B. Cooper; M.O., Lieut. Lovett.

"*A*" COMPANY: Major C. M. Wheatley, Lieut. A. D. Womersley, Sec.-Lieuts. A. J. Beard, H. G. Sheldon, J. V. Jacklin, J. W. Dalton, and J. E. Osborne.

LIEUT.-COLONEL B. O. FYFFE.

Archibald : Evans : Hudson : Chell : Ridley.

"THE PRUSSIAN GUARD."
"C" Coy. officers before embarking for active service.

"B" COMPANY: Lieut. A. S. Tween, Lieut. R. T. F. Hedley, Sec.-Lieuts. H. D. Burton, D. C. Tollworthy, A. M. Byerley, A. E. M. Corke.

"C" COMPANY: Capt. J. L. Lewis, Lieuts. C. M. Ridley and R. A. Chell, Sec.-Lieuts. J. D. Archibald, H. E. Hudson, and T. A. Evans.

"D" COMPANY: Capt. F. J. S. Wyeth, Capt. F. Western, Lieuts. H. E. Hawkins and G. J. Thompson, Sec.-Lieuts. T. M. Banks and W. G. P. Hunt.

We arrived at Boulogne about an hour after midnight. Disembarkation started at once, and was soon finished. Rain was pouring down in torrents now, and our first acquaintance with wet pavé was none too pleasant. Everyone had had his heavy boots nailed in readiness for campaigning, and more than one went down full-length on the cobbles. The march through this dark French town and up the hill to the rest camp was so novel on account of the environment, that we forgot the rain and the loads we carried. But fatigue claimed most of the men before we could get blankets to them. When we took these round to the tents few men showed any signs of life, and, for the most part, the blankets were found in heaps at the tent entrances in the morning.

That morning was gloriously sunny, and after an early breakfast, one and all set about the task of "drying off." This was accomplished successfully by midday, and after an early tea we marched down to the town to entrain for an "unknown destination." We marched well to the strains of the band, and the inhabitants were quite enthusiastic. One very fat lady, however, was heard to remark, "Good marchaires, mais bad fightaires." The replies she received from the men are left to the imagination of the reader.

The train which received us did not compare

favourably with those in which we had travelled in England on the preceding day. In England it takes two trains to move the personnel of an infantry Battalion; in France a whole Battalion is easily moved by one troop-train. Later we found that a good deal more than a Battalion could be moved by this quarter-of-a-mile-on-wheels. Soon after leaving Boulogne dusk came on, and there were few awake to observe our passage through Etaples, Abbeville, and Amiens. Someone, I believe the Adjutant, had a rumour at Boulogne that we were destined for the Vosges; dawn, however, found us at the tiny wayside station of Bertangles, a few miles N.W. of Amiens. Very few, indeed, had the slightest idea as to the Battalion's location, and when, with the yawn following a too early disturbed slumber, we fell in, we didn't in the least know whether it was a question of an immediate assault or billets!

It must have been about 3.30 a.m. when we started to march. The Brigade Commander (Brig.-Gen. W. B. Hickie) had met us, and given some responsible persons a map, but the majority of us followed along in blissful ignorance. We were heartened by the look of the country. Undisturbed fields of corn—some mown and in shocks, some still standing; roads lined by fruit trees—apples and pears for the most part; compact villages nestling in trees—these were our first impressions of the Somme country. It was a long march to do on an empty stomach, and each was carrying the maximum of impedimenta. The band was particularly laden, for every musician had his instrument in addition to the usual infantryman's kit. The man who perhaps bears the palm for enthusiasm in this line was a Private Hatchett of Banks' platoon, who was discovered to be carrying a puppy in his mess-tin and taking it out of his pack for feeding at the halts. My company was in rear, and I was tail officer of the company. My most vivid memory of that march is the carrying of a kettledrum for one bandsman, and of a rifle for another.

The villages through which we passed in the very early hours seemed absolutely deserted, and I frankly admit that my own first impression of these dilapidated Somme townships was that they were completely empty, and that the many perforations to be seen in the whitewashed mud walls of the barns were due to bullets and shrapnel. At 7 a.m. we reached our destination—Rubempré—a fair-sized village about 8 miles N. of Amiens. Here we found our transport, and we quickly settled down in the yard of our billet.

We made our first acquaintance of many French customs, habits, and institutions here. The barn-billet, the proverbial dung-heap courtyard, French flies, daily Mass were among those we noted at once. Later we found that the very dirty estaminet, dedicated "Aux Réunions des Amis," had a very good cellar of red and white wines, and trade bucked up no end for the hostess. As we were nowhere near a river, and we were the very first British troops to be billeted in the village, it goes without saying that washing water was scarce. But on the whole, we were "at home" before midday. We certainly wondered just for what we'd been brought to that place, but it was no use worrying. After lunch I disliked the smell of my billet so much that I took my old cushion out, and had a sound sleep beneath a hedge.

Naturally there are heaps of amusing incidents worthy of record concerning our stay at Rubempré, and most of these arose from our lack of French. I pass them by except for one of the funniest "leg-pulls" to be found in the Battalion's records.

Shortly before leaving Codford a very diminutive R.C. padre had been posted to the Battalion. He was a vivacious little man, and "full of beans," but very serious withal. Somehow or other when we left Boulogne he got a carriage all to himself, and when we arrived at Bertangles he did not waken. Now a padre is hardly on anyone's roll, bar perhaps the Adjutant's, so is it to be wondered that we moved off oblivious of his absence? And we had reached Rubempré ere the M.O. exclaimed, "Where's the padre?" We all wondered. He didn't turn up at all that day. Heaven alone knows where that empty troop-train took him. Next evening a certain waggish captain saw a lone body hastening into the village, and immediately thought he would indulge in a "real top-notch leg-pull."

"Good evening, padre," said the Captain.

"Oh! Captain, where is the Colonel and the Battalion?" asked the Chaplain.

"The Battalion is in that village," replied the Captain. "Where the Colonel is now I don't know, but he was out giving instructions to the police regarding you some time ago."

"The police!" exclaimed the Padre.

"Why man!" said the Captain. Don't you know that you're a declared deserter? Here we've been for 36 hours, and you've only just turned up"—and then kindly: "Now if I were you I'd go straight to the Colonel and explain. It's about dinner time, so he's probably not too busy."

On rushed the Padre to the Colonel's sanctum. The Colonel was in. The Padre was breathless; he forgot to say "Good evening," and began to stutter apologies for his apparent desertion. The Colonel looked bewildered. "What the deuce are you talking about?" he asked. And when the Padre explained———! The Colonel had not even noted his absence.

France, as exemplified by Rubempré, entirely failed to come up to standard. "We thought we came out here to fight, not to drill. We might as well, in fact better, be back at Codford," said the men. Every morning of our first week we had "parades" —close order drill, gas drill, route marches; and the Frenchman who wouldn't let us drill in his field was not popular.

But all things come to an end, and on August Bank Holiday, 1915, after a ceremonial inspection by Gen. Sir Charles Munro, our new Third Army Commander, we set out to march to Bouzincourt, and with that village as our base we went into the line with units of the 51st Highland Division for instruction in the art of trench warfare.

CHAPTER II.

Instruction in Trench Warfare.

Thiepval, 1915.

Probably some of our friends at home enjoyed August Bank Holiday, 1915; we got no fun whatever out of it. At 3 p.m., when we were standing in a field near the chateau at Molliens-au-Bois waiting for inspection by Sir Charles Munro, a heavy storm broke over us, and we were thoroughly wet long before we could disentangle our waterproof sheets from our packs. Marching order did not add to our comfort. A slight lull in the storm gave the powers the time for a very rapid fixing of bayonets. We presented arms, and shortly afterwards the review was over, and we found ourselves with 20 minutes in which to get tea and prepare for a 12-mile march. The sky was still very dark when we set out, and we had only been on the road some 20 minutes when a steady rain began. In Beaucourt-sur-l'Hallue we met two French infantry battalions returning from the line after relief by the British. Many mutual cheers were exchanged. Our route was viâ Contay-Warloy and Senlis, places which later we were to know so intimately. But on this occasion the British uniform was a new phenomenon to them, and we received tumultuous receptions as we marched through to the brave strains of martial music. Shortly after 10 p.m. we arrived in Bouzincourt. Everyone was dog-tired; the night was very dark; the streets were wet and congested; we were within easy range of enemy artillery for the first time. Our guides met us promptly, however, and we soon had everyone in billets. As we passed along the streets we met several teams of artillery horses returning from taking up their guns to action. The sight of these and the occasional illumination of a verey-light some three miles away made us feel that we were very near the war.

Bouzincourt was an improvement on Rubempré. The barns were better, and there was a bigger supply of washing water. Of water passed as fit for drinking without preliminary chlorination there was none whatever. Comparing the two places by my own billets I vote Bouzincourt the better place. At Rubempré, Evans and I were compelled, out of respect for the "entente cordiale," to share a very diminutive bed in a very stuffy room in our café, and to share this room with the sickly three-year-old offspring of our hostess (and this lady insisted on the window being closed all night). We had asked to be allowed to put our valises on the floor of the loft. We were, of course, "green," and, above all, terrified of offending an ally. We had learnt quite a lot by the time we found our billet at Bouzincourt; it must have been close on 11 p.m. then. There was one tiny room containing a very old bed, and adjoining it a large room with a stone floor. Here four subalterns had to accommodate themselves. I won the toss, and had the windows open. My victory was of short duration. There were apparently few other beds in the village, so my Company Commander commandeered this one on the morrow, and then there were four little subalterns on the stone floor.

But Bouzincourt was not a very cleanly village, and the smells were an offence to our nostrils. One "dear old soul" where Byerley lived was particularly objectionable in this respect until someone hit on the happy idea of spraying her with cresol from a knapsack-sprayer, to the lady's intense delight, since she thought it was some new form of English scent.

Tuesday morning was rife with speculation—who were to be the first to go "up the line" to look round? Again my luck was "in," and when shortly after noon my Company Commander took me off with him, more people wished me "good luck" than at any other time in my life.

The party of about 10 rode across the fields to Martinsart, thence through Aveluy Wood to the Ancre Valley, where it turned north, and rode right into the tiny village of Authuile, dismounting about 800 yards from the front line. A more ideal covered approach is hardly conceivable. Several old inhabitants still remained in Authuile, and the village was not entirely "ruined." The Somme-Ancre front had been quiet for many months. We had our surprises every day and all day these first few weeks. We hadn't overcome our bewilderment at finding civilians in the village when we ran into a cow chained down inside a dug-out at Battalion H.Q. on the hillside—the much envied source of fresh milk supply for one of the battalions we were told—and on our left we saw a large number of Scotchmen enjoying water sports in Ancre backwaters.

Up a long trench and into the front line—we might almost have been back at Codford. We were made very welcome by the battalion and company commanders of the 6th Argyll and Sutherland Highlanders and the 6th Seaforths. "Nothing ever happens here," they told us, "and, after Festubert, it is mighty tame."

The line we visited was the part of the front facing the western edge of Thiepval. The Hun had all the higher ground here, and could overlook the country for miles around. While we were being "taken round" the French heavy artillery put down a small bombardment on that part of Thiepval Chateau which was still standing. They made good shooting. How impressed we were with the "whistle" and "crump" of these first few shells I leave you to imagine. I am certain that the majority of us thought we were under a heavy German bombardment until we were enlightened by our hosts.

After a very pleasant afternoon we returned quite unscathed to our billets! At the time this appeared quite wonderful to us, and I'm sure it seemed still more wonderful to those who hadn't been up! In the course of the next 24 hours officers' "trips round the line" were completed, and then began instruction for all.

This was all so well arranged that I think it should be set on record, for we have heard that the Army's staff was far from competent in 1915. We cannot say; we only know that, speaking generally, we didn't strike up against "nasty snags." The first trip in was for 48 hours, and was for individual instruction. Each platoon commander took his platoon up, and spread the men through a company of one of the battalions of the 51st (Highland) Division. Thus one Essex man was attached to one Highland sentry group, and was "extra." In fact we were "all extra" that first trip, and Essex officers were never on duty alone. We couldn't have been sent to better instructors than those Highlanders, and they were very charming hosts. On the second trip of 24 hours, our platoons functioned as such in Scottish companies, and we thus gave 25 per cent. of the Scotchmen a spell "out." On our final trip, our company was on its own as part of the A. and S. Battalion.

We enjoyed those days' instruction in the line before Thiepval. For the most part the weather was good, and never once was the Hun hostile. The greatest excitement by day in the business of war was shooting at the enemy's periscopes. This fascinated me for hours, and almost made up for the loss of August Bank Holiday. Apart from actual business, there was the daily swim in the Ancre back-waters in the valley below (incidentally our bathing pool was within 500 yards of the German front line). At night there were listening saps (sally-ports) to visit, in addition to the sentry posts in the front line.

Another form of amusement for (what we then considered) the particularly daring was essays at patrols into No Man's Land. Hawkins was misguided enough to start out once with a lighted cigarette. And his companion Hunt's remarks when he looked back and discovered it were pithy, expletive, and distinctly to the point.

Of casualties we had but one (again I trust to memory). One or two enemy trench mortar bombs which came over during our final tour exploded, and a minute fragment of the bomb cut Sergt. Jagg's thumb. He was not reported wounded. In later days he certainly would have been.

We, one and all, went into the line quite prepared to do or die. There was quite a whisper one of the afternoons as we took over that an attack was to be made at dawn. This, of course, was only a rumour. What we should have done had we been ordered to scale our own parapets at a moment's notice, but few had wondered. Those four days' instruction were invaluable to us. They got our perspective right and enabled us to commence thinking in terms of the possible. Doubtless we had been very serious in our training in England, but we had thought of, and often acted, the impossible. We left oppressive seriousness and unbalanced plans buried deep in the trenches at Thiepval.

The Essex men and the Highlanders "hit it off" splendidly together. Perhaps towards the end of our four days we had had a slight excess of "Festubert," but as guests we were sufficiently good mannered not to show it. I remember that the good folk of Paisley had just flooded the A. and S.H. with comforts, and many of our men received huge gifts of tobacco from the Scotch superfluity.

At the end of the fourth day's warfare we returned to Bouzincourt where we " shook down " as best we could for the night (our billets had been " jumped," and it was too late to oust the jumpers). Next day we marched back to the village of Daours—a large village just west of the confluence of the Ancre and Somme. Here the Brigade rendezvoused from its instruction, prior to taking over a brigade sector on its own.

One incident to show the thrill and enthusiasm of these first days: My platoon had just left the communication trench on its return from the line, when a shell (shrapnel) burst overhead. Nearly the whole of the case banged on to the ground about 20 yards ahead of us. A man of about 40, physically one of the weakest in the platoon, rushed at it as a souvenir. He burnt his fingers ; the platoon laughed. He kicked water on to the missile from a handy puddle, and then carried this pound or more of iron in his hand to the first halt. Here he carefully put his first souvenir away in an already overfull pack. He went sick next day, and took his souvenir with him. He was too old for war, and never returned to us. I often wonder if he still has that lump of iron !

CHAPTER III.

THE LINE BEFORE MAMETZ.

The weather really favoured us for our trek from Bouzincourt to Daours, and there were few with heavy hearts, though we all had heavy-laden packs, when we set out at about 3 p.m. on the afternoon of Friday, August 13th, 1915. Our route was by way of Millencourt, Laviéville, and Bresle—three villages with which we became more intimately acquainted in May and June, 1918—thence by the "Route Nationale" to Pont Noyelles. This was our first acquaintance with a Napoleonic road, and the four and a half miles of it which we had to traverse were absolutely dead straight—there wasn't the very slightest kink anywhere—and this straightness made the march seem longer that it really was. Darkness had set in fully an hour before we reached our destination; in fact it was so dusk when we passed through Pont Noyelles that no one noticed the obelisk standing on the hill east of that village, to commemorate France's sons who fell in battle there in the war of 1870. We heard the tales of that battle from the local inhabitants later.

Daours was quite the best French village we had been in up-to-date. There was an ample supply of billets, and these were more permanent structures than the barns at Rubempré and Bouzincourt. The weather was delightful throughout our stay, and we made the best use possible of the Somme backwater as a swimming bath. A good diving board was made by felling a poplar across the stream, and the addition of a football gave our water polo enthusiasts many blissful hours. A few patient souls endeavoured to follow the example of sundry inhabitants in trying by the aid of a worm to secure fish for breakfast. I have no remembrance of any record catches, but I shall never forget what a restful sensation we experienced when on a hot afternoon we saw our brother subaltern, Sheldon, a liberally proportioned youngster, sauntering along beneath the riverside poplars, rod in one hand, worm pot in the other.

These days at Daours were not hard, for no Battalion or Brigade training was attempted. Platoon Commanders had platoons "at their disposal" for the most part. Such men as Mobbs, the C.S.M. of "C" Company, were invaluable at such a time. Mobbs was an enthusiastic gymnastic instructor, and the amount of stiffness he took out of our rural bodies in the course of an hour's vigorous instruction was quite extraordinary. Sergt. Silver, later an officer in the 1st Battalion, was also an invaluable "P.T." man. Various officers' promotions appeared in the "Gazette" during this week at Daours, and were duly celebrated in the officers' messes. Ridley, Womersley, and Tween became captains; Archibald and, I believe, Jacklin lieutenants. Champagne was regarded as the correct drink for such occasions, and in the mess to which I belonged, at any rate, several bottles were obtained from a local estaminet. These we later discovered cost 3½ francs each, and were of the sweet variety so dear to the palate of the Somme peasant. We had two of the newly promoted in our mess, and each had his own celebration. These came on consecutive nights. We decided on the morning of the third day that sweet champagne did not agree with us.

Amiens was only some six miles from us, and our mess cart made frequent jaunts there for shopping. Activities in Amiens were not wholly confined to shopping, however. The doctor's cart was in demand for certain joy excursions into the city, and one famous

AMIENS CATHEDRAL, 1918.

night Gilpin-ride back developed into a wild race between "Prince," then D Company's horse (Banks up) and the old grey mule with Hunt behind it and Tollworthy and Dr. Lovett precipitated into the bottom of the cart, which ended in the victory of the Maltese cart, despite the discrepancy of weights carried. Pinder-Davis, the O/C Transport, had something trenchant to say about mulemanship in the morning! We were among the first British troops to shop in Amiens, and prices were still reasonable in August, 1915.

Towards the end of our week's stay we were inspected by M. Millerand, the French War Minister. This made our second ceremonial " show " in three weeks, and the tongues of the cynics wagged bitterly. Our nine days at Daours were amongst the happiest we spent in France, and eighteen months later we were still censoring letters to members of the fair sex, both young and old, at Daours.

On Sunday, the 22nd August, we moved linewards for a second time. The 53rd Infantry Brigade was now to take over a sector on its own. This was south and south-east of Mametz, and required two battalions in the line. We arrived at Bray-sur-Somme soon after dark, to find that in the first instance the line would be held for a fortnight by our fellow battalions, the 8th Suffolk Regiment, and the 6th Royal Berks Regiment, while the 8th Norfolk Regiment and ourselves remained billeted in Bray. We did not protest. Bray was quite populous at this time, and a busy military centre, for in addition to the two battalions billeted there were two infantry brigade headquarters, several gunners' headquarters, and a great abundance of transport lines. Most mornings we had a ration of five howitzer shells from the enemy. These came lazily overhead, and landed just clear of the town. I remember no casualties, but a good deal of fuss and bother prevailed during the first day or two at " strafe time." On the Monday morning, the 23rd, just as the first shell sailed over, some very senior officer in a car who came from a long way back passed the very "juniorest" of subalterns in the street. "Get all your men into cellars at once," he shouted. Need I say more? The bother chiefly arose from the fact that Bray was not so well off as most French villages in the matter of cellar accommodation. Most of the remainder of Monday was spent in "cellar drill." After about four days our "greenness" began to disappear, and our clothes, in consequence, smelt less of cellars.

During this fortnight alternate days were devoted to digging and training. The 10th Essex always had a reputation for good digging in France, and it commenced to make it in excavating the ground prior to the erection of shelters in Happy Valley. We never used the shelters ourselves, but in days of the Somme battle of 1916 we met many units fresh from rest in them. This "Happy Valley," about one and a half miles north of Bray, must be almost as well known as "Shrapnel Corner" of the Ypres sector. During all our work we kept the strictest look-out for enemy aircraft, and as the glasses allotted to our outlook man were not over-powerful, we spent a pretty large proportion of the morning with our noses buried in the grass. The Somme at Bray flows through broad marshes. These abound with huge pools, and in these much swimming was carried on. A few old punts added greatly to our amusement. Many of the men of the London battalions attached to the 5th Division (on our right) were splendid swimmers, and a good deal of very friendly rivalry existed at the pools.

When at last, on the evening of Sunday, September 5th we marched up the Bray-Mametz road to the relief of the 6th Royal Berkshire Regiment in the left part of the brigade front we quite candidly admitted that our first six weeks in France had been a fine outdoor and varied holiday.

We were billed to hold the line for a fortnight. "C" Company took over the right, "D" Company the left. "B" Company, somewhere behind, found sundry working parties, *e.g.*, ration and water carriers, and tunnellers' mates (to remove filled sandbags from the mine shafts). "*A*" Company was, I believe, a kind of garrison company, a bit further back, to hold the fort (known as the Wellington Redoubt) to the bitter end.

Our relief was accomplished quite successfully. We took over the dispositions just as they were, and did not change them during our stay. The line we held was very "wiggled" indeed, and for the most part was quite near the Hun. The nearest points were in and around the "D-français," a small minefield started in the time of our French predecessors. The French had some nine months before been very active here. I believe they had captured and held the German front and support trenches. At any rate, old communication trenches, by now falling in, ran between us and the enemy. In one of these we had posts very near each other, and the fight for the "Timber Post" was by far the greatest excitement of this tour in the line.

Speaking broadly, the line was quiet during the whole tour. Both sides hurled a fair number of rifle grenades and bombs, and the enemy "got busy" now and then with a nasty minenwerfer and a gun or two. We were on our own for a long period for the first time, and every little incident seemed an extraordinary event. About the fourth night in, the enemy blew a mine under us. We were shaken most atrociously, and in one sap not many yards away from the new crater, two of my boys were almost nipped in by the crackerlike action of the walls of the trench. A few men were buried in the "D," but prompt action by a rescue party under Hedley soon extricated all quite successfully. My platoon was immediately on the right of the "D," and we were required to "stand-to" for most of the night.

At this time Sergt. Jaggs and myself had not acquired the knack of going on indefinitely without sleep, and, on the other hand, we hadn't learnt enough to know whether an order was foolish or not, so we kept ourselves awake by killing rats. In the middle of the platoon front a little bridge crossed the trench. This bridge was a favourite path for our night visitors (and there were hundreds of them in this sector). One of us stood each side of the bridge. Each carried a heavy stick. The rat that succeeded in crossing was very lucky.

With dawn we found that the German had blown up his own line for about 25 yards, where it approached the D-français from the valley. The crater so formed was about 50 yards from the line held by the left of my platoon, so we gave any Huns who might be on the lip a few 2-round bursts of rapid fire during the dawn. They did not attempt to do anything. The opinion of the majority of us always was that the Boche charge blew the wrong way.

Naturally the next day or two were fraught with excitement. Many visitors came up to look at the new crater, and the gunners were called upon to "strafe it." As their shell allowance was then about two shells per 18-pounder gun per diem, and they hadn't done any registering, they might as well have saved their ammunition. I had three of my best men wounded in 24 hours by our own shrapnel. One of these was a lance-corporal—J. Smee. He came back to the Battalion on two subsequent occasions, and each time was wounded after but a few days' duty.

On Saturday, September 11th, it was reported that the Timber Post had been lost, and a great fuss was made. This Post was one of many in the ramshackle maze of sand-bags known as the "D." This loss, somehow, was known at Brigade Headquarters at Bray, and General Hickie came up to the front line instanter. Now my platoon was adjoining the platoon holding the "D," and so far as we knew nothing had

THE TIMBER POST.

been lost. We were in constant touch at the right side of "D." Imagine my amazement when General Hickie accosted me in my bit of front line trench and about 50 yards to the right of the right extreme of the "D" with the words, "What's this about the "D" being lost?" "I'm sure it's not," I replied, "for I've just come from there." "Take me to the

Company Commander of the company holding the ' D,' " he ordered. I started off. It was a six or seven minutes' walk. Just as we fetched up at the shelter used as Company H.Q. a salvo of our shrapnel shells burst immediately behind us. The General did curse.

Next night we fired 30,000 rounds of S.A.A. and our gunners fired several shells, and any few inches of ground we were shaken out of by the Hun mine we reclaimed. Two platoons were detailed for the attack. Banks and Byerley had the honour of being the first officers of the Battalion to go over the top. It is true that they performed this feat on their stomachs, but we were all very green, and the black-masked Germans and their wonderful sniping invested them with a portentous prestige. Private Halsey showed himself an able sniper and observer during this period, and was subsequently mentioned in despatches for his good work. There can be few now who look back at the " D-français " operations of September, 1915, without smiling at themselves.

The general quietness of the line here is perhaps best shown by a description of the trench discipline maintained. At " stand-down " every morning the company commander and his second-in-command carried out a " trench inspection." This was exactly the same as an old " barrack-room inspection." Every empty cartridge case and every scrap of paper had to be picked up and deposited in the correct waste bag before their arrival, and we had to sweep the floor of the trench and the fire-step with trench-made brooms. Anyone with any command at all took this first period of trench warfare with an absurd degree of seriousness, and simultaneously deprived himself of a great deal of the sleep he could well have done with.

We were relieved from the line by the 1st Batt. the

Norfolk Regiment (5th Division) on the night September 16-17, and marched back to rest billets in Bray. During our tour in the " Citadel-Wellington Redoubt " area our "A" Company had dug a new communication trench, which, in consequence, was named " Essex Avenue" by the "powers." It greatly accelerated our relief!

CHAPTER IV.

INSPECTION BY KITCHENER AND THE LINE AT LA BOISSELLE.

We arrived back in Bray from the line between 1 a.m. and 4 a.m. on Friday, the 17th September. After a day spent chiefly in bed, or asleep (to use a more generally applicable phrase), we set out at dusk to march to Morlancourt, a village some 4 to 5 miles away in a N.W. direction. Strict night-march discipline was maintained. In this village we stayed nearly 24 hours, for on Saturday evening we marched by way of Ville and the Ancre Valley to Buire, a village destined to be associated with our movements for many months. So far as houses and billets went, Buire was nothing to shout about ; on the other hand it was a reasonably clean place, and the inhabitants were friendly. Up to date it had been neither shelled nor bombed; indeed, I believe it never received a Hun shell prior to the re-coming of the Germans in Spring, 1918. In 1915 it was about four miles from the line, and some three miles from Albert. What was more natural than for us to find in Buire sundry refugees from Albert? The chemist, who was at the same time "Maire d'Albert," continued to carry on his personal business at Buire, but journeyed each day in his small automobile to a house on the west side of Albert for the conduct of public matters. His daughters were very jolly folk, and their music and song brightened many a dull autumn evening for all and sundry. There were many worse villages in France than Buire.

A few hours before leaving the line at Mametz it had been whispered to some of us in the "very strictest confidence" that we were bound for La Boisselle. Of this village, where " in some parts the lines are only 10 yards apart," we had heard many tales since our first day at Bouzincourt, and many of us had been wondering how on earth sworn enemies, armed with bomb and rifle, managed to effect mutual existence in such proximity. We were glad when we were deputed to visit our friends of the Suffolk Regiment to see how it was done. We rode into Albert one fair September morning to make our reconnaissance. At the Brigade H.Q., which was in a pleasant, but slightly disturbed château, we said "Good-bye" to our then Brigade-Major—Major H. C. Jackson, of the Bedfordshire Regiment—who was leaving to take up some higher appointment. (This charming and capable officer was, at the end of the war, the commander of the 50th Division.)

A guide took us to the Suffolk headquarters, and then we went round our various bits of front. The " close bit " was in the village of La Boisselle itself, and was known as the "Ilôt"—our island of the village. We held the western part of the village street, and this jutted out on its own from the remainder of our line. The Ilôt was a queer conglomeration of shallow, narrow slits between old and new sandbags —these served for trenches—foundations of and the rubble from destroyed houses, a cemetery, and used and disused mine-shafts. As the village sloped up gently eastwards the enemy had an excellent view, at close range, of our forward trenches and the Ilôt. On the left of the battalion sector, and it was from this direction that we approached the Ilôt, the two front lines were about 1,000 yards apart. We arrived at Company H.Q. in the Ilôt, were there told all the tremendously exciting tit-bits about this sub-sector, and finally we crawled on our hands and knees behind a very capable Suffolk officer, who got us round the whole place successfully. We certainly heard the Germans guffawing very near at hand, and the rattling of a metal plate and cup seemed but a few yards away. We came back wonderfully impressed with this Ilôt.

But we were destined for other excitements prior to our relieving the Suffolk Regiment. About Thursday, the 23rd September, we were marched away for review by Earl Kitchener. This took place in a field just south of the Albert-Amiens Road, near Ribémont. About six battalions were present, and we were not overtaxed with demands for ceremonial evolutions. After the general salute the Earl had out all officers down to company commanders, and talked to them. They came back to tell us that ere many days more had passed we might expect to be called upon to take part in "big things." We went to bed wondering what it was all about. Next evening we were summoned to a conference by our company commander. He gloried in being able to give a slightly dramatic touch in handling every matter. He drew a large L on a piece of paper, then cut its arms by arrows converging on its "inside." "The arrow in the horizontal represents the French; that in the vertical the British; we come in at the apex." We were very impressed. The strictest secrecy was to be maintained. If we were told to "go," we were just to keep going and going; to be prepared to march

18 miles a day; to send back casualty reports every hour without fail; and not to weary our superiors meanwhile with unnecessary questions. Early next morning our senior officers were taken to a point of vantage by the Brigadier, and "shown things." They returned to do a rehearsal of the battalion advancing in open order. We carried this out on the fields just north of Buire, and often in 1918 when I visited trenches we were holding as our front line system, which ran through these same fields, I chuckled to myself at our 1915 expectations. At the close of the practice, officers and n.c.o.'s were assembled, and the Colonel spoke. Afterwards there was some discussion, and I remember one senior officer telling a subaltern who asked for details of ammunition supply, not to raise unnecessary difficulties. I still offer thanks that the Loos offensive in no wise involved us.

We were told that all the enemy wire had been cut by our field gunners (it was reported that they had fired from one to two hundred rounds on the Brigade front!) Reliefs from the line were postponed till further order. We were due to go in on Saturday the 25th. That morning the attacks at Loos and in Champagne were commenced. We could hear the rumblings of the Loos and Souchez bombardments in the far distance, and waited anxiously for the word "go." Apparently higher command soon made up its mind that we should not be required to go, for by noon of the 26th orders for our immediate departure for the line in relief of the 8th Suffolk Regiment were out. By about 6 p.m. we were in possession, and were beginning to taste the delights of the Ilôt. When it is recalled that anything and everything was spoken in clear over the telephone at this time, and that there were two or three telephones in the Ilôt itself, it is quite reasonable to infer that the enemy knew all about the relief. That dusk and night his snipers and machine guns were busy, and we had a large ration of "oil-drums." The latter were the most demoralising of all the missiles hurled at us. They wobbled over and over in the air, making a noise best represented, I think, by shsh-uh-shsh-uh. They landed with a thud, and then after 1 to 4 seconds exploded with a resounding crang. Any candles in shelters within a 50 yards radius were at once extinguished. At night one could see the burning fuses of these bombs for the first part of their journey, but they had burned in too far long before the bombs landed to be of any use as a guide to the "avoider." The mortars which threw these huge bombs made very little noise, for only a small charge was required, and this was fired by electric current. But they made up for their unassuming entry into the world by a perfectly paralysing exit, and we were much terrified of them at first. Later we became adept at slipping round the traverse to escape them, and they lost some of their terrors, save when the trenches were choked on the night of relief. From the regularity of their production Tommy knew them as "sausages," and a little ballad was current at the time, sung to the tune of "There is a Happy Land":—

"There is a sausage-gun,
  Over the way.
Fired by a blooming Hun,
  Three times a day.
You should see the Tommies run,
When they hear that sausage-gun,
Fired by a blooming Hun,
  Three times a day."

No. 10 Platoon was holding the very front posts in the Ilôt these first two days. Second-Lieutenant H. E. Hudson, its O.C., was a tremendous bombing enthusiast, and endeavoured, by means of a catapult, to hurl our 2lb. bombs into the Hun trenches in retaliation for their 60lb. oil-drums. He worked hard at it throughout the 27th September. At evening "stand-to" he made up his mind to locate and bomb a Boche sniper, who was worrying us from a position very near to our own front posts. It was half dusk when Hudson jumped on a sandbag and peered round him for a few seconds. He ducked down, and, moving on a few yards, jumped up again. This time the sniper was ready for him, and shot him through the brain. This was our first officer casualty in the battalion, and those of us who had been mess and company comrades to Hudson for a year felt his loss keenly. The Hun treated us to a noisy night, but we had no further casualties. We had nothing to throw back at him; all our available 18lb. ammunition had been used for wire-cutting the previous week.

Next day came the first move round, and "*A*" Company took over the Ilôt. This night the "oil-drums" did damage, for at least two landed full pitch on shelters occupied by men of "*A*" Company, and about a dozen casualties were suffered. The same platoon of "*A*" Company had several recurrences of ill luck during the campaign. About this time Second Lieutenant A. J. Beard, the battalion bombing officer, had his jaw broken by that conglomeration of springs and levers known as the West Gun. He was invalided to England.

No other incidents of importance occurred during this tour in the line, which continued till October 7th. On this date we were relieved, and went into billets at Albert. Hudson was buried in the Military Cemetery at Albert the day after his death.

CHAPTER V.

ALBERT AND FURTHER TOURS AT LA BOISSELLE.

ALBERT.
The Cathedral.

We were quite keen on spending eight days in billets in Albert, for as we passed through it on our way up the line from Buire, we saw that there were many quite good houses still standing intact. When, on the afternoon of the 7th October, we looked round our billets, we were not disappointed. About 1,200 troops all told were housed in Albert at this time. When it is remembered that in June, 1916, some 25,000 were found cover here (in the concentration for the Somme offensive), it is easy to gather that we "did ourselves proud" in these earlier days. Battalion H.Q. had the château which was General Byng's residence in 1917, when Third Army H.Q. were at Albert. There are two good reasons for including a brief description of Albert as it was in 1915 in this narrative : Firstly, it was our trench base and main billet centre for about six months ; secondly, it will be impossible for the relations and friends of the 10th Essex to ever see 1915 Albert for themselves, for it was completely destroyed in the 1918 fighting.

Before the war Albert was an industrial town of some 20,000 inhabitants. It stood on both sides of the Ancre—a fast-flowing tributary of the Somme. The river was about 20 feet wide at Albert. Prior to the British taking over this portion of the line the enemy had on one or more occasions bombarded certain portions of the town heavily—the very centre " had caught it " worst ; the cathedral and the line of large shops which faced it were ruined ; in the Singer factory on the main Albert-Amiens road we found a mass of old iron and rubble covering thousands of bicycle frames. All the factories had received pretty rough treatment, and were consequently out of action. The major portion of the town was still either intact or only slightly damaged, and some 800 inhabitants remained. Most of them carried on work of some sort or other ; all cultivated their gardens assiduously. Several estaminets were open, and did good business with the troops billeted in the town. Near the station (a very much knocked about building) some enterprising French folk ran an excellent officers' café, and this was largely patronised—especially for luncheon on the day we came out of the line. The smiles of Yvonne, the capable and vivacious hostess, were a sure draw for the young bloods of the then Army of the Somme. She disappeared later, and it was rumoured that she had been arrested as a spy.

I suppose she gleaned as many secrets as any legendary "Madelon."

One municipal institution which was of great service to us remained. I refer to the Town Baths. These straddled the Ancre near a ruined factory, and were now in the hands of the Divisional Baths Officer, and run entirely by his men. Here every man had a hot bath and change of clothes as early as possible after relief. The building wasn't as big an institution as one finds in the average town in England, and we had to put the men in two at a time to get them through at all. One bath was reserved for the use of officers at any time they cared to go! There was such a rush for booking this luxury that the Baths' Corporal's office reminded one of Keith Prowse and —leave. Another very useful public institution was the old Cinema Hall. Here the Brigade padres (the Revs. D. Fraser and F. H. Tuke, both of whom subsequently lost their lives in France) organised a splendid canteen and a series of evening concerts; on Sundays the hall was used for services. The Divisional Commander, too, found it useful for officers' conferences.

Those evening concerts are worth recalling. We had a fair amount of talent in the Battalion; the Divisional troops stationed in the town provided the rest. Private Wheeler, of "*A*" Company, was our star: we revelled in him. Like the rest of our artists, he delighted in appearing in quaint civilian attire rescued from attics and lumber-rooms of various billets. He had a merry, funny face, and was never at a loss for an apt retort, or joke, on any recent trench incident. His turn which I best remember commenced in a boisterous way with the couplet :—

"'Twas Christmas day in the workhouse,"
and then, after a serious pause—

" 'Twas Christmas Day outside as well!"
A little later we were told that at the workhouse Christmas dinner one of the inmates was indiscreet enough to say in a loud voice, "Curse the carrots, give me turnips." Wheeler was ever ready to lend a hand to any of his less talented comrades, and one night he turned a maiden effort of another man, which had about reached the "rude remark" stage, into a howling success. Wheeler appeared suddenly from behind the scenes as a lunatic one-arm boxer; the audience was immediately in good humour, and the turn lasted some fifteen minutes. Wheeler was killed in the Delville Wood fighting of 1916, and we were greatly poorer for the loss of his gaiety. He was one of the best-known characters in the original Battalion.

We had other enjoyable turns. Bandmaster Pitt's cornet solos always met with approval, and Private Sheldon, of "D" Company, one time chorister of Norwich Cathedral, sang popular sentimental songs in falsetto excellently. Polston, from "B" Company's cooker, was another performer, and his "Oi, Oi, vot a game" became a classic with the Battalion. These were very merry evenings.

During this stay in Albert the sergeants played the officers at football. I went down to the match in quite a serious frame of mind, hoping to come through the afternoon without having offended the referee too many times. On arrival at the ground we found the sergeants, led by R.-S.-M. E. W. Lawrence, rigged out in fancy costume. We were told that this was a "regimental custom." The football we played was also of the fancy dress variety. During the first half it was a mixture of soccer and rugger. The second half was completely "go as you please," and rugger tactics predominated. I am not sure that the officers won, but when it is remembered that we had Cecil

Neild and Alec Womersley on our side the majority will agree that we ought to have done so at any rate. Sergeant F. Mercer was the star of the sergeants' side; in pre-war days he had been a member of the 1st Battalion's team.

Of course we had a certain amount of work to do during this eight days' rest. Parties of us went up at night to work on the main communication trenches— St. Andrew's and Berkshire Avenues. During the mornings we worked on the Albert defences, which had only just been started. These defences took up most of our time when we were out of the line during the whole of our sojourn in the area. One morning, as "C" Company was drawing tools from Brigade H.Q. for this work, the enemy opened a shrapnel shelling on to this château—it was one of his favourite targets. C.-S.-M. Mobbs lost a thumb, and was in consequence invalided to England; Lieutenant J. D. Archibald was slightly wounded in the head and remained at duty. All ranks behaved with the utmost coolness. Brigade H.Q. subsequently changed their abode; their new dwelling was less pretentious. Occasionally we took a turn at digging a trench for the water pipe which was being laid up to the trenches. (The Albert water system still worked very well, and we always enjoyed the pure unchlorinated water we got there), and Corke was given the curious job of O.C. bricklayers who were employed in paving the main communication trenches with bricks from the Albert ruins.

On the morning of the 15th October we once more relieved the 8th Suffolk Regiment in the line at La Boisselle. This time we took over with two companies in the front line, two in the reserve line, and we changed round every four days. This arrangement was far sounder and much more comfortable than the one on which we had worked before. We knew now that, in all probability, we should share this section with the 8th Suffolk Regiment for the whole winter, so mutual plans were made for increasing the comfort of the line accommodation. Deep dug-outs were started, and in about six weeks some five of these were completed. Each would take a platoon. Everyone worked with vigour, and whatever improvements were made in the officers' quarters of the company to which I belonged they were made by the officers themselves. We all had blistered hands after that tour in the line.

From a fighting point of view there is little to record between this time and Christmas. Apart from "sausages" and mines the line was very quiet. We did eight days in and eight out, visiting Buire and Albert alternately for billets. Albert was shelled a little most nights; once or twice it received a salvo by day. In the line rat killing and partridge potting were the chief recreations. Second Lieutenant W. G. P. Hunt was a most efficient marksman and often had a brace of birds to his credit before breakfast; these he retrieved after dark while on patrol.

Our other marksman, Halsey, was now elevated from sniper to the position of Battalion observer, and as such became the confidant of Generals. The things he observed were amazing. On one occasion we were led to believe that the Crown Prince was visiting La Boisselle. On another it was reported that a baby had been heard crying there! But the limit was reached when through his telescope he detected articles of feminine underclothing hung out to dry. It was too much for the equanimity of our gunners, who thought that they had been pulverising the place to bits.

At the close of our second tour here we lost one of our musicians—Private F. Rose. He was drinking a dish of tea in the early morning while doing sentry. The Hun sniper must have been fully 300 yards away. He had been servant to Second Lieutenant H. E. Hudson, and it was a strange coincidence that both master and man should meet with almost identical deaths within such a short space of time. Up to date they were the only two fatal casualties in "C" Company.

About the 21st November, while "D" Company was holding the Ilôt, we suffered eight casualties from a mining operation. At this time our miners were busy catching up the Hun, for he had the mining initiative when the British took over this sector. Our tunnellers' chief job, therefore, was the location and subsequent destruction of his shafts. This time our engineers had planned to blow a camoflet (a charge laid to blow in an enemy shaft) at 4.30 a.m., 22nd, and our men were being warned to withdraw from the affected area at four or thereabouts, when, at 2.30, the Ilôt " went up." The Germans were ahead of us, and the mine which they blew successfully put our camoflet off too. The whole Ilôt was now one huge crater, and we had eight good soldiers buried alive. Their Platoon Commander, Lieutenant G. J. Thompson was at the moment of the upheaval returning from a visit to the forward post, and had a miraculous escape. The ground seemed to open at his very feet and shoot up like a volcano in the air, so that he expected to be completely buried when it came down. Instead the dèbris fell just short of him, though it rolled to his very feet. And when he picked himself up he found that a handful of men and himself were left stranded on the Hun side of the new crater. He disentangled what men he could and they prepared to sell their lives dearly if the Hun came over. Happily he did not do so, and here Hunt, Banks and Wyeth found little Tommy when they dashed over the top to the relief. "D" Company had a very trying time those days, and they did splendidly. Our snipers, Byerley, Halsey, and that cool young customer Catchpole, among others, did useful execution from our lip of the new crater for several days afterwards.

On October 23rd, Lieut.-Colonel J. F. Radcliffe, D.S.O., of the Devonshire Regiment, took over command from Lieut.-Colonel B. O. Fyffe, who had been given an appointment in England. He took us on at Buire and until he was satisfied with us gave us the soldiers' proverbial "hell." On the 24th (a Sunday) we had about three hours ceremonial to prepare us for inspection by His Majesty and President Poincaré on the morrow. This was our 6th ceremonial in the short space of four months, so we knew we weren't green at it, and everyone was rather sick at such a prolonged practice. As we were "standing easy" on the parade ground in the dusk, previous to marching back to billets, I heard Sergeant Jaggs whisper to Sergeant Mercer, "Wish we were back at Colchester having lectures on Duffer's Drift in the barrack room." We were cold and tired, and had only been out of the line twenty-four hours; that far-away barrack room with its cheery fire sounded more than attractive. Later on, when I knew Colonel Radcliffe very well, I sought for information about that parade. He candidly admitted that it was many years since he had done a big ceremonial "show," and he had to keep us out to drill himself rather than to drill us. He had been stationed in Egypt for a considerable time before the war, and there he was apparently free from the worries of ceremonial. The review went off very well. Snow fell and His Majesty did not arrive at the time we had been led to believe he would come. We cursed the French railways.

LT.-COLONEL J. F. RADCLIFFE, D.S.O.

A SENTRY-POST IN THE ILÔT.
(*Note the camouflaged periscope*).

Other officers joined the Battalion at this time, viz., Second Lieutenants A. D. Openshaw, L. W. Bird, and G. V. Turner. Second Lieutenant F. B. Wearne joined in early December.

It need hardly be said that when the wet weather set in in November the trenches fell in badly, that dug-outs and messes fell in, and that we lived with very wet and muddy feet. But there was some consolation in knowing the Boche were suffering similarly, if not to the same extent. At stand-to one morning a Teutonic voice was heard to call out, "Another dug-out fallen in, Tommee?" And on another occasion our neighbours over the way hoisted a board with the following inscription (in English) painted on it: "On and after the 13th inst. you can have these b——— trenches." Happily, simultaneously a compensation started too—leave was opened for the Battalion.

CHAPTER VI.

CHRISTMAS, 1915.

"The Smile of a Grim Warrior, Setting off for a Well-earned Rest."

Over many things the 10th Battalion the Essex Regiment was very lucky. The spending of Christmas was one of these, for during our sojourn in France we were never once in or near the line at Christmas Possibly we missed a unique experience, but we had so many other unique experiences that we raised no protest when we were told that we were to spend Christmas in reasonable comfort.

When one evening in early December the news of our early relief for a rest " blew up with the rations," we shed no tears. Our trenches had been waterlogged and falling in for many days. The relief was a very difficult one on account of the state of the trenches, and matters were not improved by the fact that the unit detailed to relieve us had not been in France a fortnight.

On relief we went to billets in Albert, the town which had been our trench base throughout the autumn, and which was to remain a centre of great interest to us for the rest of the war. A day or two later we paraded, as a Battalion, on the western outskirts of the town. Nine months later such a parade would have been unheard of, but these were days when two miles behind the line on the Somme front was absolute sanctuary—no bombing by aeroplane, indeed, only an odd " pip-squeak " or 4.2 ever disturbed the peace of our billet-villages.

And so we started off westwards from Albert at 9 o'clock on a clear, frosty December morning, with our Colonel at the head of the column, and the band wedged in the middle. Our route was viâ the Ancre Valley, through Treux and Mericourt l'Abbé to La Neuville, the western suburb of Corbie.

Everyone was happy and smiling. The smile of a grim warrior setting off westward for a well-earned rest is as beautiful a thing as one is ever likely to see. Rumours of heavy training for a minor operation after Christmas in no wise upset our enjoyment of the trek. And of our number two certainly were extremely happy—the Colonel and the Bandmaster.

I should like to say a few words about that Colonel.

Many a man who served with the Battalion in 1917 and 1918 probably never heard mention of him, but those who remain to-day who served under him during his brief three months' command will never forget him, and there are some who, in the light of after events, are able to realise his great value as the inculcator of "esprit de bataillon" among us. Jasper Fitzgerald Radcliffe had had some 25 years' service with the Devonshire Regiment before he came to us in October, 1915. He had won the D.S.O. at Colenso in 1899, and in that action had been badly wounded in the leg. By mid-December Colonel Radcliffe was very proud of his command, and on several occasions he avowed that he would not change it for any regular battalion—and real regular battalions still existed in those days. He pleased us very much when after about a fortnight's command he, 25 years a Devon, appeared wearing, not only Essex collar badges, but Essex buttons, too. He couldn't have paid us a better compliment. Many much younger regular soldiers commanding Battalions other than their own regiments consistently refused to wear the badges of their commands.

And when we set out for our Christmas route march the Colonel knew we should march well and keep up our reputation for march discipline. He cared not at all for the Divisional Commander's "spies," who were scattered at various points along the route to observe, themselves unseen, the march discipline en route. None of us had any idea that such gentlemen existed, yet no one made a "muff of things." Some hours after we had arrived in Corbie the Colonel received a 'phone message of congratulation from that arch-apostle of march discipline—Lieut.-General Sir Ivor Maxse.

The Bandmaster! We always called him that, although I'm sure there's no Bandmaster allowed to an infantry battalion on service, and, moreover, I believe he was really a private at the time, for we were in possession of a Sergeant-Drummer, who performed the duties of Post Corporal! But Pitt was Bandmaster, for in the days when we were training at Colchester he had collected together a number of brass instrument enthusiasts, and by a further expenditure of energy had bought, borrowed, or stolen the instruments of the Wivenhoe Town Band. From Christmas, 1914, we possessed a brass band.

Pitt was not a musical genius, but he was a tremendous enthusiast, and worked unstintedly for the Battalion. By the time we went to France we had quite a decent band, and our arrival in any of the small Somme villages was an event.

In the early days our band was excused no duties, and Pitt was to be seen on sentry or working party every day the Battalion was in the line. The band, in fact, suffered several casualties, and Pitt had his work cut out when we were resting to get reinforcements trained.

Pitt was killed during the German offensive of 1918 on the Oise front.

We marched through Corbie in the early afternoon of that December day to the tune of "Keep the Home Fires Burning," the very latest from home. Corbie is tucked away in the Ancre Valley, and coming on it from the higher ground south of Bonnay, we all felt what a charming haven it was for a fortnight's rest, and some saw visions of a final march—the Peace March home. The inhabitants greeted us quite enthusiastically, and were the best friends with us throughout our stay. We were "très gentil."

Primarily we went back to train for an operation, the object of which was the capture of a Hun salient at Mametz. The higher authorities were "training mad," for it was such a long time since they had had a whole Brigade to run round in a back area. General Macandrew—the cavalry general who met with such an untimely end in Palestine in 1919—was our Brigade Commander.

Our day was a very full one. The first parade was at 7 a.m. in the half light ; all the morning and all the afternoon were spent further afield on a specially prepared training ground; and to conclude every other day we had night work. To keep the officers up to scratch a lecture was arranged for each of the "free" evenings. But we didn't mind; we were having a healthy rest, and " Christmas was coming."

Full scale replica trenches of the scene of the proposed operation were dug about two miles from our billets, and here we put in several strenuous mornings ere we learnt that the proposed operation was " off." In the light of later experience we were thankful that the January, 1916, attack at Mametz was never launched.

And we put up all kinds of demonstrations for the benefit of our superiors. Of these, raids on the enemy trenches—on the plan of the recent Canadian raid at Petit Douve Farm—were the most stimulating. In short, we enjoyed our training, even though some power above us decreed that it should be done in marching order!

Training simply hastened on Christmas, and when we slackened off a day or two before the feast, we had our work cut out to get our Christmas shopping done in time ! Corbie can seldom have been so gay or prosperous, and the good folk who kept the shops in the street running south from the Cathedral never failed us. They had fruit and nuts and "decorations" galore. The beer, too, was plentiful, and not at all bad. By the aid of the mess cart and a limber or two we had our Christmas fare at the Dining Hall on Christmas Eve.

The girls' school at La Neuville made an excellent dining room and concert hall, and every one helped to make it gay and jolly. Few of us had experienced Christmas in a Roman Catholic country before, and during the afternoon of Christmas Eve a fair number of requests were received for permission to attend the midnight Mass. Many men attended this service with their hosts.

Christmas Day itself was fine, and the band roused us to Christmas pitch with a few carols ere it took us off to church parade. After service it played from the bandstand in the Square. "La Place" became quite a Rotten Row for the next hour. And then it marched home to the tune of "What cheer, me old brown son, how are yer." One can still in memory's ear hear the shouts of the old Battalion as that favourite tune came on.

Dinners should have been at one o'clock, but a minor tragedy occurred. There was one evil spirit in Corbie, and he was the La Neuville baker. Days before this gentleman had promised the Colonel that he would roast pork for the whole Battalion on Christmas morning. Normally he finished bread baking at 10 a.m. But during those days before Christmas we all had shown such a liking for his bread that he put on two extra bakings daily. At 10.30 on Christmas Day he quietly but firmly told the Colonel that he couldn't start on the pork till 3 p.m.! If he had only had the decency to give us a day's notice of this change of mind! What were we to do? I well remember being dragged in to reason with him in the best French I could muster. He was obdurate. We had to decide whether our Company should wait till

5 or 6 p.m. for a "roast," or take stew at 2.30 p.m. We decided on the latter course, and made the best of it. A plentiful supply of good pudding and other Christmas fare, and, above all, an unlimited supply of cheery spirit, went a long way towards smoothing things over. But it is impossible to neutralise the disappointment of dishing up another dose of "everlasting stew" in place of roast pork on a Christmas Day on service.

There were but two officers in my company at the time, so the Commander hit on the happy plan of having the C.-S.-M. and Q.-M.-S., and the four platoon sergeants to dinner that evening. We were a very merry party, and our merriness was increased by our possessing a reasonably useful piano. Of those present I remember two in particular for exceptionally fine work done during 1916—Mercer and Jaggs. Mercer was C.-S.-M., Jaggs my platoon sergeant (later C.S.M.) Both were old soldiers (re-enlisted) of the very finest type. Neither knew anything of fear; neither would tolerate a breath of indiscipline. Both were particularly cheerful souls, too. Mercer was awarded the Military Cross for bravery at La Boisselle in January, 1916, and the D.C.M. for gallant behaviour in Delville Wood in the July of the same year. He was mortally wounded in our successful assault on Thiepval on 26th September, 1916.

George Jaggs was just as gallant and determined a man. His second recommendation for the Military Medal was sent in for his good work in Delville Wood (and that time he got it). Here he was sent down during the first day's fighting with a face scarred all over with shrapnel. Next morning he was back again and "at it." For further good work in action he was awarded the D.C.M.

Byerley and No. 5 Platoon won the Brigade Football

Back Row: 2/Lts. Sheldon, Wearne, Bird, Turner, Lt. McKenzie (R.A.M.C.)
Middle Row: 2/Lts. Hunt, Byerley, Evans, Lts. Chell, Archibald, Cooper, Neild, 2/Lt. Dalton, Capt. Hawkins.
Sitting: Capts. Tween, Lewis, Major Scott, Lt.-Col. Radcliffe, Capts. Meares, Wyeth, Womersley.

OFFICERS' GROUP, CORBIE, DEC., 1915.

Cup on December 27th, and early on the morning of the 28th we set out once more for our old Albert.

On the 29th December we took over a sector of the line at La Boisselle, and that tour was a very record for mud and slush, but we had had our Christmas out, and so went on our way full of good cheer!

CHAPTER VII.

FURTHER ADVENTURES NEAR LA BOISSELLE.

We arrived back in Albert during the afternoon of the 28th December. Early next morning we left for the line. The reason we left so early—7.30 a.m.—was as follows: We were ordered to take over the right-hand sector of the Brigade front this time, and Bécourt Avenue, the main communication trench from Albert, was waist deep in mud. To reach Bécourt Château—the point about 800 yards from the front line, where we were to put on thigh gum boots and pick up our guides—we should normally have gone up Bécourt Avenue. Instead of doing this mile up a trench we were obliged to march viâ Meaulte, Bécordel, and Bécourt overland. By making this lengthy detour we avoided observation, but as our packs were full and the trenches muddy, we arrived in the front line fairly fatigued.

As we were removed but one sector south, our left company was now in the edge of La Boisselle, and, in general, close to the enemy (40 to 50 yards distant on the average). It was an uncomfortable spot of much mining and trench-mortar activity, and rejoiced in the name of "the Glory-Hole." But it was not as bad as our old friend "the Ilôt." The right-front company was a fair distance away so far as the enemy immediately to its front was concerned, but in a half-left direction (N.E.) the enemy was near, and not directly visible. Moreover, there was a considerable portion of "dead ground" in front of this right-front company. The trenches near La Boisselle were chiefly in chalk, and so held but two to three inches of mud; those further south were in a heavy dark soil, and were deep in mud. Only the tallest men were able to pass along this front line in thigh waders and get no liquid mud in their boots. The Colonel was a little man, and he disappeared in the mud to a point quite half-way up his stomach. The front line was the worst. "C" Company took on this sector for the first four days; "B" Company took the next four; Company H.Q. were under a huge mine shaft dump about 100 yards from the front line, a colossal mountain of white chalk burrowed from the bowels of the earth. This was the well-known Lochnagar Sap, which was successfully excavated at three different levels right under the enemy's front and support lines, and which shook him up more than a little when it was put up on July 1st, 1916.

At the moment there were but two old officers in the company. We took it turn and turn about to go round the line, and neither of us could push our way round the company front by day under 90 minutes. By night we could do the trip "on top" and manage it in twenty minutes. Never again did we strike a continuous front line trench so uniformly deep in mud. It was such thick mud, too, and every day that passed without rain the mud grew thicker.

The line on our immediate front was quiet throughout this tour, but on our first night the Hun bombarded and raided another battalion of the Division that was in the line at Fricourt (about one mile south of us). In the bombardment the enemy used many tear shells, and the heavy vapour from these drifted up Sausage Valley with a south-west wind, and we were obliged to wear goggles for about half an hour. This was the heaviest bombardment we had ever heard, and we had never experienced tear gas before. We had " stood to " in our goggles for almost an hour when the bombardment died down, and nothing further of interest occurred that night. Next morning some details of the raid (a success) were available. The enemy, by a clever use of " dead ground," had formed up unnoticed in the dusk; then by means of a box barrage he had isolated a tiny salient in the British lines; his infantry had rounded up some prisoners from this isolated portion, and retired with them.

Our Colonel became somewhat alarmed about the dead ground on our own front, and next night went out in front to have a look at it. The fact that a sunken road (the Bécourt-La Boisselle) ran between our lines at this point added to our worries. The Colonel next went all along our sentry posts and assured himself that every officer and man knew his job. He seemed quite satisfied. At this time an order existed in the Battalion to the effect that every soldier's rifle should at all times be on the parapet in the firing position belonging to its owner. If the owner was off duty and sleeping in a near-by shelter, he would, if alarmed, rush straight to his fire-position and rifle and get to work at once. Further reference will be made to this order later.

The only casualty I remember during this tour in the line occurred in "C" Company the morning following its relief from the front line. "C" Company had passed into reserve in Dundee Avenue, a trench some 600 yards back and well down below the spur. Here its chief duty was ration carrying. On this morning the breakfast ration carriers had barely paraded under Sergeant Blowers, when an odd Hun bullet coming from a great distance struck the sergeant through the heart. Such a casualty would have appeared impossible the day before—it was the very foulest luck. Blowers was a good soldier and an excellent carpenter (his civil calling). When out of the line he had put in nearly all his time at working out improvements to the men's billets.

On New Year's Eve we had a little excitement. The Boche blew a mine under the Glory-hole in the morning, and then, as if to wish us the compliments of the season, put down an intensive strafe along the front for five minutes at 11 p.m. (12 midnight German time). Our guns had their own back an hour later. But the Scotties, of the 51st Division on our left, really let themselves go, and the night was hideous for hours up there with high explosives and (tell it not in Scotland) with bagpipes and Scottish songs.

After eight days we were relieved by the 6th Royal Berkshire Regiment and returned to Buire. A very ordinary eight days were spent there, the one little bit of excitement introduced being a trip to Amiens for officers, so that they might visit the "School of Camouflage" recently opened there. (The word camouflage became a common military term at this time.) Some well-known French artists were at work there, and we really had our eyes opened by some of their demonstrations. Our insularity was brought home to us when we were told of the length of time it took the French authorities to get the British to take up camouflage work seriously. One other incident was provided by Cooper, now the Battalion Quartermaster, who broke his ribs in a tussle with "Bronco" and had to go home for a bit.

We next went into the line for eight days, and as

the weather had improved somewhat, the right sector wasn't quite so bad. On relief (and on all subsequent reliefs in January and February, 1916) we took up billets in Albert. After seven days in Albert we again took over the line (January 29th).

All "old" 10th Essex men will remember January 31st, 1916—the day on which our "*B*" Company was raided and Colonel Radcliffe killed. We noticed enemy artillery activity on our front as soon as we went in: he was obviously registering. In addition he had a very big mortar up against us. The bomb this fired was much larger than the "sausage" previously referred to, and was fired from a greater distance. We were all on the alert, and I myself was particularly so, for my platoon was holding that portion of the right front, before which was the dead ground (already referred to). The first two nights in we patrolled vigorously, both along the sunken Bécourt-La Boisselle road and the enemy wire. We encountered no Huns at all. Between 2 and 3 p.m., 31st January, inter-company reliefs took place, and my platoon by 4 p.m. was resting from its two hard days in the front line, and simultaneously carrying rations, etc., from Bécourt Chateau to all the companies. About 5 p.m. the Hun artillery woke up. Shells fell on adjoining sectors first, and our previous knowledge of the next sector to the north enabled us to take a keen interest in the shelling put down on the 8th Suffolk Regiment, who were then there. After a few minutes shells came down on our own front, and the rate at which these fell rapidly increased, till twenty minutes from the firing of the first shell into the Suffolks, we ourselves were suffering a really heavy bombardment—our first. In reserve, we "stood to" immediately, and so we remained for a couple of hours; we got no further orders at all.

What really happened is not clearly known, but officially the raid was accounted for somewhat as follows :—The enemy put down a very heavy bombardment on our right front line immediately before the hour of evening "Stand to." Under cover of this bombardment a party of from 30 to 40 Huns left their trenches and formed up in the dead ground. All our troops in the front line at once manned fire positions. The only exception was one section of "B" Company, which lived in a dug-out in a communication, trench, and about 15 yards from the front line. One of the earliest H.E. shells struck the only exit to this dilapidated shelter and more or less blocked it. The first man crawled through the little hole that was left to find a burly Hun awaiting him. The remainder of the men entombed were without weapons. Half an hour before their rifles had been standing on the fire step—beautifully clean and bayonets fixed, ready for anything. They were now deeply buried where the trench once was. At the close of the operation 11 men were missing; the front line trench for about 100 yards had been blown in: all telephone wires were cut, and—our Colonel was dead. The shell which struck the Battalion H.Q. dug-out brought a heavy beam on to his head—a beam so heavy that the Colonel's head was crushed in. The other officers and signallers present were very badly shaken, but there were no other casualties.

Parties at once "got busy" re-digging our front line and the trenches leading thereto, and many hours' work had to be put in before we had anything like a front line trench. Next day we excavated the poor, battered, raided dug-out. One dead body was found; the 10 men still missing were prisoners of war. One of the men taken prisoner was a traffic control man from Albert, who had come up to the trenches to take tea with his brother! Truly every active service incident had a certain amount of humour wrapped up with it!

We hated having lost men as prisoners, and for a time we were disliked for our misfortunes by those in authority. This was particularly galling, after being complimented but a short time before by the G.O.C. as the best battalion in the Division. But the German "travelling circus," as the party who performed these stunts up and down the line was called, was the temporary grave of a good many reputations. Several months afterwards it was agreed at a big conference at the Third Army School that it was well nigh impossible for a unit to protect itself against these well-organised and executed incursions. In our case the "rifle-on-the-parapet" order rendered any men shut in a dug-out or shelter entirely defenceless.

There were one or two remarkable features which show the careful preparation which the Hun applied to these performances. The majority of the German participants could speak English, and orders, such as "Reinforcements coming over the top," were shouted by them to put the defenders off the scent. A good many of them, too, were clothed in British uniforms. But strangest of all was an elaborate and carefully-worked banner which they brought over with them and left planted on our parapet, bearing the words:

"Brave British Boys."

"*Why will you fight for your bloated capitalists, who sit at home in armchairs and send you to death?*"

We continued to hold this sector till the end of February (8 days in and 8 out). A good deal more general activity prevailed than we had experienced before Christmas. Our billet days were full of work on the Usna and Tara Redoubts—the forts of the front line systems, designed to hold Battalion H.Q. and one garrison company of each front line battalion, but destined, as events turned out in 1918, to become a stronghold for the Germans from which the 10th Essex had to expel them with the persuasion of the bayonet. Perhaps we would not have worked so hard if we could have foreseen this development!

February, 1916, was a cold month, and there was a good covering of snow on the ground most of the time. On February 29th we marched back some six miles along the Albert-Amiens road, and took billets at Franvillers. The 53rd Brigade was relieved by a Brigade of the 32nd Division. These moves may be regarded as among the earliest made in the concentration for the Somme Offensive of 1916.

CHAPTER VIII.

FRANVILLERS AND THE LINE AT MARICOURT.

Franvillers had struck us as a reasonably clean and attractive village when we passed it on our trek back to Daours in August. At that time troops of the Indian cavalry were billeted there, and, as we marched by, these had rushed down to the main road (for the village lies some 200 yards to the north of the Rue Nationale) to exchange mutual greetings with us. When we had "shaken down" and looked around on this afternoon of 29th February, 1916, we found that Franvillers wasn't at all a bad place. The billets were nothing to make a song about—they were a little above Somme average—and the inhabitants were very friendly. For the first part of our twelve days' stay the weather continued to be wintry, but during the latter part we had some glorious spring days. Mornings were spent in training, afternoons in recreation. To be frank, we were surprised that we were allowed to stay as long as 12 days, for when orders were issued to us late on the night of February 28th, we were told to be prepared to march to an "unknown destination" on the morrow. We had visions of Verdun, and for a few hours rumour was rife. Little did we dream that we should be left in

LIEUT-COLONEL H. L. SCOTT.

Thompson : Byerley : Hunt : Chell : Tollworthy,

EMERGING FROM A SPELL IN THE TRENCHES.

peace in this little village of Franvillers, which some of us had passed so often on our way to and from the Field Cashier at Querrieu (X. Corps H.Q.) This move, however, synchronised with many moves of troops in the southern portion of the British area. Our Third Army moved northwards to relieve the French still in the line before Arras, and those British toops left on the Somme passed into the Fourth Army, which was then being formed under General Rawlinson.

Various changes in officers took place while we were at Franvillers. Major H. L. Scott, who had fostered the Battalion from its weaning-days, was appointed commanding officer, and promoted lieut.-colonel. We were all pleased at this, for he was an Essex regular, and we knew him and understood his ways. When the real business of war began we all got to know him much better, and our admiration for him increased daily. Captain J. L. Lewis now moved from "C" Company to H.Q. as second-in-command, with the rank of major, and Captain F. J. S. Wyeth left us to take up the newly-made job of Divisional Gas Officer. Captain A. D. Womersley had been invalided home in January. "A" Company was now taken over by Jack Dalton; "C" Company by Ridley; "D" Company by Banks. Banks (who had become a lieutenant in November) was shortly afterwards promoted captain, and Dalton received acting rank. Jacklin, who had been invalided home with dysentery in October, rejoined us, and brought with him Second-Lieutenant J. L. D. Howitt, an officer we had left behind in England when we embarked. The most noteworthy joining, however, of these 12 days' rest, was that of the man destined to be the padre of the 10th Essex Regiment for the remainder of the war. He was a very meek and mild Welshman, intensely shy, and so very afraid of "putting his foot into it" when he came to us. He had spent the major portion of his life in some far-away Welsh village, with angling and music for his hobbies. He was punctilious in calling subaltern and private alike " Mr. So-and-So." What a joke he was those first few weeks!

Capt the Rev D·RANDELL·M·C

As soon as he came into the mess everyone took on another manner. And it was not till real war came in July that David Randell found his feet. On the 1st July the colonel wouldn't let him come into action with us, but sent him back to the advanced dressing station. Early on the morning of the 2nd July David was up in the line to see us. He came every day, and next time we went into action he came with us.

Further reference will be made to some of his work. Whenever I think of Franvillers I think of the arrival of our padre.

The changes at H.Q. had their comic element, for there was some delay in announcing the C.O.'s appointment, and with Scott away temporarily on a course there was a confusion as to who was the senior officer. For a certain time we were divided into two factions, and each side issued its own Battalion Orders; and on the memorable day when Scott came back he issued a third set cancelling the other two! The Adjutant, Meares, deserved a C.B.E. for his services in keeping the balance in these thorny days; and one wonders what Rippengill, the Orderly-Room Sergeant, thought about it.

Nothing of moment occurred during this rest. Training went on quite smoothly, and a certain percentage of all ranks was allowed to visit Amiens each day. In addition, there was the café at Heilly, where the three graces, Suzanne, Marie-Therèse and Lucienne, charmed the cares of battle away in a wonderful way. Plucky girls these were. They had been driven out of their home near Brussels in the first tide of invasion, and with their parents they instituted this little oasis for the weary sojourner in the land of Somme, to keep the pot boiling until the evil times were past.

We were all deeply interested in the progress of the battle at Verdun, and this interest was quickened by the personal connection of many of our hosts with this battle. Some had already lost sons, some husbands, some brothers; but with a gesture and tears in their eyes they merely said "C'est la guerre," and carried on with their ploughing and their cobbling.

On the last day of our stay we had our first battalion athletic meeting. Events were provided for both the serious and the humorous. The first had their flat races; the latter bare-backed mule rides. I regret to say that I remember no specific incident to record with regard to these sports. The inhabitants were very much to the fore as enthusiastic spectators.

On March 12th we marched south-eastwards till we reached a camp in the Somme valley near Etinehem. Here we stayed till the 14th, when we marched at dusk to Maricourt, and took over the line there. While at Etinehem we experienced our first night air raid in France. About 9 p.m. when the moonlight was at its best we heard a great buzzing, and rushed out of our tents to see an enemy plane pass over, low down. It did nothing at the moment. A few seconds later we heard it turn, and then, after a few more seconds, two or three bombs exploded about a mile away. At this time there was no such thing as anti-aircraft discipline, and when one recalls the fact that candles were ablaze in every tent, and that a big incinerator was flaring up a hundred yards or so from the camp, one must admit that we were very lucky not to receive those bombs in our midst.

We relieved the 2nd Bedfordshire Regiment (30th Division) at Maricourt, and thereby took on the task of holding the right-angle bend the salient made here. Our front line ran along the north and east edges of Maricourt Wood. From the apex of our right-angle, i.e., the N.E. corner of the wood, a sap some 70 yards in length ran out towards the Hun line. This sap was known as A.P. (advanced post) 1, and was the chief scene of activity in this sector. It stretched a good deal more than half-way across "No-Man's-Land," and its furthest end was broadened out and held by three sections of a platoon. This little garrison was very much on its lonesome, and only some 30 yards from the enemy. The Hun had attempted to raid some of the 30th Division troops here, but with no success. He did not try that on us, but instead shelled the base of the sap so as to close its trench line of communication. We had a few casualties where the sap joined the main trench, and very soon our Brigade commander ordered a revision of dispositions, which thinned out the garrison of the advanced posts and the front line. Corporal Shaill was one of the first to be wounded at the base of the sap. As we were living in a wood the shelling sounded perfectly awful. Apart from A.P.1 the line was quite respectable and fairly healthy. Just behind the front line, about the middle of our sector, we had two wheat stacks. During our stay machine guns were emplaced in them.

At the further end of our line Machine-Gun Wood represented the last word in front-line peacefulness, and the trenches here rejoiced in such idyllic names as " Honeymoon Lane " and " Cushy Corner." Other trenches which we found unnamed were christened after familiar Colchester landmarks like " Long Wyre Street," " Lexden Road," and " Abbey Fields."

One of the popular sports in the quieter parts and times was hunting the ubiquitous rat, and our local sportsmen would invite their friends from neighbouring companies for a shoot in the evening at " stand-to." This pastime was not without utility, but when in the exuberance of the chase E. de Q. one dusk mistook a sentry's tin hat for the brown rodent and inflicted a deep dent in it, to the considerable annoyance of the occupant, sportsmanship received a severe check and was strongly discountenanced by Company H.Q. Battalion H.Q. was in a house in the village, and only about 800 yards from the line.

Until the battle of Frise on January 29th, 1916, this village of Maricourt had been but little damaged, and civilians had remained there, keeping their shops and cafés open. In March we found the northern part fairly badly smashed, while the southern part was reasonably intact.

Here we lived when the Battalion was in support and lived really in good comfort, even essaying quite a lot of inter-company entertaining. The trouble for the late-night visitor on his return home was that he usually encountered a stream of machine-gun bullets around the corner of the village street. But for that we might have been many miles away from war.

The spot billet was the old Maricourt chateau standing within 400 yards of the line, but so solidly built that we thought it immune from danger, and lived in luxury on the ground floor in an old-fashioned kitchen with an open hearth. Harold Sheldon had a comfortable cellar residence, which was a rendezvous at times when we were slack in the line. He had a free-lance job as M.G. officer, and one of his amusements was to walk along the front line with an old top-hat he had unearthed in the village on the top of a pole, shouting "Vive Poincaré," and at intervals making noises like the Marseillaise. This praise-worthy effort was supposed to delude the Boche into the belief that the French were holding the sector and receiving visits from their President. We never heard the measure of its success. But Halsey rapidly introduced a counter in the shape of a report that he had observed the Kaiser in Montauban!

From our front line we looked slightly uphill to the village of Montauban and Bernafay Wood. On our right front lay Hardecourt, Maurepas, and Favière Wood. Both villages and woods were untouched, and the trees were just commencing to burst into leaf. In our own little Maricourt Wood the foliage was so dense that we could roam about by day, immediately behind our front line trench, in search of primroses, bluebells, and willow catkins. Men off duty snoozed behind trees. The men had more time than usual on their hands here, and some amusing efforts resulted. In one case a German shell, which had lodged in the parados and failed to explode, was made the object of an elaborate wooden cross, with the inscription, "In memory of one of Kaiser's pills.—R.I.P."; and underneath :—

"Here lies the body of a German shell,
It hoped to send us all to Hell.
But it didn't explode and did no harm,
So we covered it up to keep it warm."

The cycle of arrangements in this sector was as follows :—Line 6 days, Maricourt defences 6 days, line 6 days, Etinehem 6 days,—line again. There was always a heap of digging and wiring on hand here, and sundry raids on and by our neighbours kept us on the "qui-vive." We carried out the cycle twice, and then went back to billets at Bray. Most of the days were uneventful. Second-Lieutenant D. C. Tollworthy was wounded through the arm when out on patrol one night. Towards the end of March Second-Lieutenant F. B. Wearne was appointed scouts' officer, and he was given a number of picked men from each Company to train. Of their deeds more anon.

We moved to Bray for work—the preparation of ground for a railway line. Early in May we marched back by way of the Somme valley to Longpré-les-Amienois to carry out our actual tactical preparation for the coming offensive.

CHAPTER IX.

TRAINING AND PREPARATION FOR THE SOMME OFFENSIVE.

We knew for certain as soon as we had settled down at Longpré, that ere many weeks had passed we should be engaged in big offensive operations, and thrills similar to those we had experienced on first landing in France came to us again. No more monotonous trench warfare, with its attendant physical discomforts! Our chance to "do or die" on the magnificent scale was at last coming!

Authority had put us into the best billets we had seen since our arrival in France. Longpré was a very pleasant suburb of Amiens, and lay some mile and a half to the N.W. of that city. It was easily reached by electric car, and the village itself had electric light. The inhabitants were, as usual, most friendly, and we enjoyed our times off duty thoroughly. The secluded square in front of the church made an excellent spot for band performances, and the populace attended these in large numbers.

What of our training? The whole of the 53rd Infantry Brigade was concentrated in the area N.W. of Amiens, with Brigade H.Q. at Ailly-sur-Somme. Here our new Brigade Commander, Brig.-General H. W. Higginson, D.S.O., Royal Dublin Fusiliers, lived and worked; and, working harder than any Brigadier we had experienced in the past (or any that we ever met at all for that matter), he got no end of work out of us. At this time breakfast at Brigade H.Q. was at 6 a.m. each day. General Higginson was another regular soldier we grew both to respect and love, but it took a week or two to get used to his methods.

For the first few days we were marched to the training area to dig. The ground selected for our rehearsals was the open ground around the wayside station of Bertangles, at which we had detrained in July, 1915. Except for a small copse here and there the country was rolling plain devoid of cover. The Royal Engineers taped out a certain trench system, and each morning from 7 a.m. we worked our hardest to dig this out. May, 1916, was a glorious month. The country we were in was at its best; we were very keen; everything and everybody encouraged us, and so, before many days had passed, this full-scale replica of a certain system of Boche trenches was completed. These mornings of continuous digging were not entirely devoid of amusing incident. On more than one occasion a hare put up by a party of diggers found itself in an area of about two acres from which there was no exit, for a whole battalion encircled it. One shout sufficed to raise every spade from the attitude of industry to that of destruction. Very few hares escaped. Of course, it was close season, but—well, there was a war on, and we'd had such a lot of bully and stew; that must be our excuse.

When the trenches were dug to a sufficient depth they were named by notice boards, and we were all bidden to learn these names without delay. Mine Alley, Bund Trench, Bund Support, and Popoff Lane conveyed nothing to us, but Montauban Alley did give us some indication of the area in which we could expect to give battle. And now began the business of training proper. Of the 4 battalions of the Brigade, 2 were to assault, 1 to support, while the fourth was to remain in reserve. We were exercised in both assault and support, and towards the end of our training it became clear to us that we were to be support battalion in the first day's battle. As support battalion we practised sending forward "mopping up" platoons with each of the assaulting battalions; sending other platoons forward a little later to open up the main communication trenches; sending a third company forward in support of points in the main attack, whilst our last company carried up ammunition, etc., to the assaulting troops. We soon got the hang of our commander's instructions.

"Mopping up" was quite new to us, and the idea was based on the most recent French experience at Verdun. Major-General F. I. Maxse, C.B., C.V.O., D.S.O., our then divisional commander, had no insular notions on the subject of adopting French ideas and methods if he considered them sound, and our success as a Division on the 1st July, 1916, was in large measure due to our "mopping up." On that day the majority of British troops did not attempt this recent development of the assault. "If a battalion is detailed to assault and capture three successive trench lines," said General Maxse, "it will not clear up the first thoroughly before it goes on to the second, nor will it clear the second before it goes on to the third. Men of one battalion hang together. We therefore will detail a special party from another battalion to move forward with each wave of the assaulting battalion, so that it can squat down at any given point where we know there are dug-outs, and proceed to mop these up." The direct result of our training in this very attractive job of encouraging Huns out of dug-outs was a minimum of "shot through the back" casualties among our assaulting troops. At this stage, too, assaulting troops were trained on the "right-through" system. This meant that the line of troops to rush the first objective subsequently carried on as "first line" to the second and final objectives. In the light of the results of the "leap-frog"* tactics of 1918 some may criticise General Maxse for insisting on this older method of assault. As an apology, I would submit that we were not sufficiently skilled or practised in modern warfare successfully to carry out the difficult movements involved in "leap-frog" tactics as early as July 1st, 1916. Results certainly were in favour of General Maxse's methods.

Our training was never once monotonous. Some mornings aeroplanes worked with us, and the elements of contact work in battle were demonstrated to us. Another day the Divisional Gas Officer, Lieut. R. J. Thompson, came along with a limber-load of smoke candles, and "P" (Phosphorus) bombs, and, with the help of sundry Battalion Gas Officers and n.c.o.'s, completely upset the right wing of the Brigade attack. Just as the assault was reaching the railway line a most terrible smoke cloud was started up from the railway embankment. The average private either lost direction, or was so interested that he forgot to carry on.

We enjoyed Amiens during our spell back, but it was out of bounds to all British troops for a week of our rest. These weeks of "close season" came along periodically in 1916 and 1917 to allow a general round-up of suspects and odd deserters in Amiens.

*In "leap-frogging" tactics the troops which take the first objective stay there, mop it up and consolidate it, while troops following close behind pass over them and make for the second objective. Elaborate this plan and you have the method on which the big advances in summer and autumn, 1918, were made.

On Sunday afternoons there were most excellent band concerts in the park, and the occasional vocal items were jolly good, too.

During this stay back we were all inoculated against typhoid once again—our Colchester dose was reported worn off—and I succeeded to the Adjutantcy, Captain G. K. Meares, who had been our adjutant since the formation of the battalion, joining the 54th Infantry Brigade H.Q. as a staff-probationer. As a company officer there had been a certain amount of free time for me to spend as I wished—reading, joy-riding, reflection, football. Now I found I had mighty little time at all; even the usual letter home became curtailed. And if from now onwards I record fewer amusing incidents and matters which really interest you, please try to remember that I had less time in which to fix these in my memory. Events, too, began to move so rapidly from the time of our next move linewards that no one memory can possibly hope to provide more than a few very outstanding facts.

On Monday, May 22nd, we marched via Daours to Corbie. Here we found a large number of troops of other divisions, and prices very much higher than they were at Christmas, 1915. Officers and men spent the evening visiting old friends in La Neuville; we had warm receptions, and much hospitality was proffered. Our next day's march was a long one—to Bronfay Farm and Billon Wood. As the last four miles or so of this march had to be carried out by night we did not leave Corbie before 4 p.m. Our route was via Bray, so for some 6 miles we covered the road along which we had moved during our forward march of August, 1915. A good deal of rain fell on this evening, and we were a wet and weary band when we reached our destinations. Battalion H.Q. and "*A*" and "*B*" Companies went into billets and dugouts in and around Bronfay Farm, while "C" and "D" Companies took over shelters in Billon Wood, some half a mile to the east of the farm. Bronfay Farm had been one of the few isolated Somme farms before the war, and so was a set of buildings of considerable dimension. These enclosed a courtyard. This farm, though lying on the Bray-Maricourt road, and barely 1½ miles from the front line, was, I believe, quite intact. Enemy shells, when they had come, appeared always to have missed the buildings. Tiers of rabbit wire beds had been erected in all the barns, and so long as it pleased the Hun to remain quiet, this farm was a reasonably comfortable and dry spot. The shelters in Billon Wood were good too. Both the farm and the wood will be full of memories for us for ever. From them and in them we began our active preparations for the Somme offensive. During this last week of May our energies were chiefly concentrated on the digging of a new broad communication trench from the heart of Billon Wood to Carnoy. The sappers supervised our work, and took on the tunnelling required to pass under the Albert-Peronne road. "Spring Avenue" was a fine trench. When the concentrating of troops into actual battle positions was on, it was used for "up-traffic only." With all its winds and wriggles it must have been over a mile in length.

Some of us had a good deal of office work to put in, too, for many " preliminary instructions " were issued, and there was always a heap of returns to get out.

Bronfay Farm in these days was a veritable "house-of-call," and Major Lewis was an able dispenser of hospitality. Remember that this was the one and only house between Bray—a good two miles away—and the line; that, indeed, it was the most advanced outpost of civilisation, and you will understand the popularity of our hospitable Battalion H.Q. in residence at Bronfay Farm. We were about to get our Pioneer-Sergeant Heyward to make and erect some such sign as "The Three Balls," when, on the 31st May, we moved forward to Carnoy in relief of the 8th Suffolk Regiment.

CHAPTER X.

June, 1916.

We went into the line at Carnoy so that we might get acquainted with our "battle front." As we were not an assaulting battalion, we held the line immediately to the right of the sector from which the 53rd Infantry Brigade was to "kick-off," but all ranks visited this sector both by day and night and mastered the "lie of the ground," etc. And we held the front line quite earnestly, too. The Hun was kept under keen observation; our snipers were active, and one night Wearne and some of his now expert scouts caught our very first prisoner—the first to be taken by the 53rd Brigade. When one remembers that we had been out nearly eleven months then, one realises how comparatively tame and bloodless our time had been. F. B. Wearne was a wonderful scout; he was brave, daring, and had a head full of brains. The youngsters he took on—I remember Corporals Meager and Cooper particularly—would follow him anywhere and respond correctly and immediately to his tiniest sign. The Hun had no chance. He was cut off, rounded up, and brought back senseless. Excitement ran high. A special party pushed him down on an old trolley which worked along the narrow gauge railway in the Talus Boisé valley, and an ambulance was sent up from Bray to take him post-haste to the Intelligence Officer. General Higginson thanked Wearne and his men next day. A few days later Wearne became my assistant adjutant, but he was soon away wounded (July 3rd). No one in the 10th Essex was surprised when he read in 1917 that F. B. Wearne had won the V.C. with another Essex battalion, and at the same time had lost his life. We were more than disappointed that he had not returned to us on recovery.

Each night during this tour we had every available man at work. There was so much to do that Battalion H.Q. had to send nearly every man out to carry up food and ammunition for the Brigade dumps. Mercer, who was acting R.S.M. at the time, paraded all servants (including the Colonel's), runners, clerks, sanitary men, cooks, etc., about 10 p.m., and with them moved up the night's contribution to the rapidly-growing battle dumps. What a thrill it was to be preparing for the "real thing" at last! There was no shortage of guns and ammunition, trench mortars and grenades, gas and smoke any longer, and many of us were quite convinced we'd have the Hun asking for peace by the end of July!

This time we were relieved by the 8th E. Surrey R., of the 55th Infantry Brigade, and marched to billets in Bray. Here we had barely settled down to work in the town and at the canal landing stages, when two companies were ordered up to Carnoy for more work there. June 8th to June 25th was for the men a period of extremely hard and tiring manual labour. Officers, in addition to helping with and supervising this work, had to attend and also to hold many conferences. Some of the Brigade conferences were most protracted. I well remember the Colonel and myself riding from Bray to Sailly Laurette, a distance of some six miles, for a conference beginning at 3.30 p.m.; we left at 8.15 p.m. General Higginson was very thorough.

Small drafts of officers and men joined us about this

time. The men were at once absorbed by companies, for we were still under strength. Among the officers who came at this time were Second-Lieutenants C. H. Walker, A. Carpenter, I. H. Linford and H. S. Gray. In the last week of June a tall Scotchman, with a long, dour face, and wearing a feathered bonnet, turned up —we were established at Carnoy at the time. He came to take over the duties of Transport Officer. We had hoped that this job would fall to R.S.M. Lawrence, who had been acting as T.O. for a month or so. Authority, however, declared him too old for a temporary commission, and after a few weeks' attachment our Scotchman—Lieutenant Robert Forbes— took over. Forbes belonged to a kind of Corps of Transport Officers, and was eligible neither for promotion nor for any other duty. What restrictions to set about a great man! When, in 1917, Forbes was wanted for adjutant, we were able to obtain a special dispensation from the War Office and get him out of the Transport Corps. The history of the Battalion for the autumn of 1917 and the whole of 1918 will bear testimony to his capabilities and his gallant leadership. In passing, let us say that those of us who thought at all soon realised that a great man had joined us.

The discipline in the Battalion was always of a high standard. Probably the Essex temperament is as ideal as any possible for a soldier to have. Ordinarily we had no crime sheet for the Colonel in the morning; now and then, however, someone had to be brought up. In June, 1916, we had two interesting court-martial cases, which I propose to record for various reasons, but especially for the purpose of showing that in our Battalion, at any rate, we did our best to administer military law with justice, kindness, and a sense of humour.

Private X had been up before his company commander and Colonel on several occasions in 1914 and 1915. This time, while in the front line at Carnoy he had just refused point-blank to go on sentry duty—it was a case of occasional fits of sullen obstinacy, I think. The Colonel went up to the front line to hear the case, and remanded the man for F.G.C.M. The evidence was overwhelming when the case was heard at Bray, and Private X. was found guilty and sentenced to a year or more of I.H.L. (imprisonment with hard labour). The Army Commander suspended his sentence, and Private X. returned to his company with the advice that he should make good in the coming battle. He was detailed for carrying with an assaulting battalion, and worked fearlessly and well till he was wounded, fairly severely. He had made good, and one of the Colonel's first acts on our relief was to forward a recommendation that Private X.'s sentence should be remitted, and higher authority agreed.

Private Y.'s was rather a different case. While back at Longpré he had enclosed information concerning the coming battle in a letter to his wife. In addition, the silly fellow had dotted under individual letters of words in his screed so as to spell the name Carnoy. The Base Censor caught him, and knew his brigade from the field post-office stamp. One afternoon, while we were at Bronfay Farm, I was asked over the telephone if we had a man named "Y" in the Essex. As "Y" was formerly in my platoon, I couldn't deny his existence. Such a serious case naturally had to go before a court-martial, and for hours I racked my brain for some defence for "Y," who was a good hard-working soldier, though somewhat of a babbler.

One night I had him into my dug-out at Carnoy to

help him with the defence. There seemed no hope, when he suddenly said, "I don't believe I signed the envelope at all. May I see it?" I showed it him, and he confirmed his suspicion emphatically. I had by me a duplicate copy of his signature in a recent pay roll: this was quite different. "I remember now," he said, "that one day I left a letter on my bed at the billet, and when I came back the letters had been collected. Sergeant —— told me he had signed and sent mine, as it was a shame to let it miss the post." Someone at G.H.Q. had laid down the charge for "green envelope" cases. It read something like this: ". . . . signed a solemn declaration that no information of value was contained in the envelope, well knowing that such was not the case."

The trial came on almost at once. The Base Censor gave his evidence; the C.Q.M.S. produced the duplicate pay roll. The accused then gave evidence on oath in his own defence. His point just was that he didn't sign the envelope. He admitted writing the letter, and proclaimed his sorrow for having offended. The court was a little dumbfounded, and couldn't decide right away. Next morning Private Y. was released. We never had another "green envelope" case. Private Y. was wounded in July.

On June 25th, when the "big bombardment" began, we were concentrated in trenches in and around Carnoy.

We were just in reserve at Carnoy; none of our troops were in the front line. The noise went on all the time—all day and all night—but it was not the continuous thunder-like roar that some had expected. The Hun retaliation was almost nil. All forms of artillery worked to one programme. When the 18-pounders had finished the 4.5's took up the ball; then the heavy mortars would have a go, and the big, merry

French gunners in Billon Wood would swell the chorus with huge shells from their ancient pieces. On Monday, June 27th, we went back to this wood for a few days' final rest, and our shelters in the valley were about 120 yards in advance of these French gun positions. These funny little howitzers they were firing day and night were made in 1872, had no recoil action, and were emplaced on inclined wooden platforms in the sloping chalk bank on the south side of the valley. The gun pulled into position by means of ropes, two Frenchmen ran up with a shell on a little stretcher, and threw it into the breach. The gun was laid by various crude devices. Another second, and with a loud "Tirez" from the n.c.o. in charge, the gun was fired. The noise was colossal, and never before nor since have our ears been subjected to such a strain. In our huts on the other side of the valley we were not only deafened, but singed by the warm blast of the discharge. During the day the shell could be followed easily for the first minute of its flight! Perhaps what amused us most about these guns, however, was that the shell protruded from the muzzle of the loaded gun! The dear, happy Poilus, who loved to get us over to "tirez," are another of our happy memories. Montauban was their target, and they smashed it up successfully.

Originally June 29th had been selected for "Z" day, but for various reasons the assault was postponed two days. On the evening of June 30th we moved up viâ Spring Avenue to battle. "It was a glorious evening," *but* "our work was scarce begun." Carnoy and its surrounding trenches were full of eager, almost excited men. The sides of Brick Alley—a main communication trench—were covered with men laughing and singing in anticipation of the morrow. All were now fully equipped, and each carried two bombs and extra ammunition. Our companies rested in the old Carnoy defences for the night, but Battalion H.Q. moved up to its " battle-shack " in the front line. This was a poor place, and already more or less full of Berkshire officers. The hour was about midnight when we arrived, and Colonel Scott would not hear of the Berkshire subalterns moving out. "You are assaulting in the morning," he said; "get all the sleep you can." They did; so did we. We sat round the edges of two wire beds and snoozed off and on from 1 a.m. till 5 a.m. Colonel Scott read his novel—he always took one into action—till he fell off. At 5 a.m. we all had breakfast, and I remember that tinned sausages from the canteen played a prominent part in this. We then went our respective ways. In three hours' time three of the four Berkshire officers had been killed!

The order of battle on July 1st was as follows :—

Headquarters : Lieut.-Colonel H. L. Scott, Major J. L. Lewis, Lieut. R. A. Chell (adjutant), Lieut. D. B. Cooper (Q.M.), Captain W. A. Coates (M.O.), Second-Lieut. L. W. Bird (Signals), Second-Lieut. F. B. Wearne (asst. adjutant).

"*A*" Company: Lieut. J. V. Jacklin, Second-Lieuts. C. H. Walker, J. L. D. Howitt, A. D. Openshaw.

"*B*" Company: Captain A. S. Tween, Second-Lieuts. W. G. P. Hunt, H. D. Burton.

"*C*" Company: Captain C. M. Ridley, Second-Lieuts. T. A. Evans, A. C. Pochin, H. S. Gray.

"*D*" Company: Captain T. M. Banks, Second-Lieuts. A. M. Byerley, E. de Q. Mears, R. A. Cotman.

The remaining officers were in reserve either at the Transport Lines near Bray or the Divisional School near Corbie.

CHAPTER XI.

JULY THE FIRST, 1916.

OVER THE TOP!

About 7.20 a.m. our hurricane bombardment became a veritable whirlwind. All our lighter artillery and Stokes' mortars played to their utmost on the front line and close-support trenches of the enemy system. This was the first time Stokes' mortars had been used "all-out," and their effect was at least spectacular; the air was full of toppling and turning cylinders at various stages of flight. And yet other noises and excitements were in store for us in that 10 minutes which preceded our zero hour. At 2 minutes to zero our tunnellers blew strongly-charged mines below the old minefield on our right front and below "Kasino Point," slightly to our left; sappers simultaneously blew the charges to open the Russian saps they had made in preceding weeks, as communication trenches with the enemy front line. Kasino Point filled the air around us with lumps of chalk of varying sizes, and a fair number of our men were injured by them. Our little shack was on the trench level, and was quite open on the west side. Several hunks came into this den, and the colonel's servant, Hodges, who was standing at the opening, was almost stunned. He suffered badly from concussion for the rest of the day.

As soon as the mines went up the assaulting troops went over the top, and halted for a few seconds to get their line straight. The barrage lifted, and forward they all went with cheers and yells straight for the Hun. The line 100 yards away was invisible for a time—there was so much smoke.

Two platoons of our "*B*" Company accompanied the 8th Norfolk Regiment, two platoons of "*C*" Company the 6th Royal Berkshire Regiment. The remaining two platoons of each of these Companies advanced an hour or so later to open up the two main communication trenches—Mine Alley and Popoff Lane. As "*A*" Company was carrying and helping the sappers, Colonel Scott was actually left with Battalion H.Q. and "*D*" Company as a command. Battalion H.Q. was in it from the start. Bird and Coates (the M.O.) stood on a knob just outside the shelter and yelled news to me; Colonel Scott examined prisoners. The first of these arrived about 7.35. He was an awful-looking object, for he had been under our 7 days' bombardment without relief, and had had no wash or shave and very little food. I 'phoned his regiment, etc., back to the brigade. What a lot of 'phoning and message writing there was to do that day!

The battle went on well, particularly on the left. The 6th Royal Berkshire Regiment was in splendid form, and nothing could stop it. Its casualties were many in number—in officers extremely heavy—but it meant to get home, and it did so. On the right the Huns seemed more troublesome, and there was a hang up in Mine Alley. Certainly the Huns were thick there. Our moppers-up and trench clearers helped enormously here, for Tween, their company commander, was on the spot, and he was always a sound man at handling a situation rapidly and efficiently. Every trench junction was a veritable "strong point," and the enemy contested every yard of ground. His officers at this time were of the finest that the Hun military machine ever produced. They fought skilfully, and with magnificent bravery, and several inflicted heavy casualties on us by sniping from points of vantage in the rough weed-strewn ground between trench lines. One of them, outwitted at length and caught, absolutely refused to surrender.

The "hang up" on the right did not last long. The progress on the left and the help from our supports enabled the 8th Norfolk Regiment to get its second objective and capture many prisoners. The C.S.M. of "B" Company, Hammond, I think, by name, and two n.c.o.'s viz., Sutliffe and Cox, were amongst those mentioned by Tween for doing excellent work. On the left Ridley had sent Evans and Pochin to mop up with the Berkshires. Evans was wounded at the outset, Pochin a little later; Ridley himself was wounded during the morning whilst supervising the work of his company. "C" Company was thus for a time in the hands of Gray, an officer who had joined us but 10 days before. Gray, with that veteran Sergeant Jaggs as his acting C.S.M., carried on calmly and untroubled, and at 4 p.m. we found him on his correct line (Pommier Trench).

Cotman, full of Latin enthusiasm (he hailed from South America) was a little disgruntled by the fact that he had a fairly easy initial passage. So, entirely unsolicited, he took his platoon off to help the Middlesex take Pommiers Redoubt. Here he had a very satisfactory fight and did some useful work, and returned to his Company with his platoon later in the afternoon profoundly pleased with himself.

At this time the Berkshires were still fighting for their last objective, Montauban Alley, the last trench in the Hun first system of defence. By now they were almost without officers, and their commander, Colonel Clay, and their adjutant, Rochfort, were taking it in turns to go up and organise bombing stunts to dislodge packets of Huns. At this stage our "D" Company, under Banks, came along and rendered a great deal of assistance, for which the Royal Berkshires were profoundly thankful. Of course, it was our duty to do this, but the execution of duty even in war is liable to be accelerated or retarded by personal feelings. We always got on well with the Berkshires. Colonel Clay expressed a wish or suggestion; Colonel Scott, without any more ado, carried it out or backed him up as required, and vice versa. By about 6 p.m. the fighting on the brigade front was over and our "D" Company stalwarts came back smiling, and we set about sorting ourselves out thoroughly. Our job now was to consolidate and hold the Pommier Line (the Brigade's 2nd objective in the morning), as the British second line. The Hun did not interfere with us, for we had penetrated his front to such a depth that what guns he had not left behind in our hands he had had to withdraw, and these were not yet again in action. One gun from Delville Wood (to the E.N.E.) fired at Pommier Trench occasionally, but on the whole a quiet night was passed on our front, and by 9 p.m., 1st July, the battalion was thoroughly reorganised and settled down. Archibald had come up from the transport and taken over "C" Company, and one or two others had taken it on themselves to come up off their own bat. Colonel Scott was kind enough to let them stay up.

At 5 p.m. Bird had found a huge Boche dug-out in Mine Alley for our new Battalion H.Q. As we were still in support we might as well have stayed in our old position, but we all wanted to be up and residing in territory so recently Hun. This was one of the great thrills of this day. What a satisfaction it was to drag out all the German uniform and filth from that old dug-out and set fire to it. Later, when we had dinner (about 11 p.m., I think), we had excellent Hun sparkling water with our whisky. Everyone had endless chocolate.

Our only officer killed on July 1st was Captain H. E. Hawkins. He was in charge of the main brigade dump on the Carnoy-Montauban road, when an enemy shell exploded very close to him. He was killed instantly. Openshaw, Sheldon (attached M.G.C.) and Osborne (attached T.M.B.) were among the wounded.

About 7 p.m. General Higginson came tripping across the battlefield, and, having seen our dispositions, went on with Colonel Scott to visit the Norfolks and the Berkshires. He gave his congratulations and thanks to every one he saw, and was as genuinely and enthusiastically happy as a boy who has just won a school championship. Next day our corps com-

With the 10th Essex in France. 121

mander, General Congreve, came round the whole front; indeed we had a superfluity of visitors!

The 1st July was full of tragedy for the majority of British divisions—Regular, Service, and Territorial. For us of the 18th Division, who were not "blooded" before that day, it was a magnificent victory. Countless reasons may be adduced to account for our success. Apart from the courage and efficiency of our officers and men, their wonderful enthusiasm and esprit de brigade, I would emphasise the untiring devotion of our commanders to their respective jobs. Those of us still remaining salute Maxse and Higginson for the training they gave us and the preparations they made for the battle. In every case the soundness of their respective decrees was established.

Battalion H.Q. was reasonably comfortable, but not clean in the soldier's sense of the word (I caught the first louse I ever saw there). I felt so concerned that the enemy might counter attack that I sat up all night. We were all over-anxious in this our first battle; we couldn't bear the idea of anything going wrong for the want of any little personal effort or sacrifice. A good deal of the time that night was spent answering a host of those fatuous enquiries peculiar to base and regimental paymasters. This fact should show how very thoroughly we were established in this new line!

Wearne was very useful now. He took on most of the morning duty, and I expected a reasonable time. On the morning of the 3rd, however, he thought he might as well go out on his own on a little exploration towards the Hun. He took Howitt with him. Where they went I never found out. A signaller woke me to say both had been fairly badly wounded, and evacuated. Wearne never came back to us; he was a great loss.

About half a mile in front of the brigade front line

was a long strip of wood running parallel to our front known as Caterpillar Wood. The valley on whose southern bank this stood was very steep on this side. Consequently we couldn't see the wood from our front line. On the evening of 3rd July higher command made up its mind that this wood might as well be added to our territorial gains, and so just about dusk we were warned by 'phone that probably the Essex would be required to do the job at dawn on the morrow. The wood was reported held by snipers.

What a hustle and a bustle we had in getting reconnaissances done and "B" and "D" Companies in position in time! These two companies were considered an adequate force for the task, and were hurried up from the Pommier Line to positions in front of Montauban Alley and astride Caterpillar Alley (the communication trench from Montauban Alley to Caterpillar Wood). The night was dark, and we encountered many working parties returning from wiring and digging as we went up. No time was fixed for our "assault"; no bombardment preceded it. Three platoons of "B" Company were lost for a short time in the approach march, but dawn had not passed into daylight when our troops started out. "B" Company was on the right of Caterpillar Alley, "D" Company on the left. Each company had two waves. Colonel Scott, the Brigade-Major, and myself walked down Caterpillar Alley. We didn't know in the least what we should find, and it was nervy work, for we were advancing in close-packed night formation, and already it was nearly fully light, and every moment we expected to be pulverised by shells and decimated by machine-guns. But nothing happened. Our victory was quite bloodless! A wood empty of enemy, seven or more abandoned guns, and heaps of artillery ammunition were amongst our captures.

This wood had been the haunt of German artillery before the 1st July, and its shelters were well furnished. Here, on this lovely July morning, our two isolated companies (for divisions on right and left were not up to this line) had a great picnic. Byerley, we heard, gave a grand concert, as the piano found in one of the shelters was in quite good condition. A sound outpost position was taken up on the south edge of the wood, and sentries here had an excellent view of the southern edge of Mametz Wood on the left, the approach to the Bazentins on the ridge ahead, and the valley to the right. The troops to man this position in case of attack rested in the valley in front! Here they were well hidden and covered, and, above all, could dress up in the silk underwear left behind by the Huns, collect the numerous abandoned pickelhaubes, and sing to Byerley's music.

We were relieved next night, and moved back to the old trenches at Carnoy, Battalion H.Q. taking up its old Battle H.Q. as residence. "D" Company made some strenuous efforts to bring some of the captured guns out with them as souvenirs, but got bogged en route. Captain Banks unfortunately sprained his ankle badly during this relief, and had to be invalided away as a result. The next two days brought nothing very exciting. A bit of the case of an enemy lachrymatory shell went through the brain of one of our best signallers who was walking along an old trench near Battalion H.Q. His name was Warwick; I remember him well, for he had been on duty at the 'phone most of the night, 1st-2nd July. A war correspondent visited our "A" Company, and I believe they lied liberally for his benefit. On the evening of 7th July we were relieved by a battalion of the 3rd Division, and passed back to Bronfay Farm, by now a distant rest camp, and surrounded by hosts of bell tents. On the afternoon of the 8th our band "came up and called for us," and took us swaggering down to Bray. En route we passed two or three regular battalions, which had not yet taken any part in the offensive. There were mutual cheers and jokes.

CHAPTER XII.

JULY 8TH TO JULY 18TH, 1916.

We had never before felt quite so bucked with ourselves as we marched back from the line. All and sundry were carrying trophies from the old Hun lines —pickelhaubes, soft round caps, rifles, flare pistols, miniature shovels. At Bray we found our rest camp still in the course of erection. It was to consist of three or four huge canvas shelters, each to hold some 200 men. Of tents and huts there were none at all. What did we care? The weather was glorious; we were almost as pleased with ourselves as authority was satisfied with us; we had heaps to talk about. With a little help from us the sappers finished off our shacks by evening, and we settled down to " make the most " of a short respite. Each one of us had his own idea of this making the most of rest, and probably the one with the most fixed ideas on the subject was our quartermaster—Lieutenant D. B. Cooper. He served us admirably in the matter of refitting, and he hustled those concerned to such an extent that he had us ready for action again almost before we had had a night's rest. Probably good feeds, good sleep, a chance to read the newspapers, have a decent smoke, and write a long letter home, represent the average soldier's idea of making the most of a rest.

On Sunday morning we had a short service in the little quadrangle around which the shacks were built. What a difference our 150 casualties made to the appearance of the old battalion! The singing was lusty; it gave each just the chance he wanted to get a certain feeling off his chest. After "God Save the King," sung as soldiers on service alone can sing it, Colonel Scott addressed all ranks on the good work recently done. We were all pleased exceedingly, for we knew how very genuine this colonel of ours was.

In the afternoon we had the tarpaulins thrown away from the sides of the officers' shack, and took our tea alfresco. The wooden boxes in which rations had come up served as chairs and tables. We had barely started our meal when the Divisional Commander arrived, accompanied by one A.D.C. General Maxse always did the right thing on these occasions; indeed, one might say that he was at his very best when paying these informal visits before and after battle. He could say, "How are you, boys?" as no one else could say it. This he followed with his "Gather round, boys, and I'll tell you what's going on." We may have called him "the Black Man" in our early days at Colchester, and taken just a month or two to get accustomed to the frank and hearty cursings he gave us on field days, but we knew we had the right man over us now, and went into battle full of confidence when we knew we were fighting under our own Divisional Commander. The period of active operations I shall cover in these pages tells of only one engagement which was not an unqualified success, and for that fight our Brigade was lent first to one division, then to another.

After tea with us the General dodged round the men's shelters. A group of men studying a large-scale marked battle map attracted him, and he immediately set to and held forth on the general situation to them. He told us, too, that we were not going away from the Somme front. Reinforcements would begin to arrive on the morrow, and after a few days we should be up and at it again.

With the 10th Essex in France.

Reinforcements certainly came, and came quickly. Each batch contained an assortment from about three different regiments. We had Hertfordshire and Cambridgeshire Territorials, and men of the Leicestershire Regiment becoming 10th Essex men at the twinkling of an eye. We were soon reasonably strong, and a little training each morning made our newcomers accustomed to our methods of working. We were warned to be prepared to exploit in the next battle, so forming up on a tape, instead of in a system of trenches, played a great part in our training. Afternoons were free.

All these days the Hun was busy reinforcing his front and strengthening its defence by increasing his artillery support. Back at Grove Town Camp we had evidence of this, for each day he shelled the important cross roads and road junctions near by with his long-range guns.

We knew another big attack was soon to be made, and did not mind much when. On the 13th reconnaissances were ordered, and Colonel Scott and myself had a long and tiring morning in and around the front line of the 55th Infantry Brigade and the French, with whom they joined on their right. This was the day of the bitter fighting in Trones Wood; we knew all about it from close contact! On our return we rode to Brigade H.Q. for instructions. The conference was long, and all kinds of possibilities were considered. The whole thing, however, really came to this: The Fourth Army would continue its northerly advance on the morrow, and the 18th Division was to hold the right flank of that attack, building up the "defensive flank" and exploiting as required. The 53rd Infantry Brigade was first for action, and of that brigade the 10th Essex would go first. Just after midnight we received orders to march off between

3.30 a.m. and 4 a.m. to a valley in Billon Wood, whilst the Colonel pushed on ahead for instructions. Dawn had barely commenced when we fell in. I do not remember any parade in France which impressed me more than this one at dawn on the 14th July, 1916. The skies to the east and north-east were ablaze with gun flashes and alarm signals, the roads beside our camp were thronged with Indian cavalry moving forward to uncertain tasks, and amongst it we moved off as the van of the 53rd Brigade.

We moved rapidly to our rendezvous, marching by "overland tracks" all the way. On arrival packs were dumped and extra fighting kit issued (rifle grenades, two bombs per man, etc.). These little movements took but a few minutes, so when Colonel Scott returned with instructions we were able to move off at once. We marched viâ Carnoy, and it gave us some satisfaction to be able to do this "on top." Spring Avenue was quite superfluous now!

The 9th Division had attacked on the right that morning, and their South African troops had taken the greater part of Delville Wood. Our job was to hold a line covering their flank. British troops already held Trones Wood, and so our dispositions were Trones Alley (a trench running from the N.E. of Bernafay Wood to the N. apex of Trones Wood), and the eastern edge of Bernafay Wood. "A" and "D" Companies held these lines, and "B" and "C" Companies were in reserve in Bernafay Wood. Battalion H.Q. was established at the N.W. corner of this wood.

By about 8 a.m. we had taken up our dispositions, and we then commenced to have a hectic day. True, our approach march had been somewhat uncomfortable, for the Hun was shelling us from a flank all the time, but it wasn't as bad as it was later. His guns in and around Leuze Wood pounded into the lines we were holding all day long. Ahead of us (to the north) we knew British troops were fighting, but for a long time we knew nothing of their fate. Longueval was burning fiercely. About 10 a.m. orders for assaults commenced to arrive. These were all " in the event of this and that." The first batch was cancelled, and others substituted. We were " on edge " all the time, but in the end we were ordered to just hang on to our positions. The main attack, though successful, had not been on such a large scale as to make the Hun think of relinquishing such strong positions as Guillemont and Ginchy without a tremendous fight. Had we been put at either of those villages on this day " to exploit " we should have been obliterated. As it was, we had a good many casualties—Second-Lieut. E. de Q. Mears, of "*D*" Company, was killed; Captain W. A. Coates, our M.O., was wounded. Mears was a keen, lively officer, and his death removed a good and ill-spared leader. Byerley had left him but a minute, and when he returned he found Mears' servant, Shelton, sobbing over his lifeless body. Out of the line we knew him as a poet, and he was always ready to read one of his lyrics to an appreciative mess. During this day and the next some 80 other ranks were killed and wounded. These casualties were mainly amongst "*A*" Company in Trones Alley, though we had some at Battalion H.Q. A most faithful soldier, Private J. Bollister, of our Pioneer Section, was killed, and he and Mears were buried together just across the road from our Battalion H.Q. When in September, 1918, I went to look for their graves, I found a trench railway track over the spot, nor could I find their crosses in the cemetery near by.

"*A*" Company certainly had a rough time. The shelling was vile. It seemed to attract our padre,

David Randell, who spent most of his time there. He did well in these days. By day he was in and around the trenches, by night he buried the men killed on previous days. This was his first battle at first hand, and he very much more than justified his presence in the line.

The idea of a further attack by the 53rd Brigade was still current, and early on the morning of the 16th General Higginson conducted a "staff tour" round parts of Delville Wood. All battalion and company commanders of the brigade attended, and the General showed how and where the 8th Suffolk and 10th Essex Regiments would form up in the south part of the wood, and attack in a S.E. direction from it, and so take Guillemont largely by surprise. During the afternoon tapes were put out, and we were led to believe that as soon as we had been relieved by certain Bantam troops we should go forward and form up on these tapes. The general situation, however, did not warrant this, so when we were relieved on the evening of the 16th we trudged back to Billon Wood. Rain was falling now, and the going was very heavy. We expected to be moved up on the evening of the 17th for our Guillemont fight, but the move was postponed. Again, on the 18th, the same thing happened. By this time our plans for the job were as definite as they could be. We were anticipating another easy night in Billon Wood, when, at 7 p.m., 18th, we were ordered to move at once to Carnoy, and from the time of our arrival there to be prepared to move at a moment's notice.

All was not well in Delville Wood, and we might be required to do a counter-attack in the morning. We trudged to Carnoy with all possible speed, and squatted down in empty trenches and shelters in the Talus Boisé Valley.

CHAPTER XIII.

DELVILLE WOOD.

"THE ABOMINATION OF DESOLATION."
(*An impression in* 1918).

Our rest in the Talus Boisé Valley was but a short one—from 9.30 p.m. (18th) to 12.30 a.m. (19th). Our shelters were quite comfortless: they contained no ' furniture " whatever. Two of these bare places were allotted to the officers. Some snoozed, but the majority had not had a very strenuous day on the 18th, and the afternoon nap, followed by the excitement of a sudden move, was sufficient to keep them fresh till midnight. The sleepless ones, led by Byerley and Archibald, our two "sweetest of musicians," sang well-known old glees till such time as they were roused for the next move. "Annie Laurie," "Sweet and low," just made us forget for the moment what we felt certain we should be up against in the morning.

The Brigade Major (Major J. C. Markes, of the Leinster Regiment) came to us from Brigade H.Q. at 12.30 a.m. His instructions were for the Colonel to ride over at once to Maricourt to see General Higginson, while the Battalion moved forward viâ Montauban to a rendezvous in Caterpillar Valley. We did not stop to argue about the need of hot breakfast, but got under way at once, and were in position on the northern slope of the valley, some 400 yards west of the north-west corner of Bernafay Wood, by 2.30 a.m. Here we awaited the arrival of the other three battalions of the Brigade and our orders. The other troops and the colonels came along in due course, but not in sufficient time for the brigade to launch its counter-attack at dawn, as had been intended.

Our Colonel gave us the reputed situation and our orders verbally as soon as he arrived. Those concerned sat round the edges of a huge shell hole to hear him. The troops in Delville Wood and Longueval had been heavily counter-attacked on the afternoon of the 18th and driven out of almost every bit of the Wood. The 53rd Brigade had been "lent" to the Division responsible, for the purpose of getting the wood back, and it was told to get the job done at once, forthwith, instanter!

Delville Wood is more or less rectangular in shape, the longer sides being the east to west ones. At this time the wood was more or less divided into equal north and south parts by a ride running slightly north of east from Longueval, and this we had named

Princes Street. The ride running along the south side of the wood was South Street. The 53rd Brigade plan was for the 8th Norfolk Regiment to sweep that portion of the wood south of Princes Street in an easterly direction and hold the southern portion of the eastern edge, while the other three battalions, following on its heels, wheeled, and, forming up on the Princes Street line, advanced in a northerly direction to clear the northern half of the wood, where the Huns were in much greater force. The 10th Essex followed immediately behind the 8th Norfolk, and so had the extreme north-east part of the wood as its task. This operation sounds complex, and it was complex. Remember, too, that we had but hasty orders; no time in which to determine the situation for ourselves; to complete our approach march in broad daylight, and for the most part under direct terrestrial observation from the enemy; and finally to operate in a dense wood with the foliage at its maximum. What a test for leadership! The artillery was not that we had been working with previously, and throughout the 19th we received practically no artillery support whatever.

What happened? The Norfolks started off at 5.50 a.m. in single file up the sunken road leading to Longueval. Colonel Scott, seeing that his company commanders knew their jobs as far as he was able to tell them, decided to push on ahead with the Norfolks to get in touch with the situation, and so, if possible, help his troops. We had a fairly rough passage up to Longueval, for the enemy gunners were making good shooting at the sunken road. We went up a part of Longueval High Street and turned off through a farmyard into the western outskirts of the wood. Here we found a telephone of which the Brigade Major had told us, and we were able to speak back to Brigade, now at Montauban. We could only report that things were going slow; that we were up in touch with the remnants holding the line (a signal sergeant appeared to be commanding the battalion we bumped against); that any barrage our gunners had put down in the early morning had long since been lost. Company commanders kept us informed of the rate of progress of the forward movement. Hours seemed to pass before any of our troops got into the wood. All the time the enemy subjected those parts of the wood and the village in our hands and the approaches thereto to a heavy machine-gun and rifle fire ; nor did his artillery fail to speak. Things were "sticky" in the south-west corner of the wood, so Colonel Scott issued orders for our companies to render the 8th Norfolk Regiment every possible assistance in getting the first round-up completed.

We hadn't been up in the wood long before Colonel Clay and his adjutant came to confer with us (the 6th R. Berks R. was following on our heels). The four of us had stood together in the wood about five minutes, I should think, when a shell burst in the air some 200 yards away. It was a "White Hope"— really an H.E. shrapnel. A second later, a whizz, a small, dull thud, and Colonel Scott had toppled over into my arms. A small piece of shrapnel had entered his head just over his eye. The superb coolness of the man ! While reclining in my arms his first act was to test the sight of his injured eye. He placed his hand over the other eye and found he could still see. Our doctor was at hand, and the Colonel was taken to the shelter which had been fixed on as an aid post. I got on the 'phone to tell Brigade of the casualty, and was told that the Brigade Major had just been killed. The General arranged to send up Major Lewis, who was acting as our liaison officer with the Brigade, to take over command. Reports of casualties and calls for stretcher-bearers came in from all sides. The evacuation of the wounded was a dreadful business, for the only line was the one by which our troops had approached. Jacklin, commanding "A," was wounded; Archibald, commanding "C," was mortally wounded, and died at Corbie next day; Byerley, commanding "D," was wounded. Other officer casualties were: Pearson killed, and Pinder-Davis, Bird, and Corke wounded. We lost over 200 other ranks in this engagement. The company-sergeant-majors of "A" and "D" Companies—Gaster and Palmer—were killed; so was Sergeant Ager, our chief Lewis gun n.c.o.

I do not propose to give a long and heartrending account of those two dreadful days in Delville Wood —they were certainly the most trying days I myself have ever experienced. During the first day the 53rd Brigade cleared most of the southern part of the wood —originally set as the task of the Norfolks. The other battalions lost as heavily as we did. Everyone found the place nerve-racking; the senior company commander and the adjutant of another battalion were sent down complete nervous wrecks.

For a long time it continued to be difficult to get wounded away, but things became a bit quieter in the late afternoon, and certain bearer parties of dismounted cavalry came up to help our stretcher-bearers. About 4 p.m. our padre carried Colonel Scott down to Bernafay Wood. It was a difficult deed well done, and one never to be forgotten by the survivors.

The night 19th-20th was somewhat noisy, and a noisy night in a wood is not at all restful. Isolated Huns, both in Longueval and the wood, put up streams of multi-coloured lights, and so gave us a veritable Brock's benefit. Here and there little scraps took place, and at one stage of the night the enemy threatened to rush our headquarters. Sergeant-Major Mercer deployed the servants, signallers, and runners with such wondrous speed that we had ample defence.

On the morning of the 20th other troops were hurried into the wood to continue the attack. They had to form up in the dark in the middle of the wood. Their task was more difficult than ours had been, and their success was less. Almost a month passed before Delville Wood was completely cleared of the Hun! He could not be hustled out; a carefully planned, systematic attack, supported by artillery, was required, and somewhere way back someone lacked the patience or intelligence to bring this about. Our men were wonderful. The majority of all ranks who went into Delville Wood were "original" 10th Essex. It was a very meagre skeleton that came out.

Of those whose deeds in the wood will ever be remembered I would name first Captain A. S. Tween. He was the only company commander not knocked out, and he took charge on the spot of all four companies. For his bravery and leadership here he was subsequently awarded the D.S.O. He was ably backed by Second-Lieut. W. G. P. Hunt, who was the senior officer left in "C" Company after "Archie" had been hit. Hunt had a most tranquil temperament in action, and of all the Battalion he probably felt the least strain in the wood. Every officer and man, I honestly believe, did his very best to carry out the task originally allotted. We just hadn't a dog's chance.

The 20th was another day of machine-gun and rifle fighting. On the night 20th-21st we were relieved by troops of another division. These suffered heavy casualties from enemy artillery fire while on their way up, and arrived too weak to take on the whole front. "C" Company, under Hunt, had an extra day to do in consequence. The relief itself was no easy matter. Sergeant Culver helped me very greatly in handling our guides. We had a good handful of these, as we were responsible for the guides of two other battalions of the Brigade, and the relieving troops were over two hours late.

Going out we suffered further casualties. Chiefest of these was our orderly-room clerk (Corporal Carter). He was with Mercer, when a shell, exploding close by, blew off his legs. Mercer put on two tourniquets and got the boy down to the nearest ambulance wagon, but the shock was too severe, and he died at Corbie either that day or the next. A very cheery boy and a most efficient clerk—we missed him very much. His brother had been one of the eight buried in the Ilôt the previous November. Such was the ill-luck of some families!

What a little band it was that collected in the Talus Boisé Valley that Friday morning! Cookers were waiting there with hot food, and we enjoyed, so far as exhausted men can enjoy, what they gave us. After a rest we marched on to Bray.

The 53rd Infantry Brigade's counter-attack in Delville Wood was the most miserable and at the same time most costly operation in which the Battalion took part during the time I was serving with it, and I believe no one will contradict me if I say that the Battalion never again played a part in any battle anything like so unsatisfactory as this one.

CHAPTER XIV.

A Holiday in the North.

Mont Des Cats.

A Trappist monastery, the scene of a cavalry action in 1914, in which one of the Kaiser's sons was killed. In 1918 this peaceful spot was devastated by shell-fire.

Our small and weary battalion rested in the fields near Bray for the remainder of the 21st of July. We were warned that a move by train was imminent, and very early next morning orders came for our personnel to march to Edgehill Station—a siding in the fields between Buire and Dernancourt—for entrainment. The hour fixed for this was 7 a.m. We started out from Bray about 5 a.m., and at 1 p.m. we were still lying in the fields around the siding. We didn't mind much how long we stayed there. We were in country we knew well; the day was fine; and we could bathe in the Ancre near by. But when afternoon came we thought we had better get a move on if we were to have anywhere to sleep that night, so we set to and off-loaded a supply train, and this then took us back. We were so small a battalion that there was no need for us to travel with the traditional " 40 hommes " to a carriage. Doors on the safe side were kept open, and we sat on the floor and dangled our feet outside. Passing through Corbie and Amiens we received tremendous cheers from the inhabitants. The German caps, pickelhaubes and other trophies displayed by us, as well as our general appearance, could leave no doubt in the minds of the civil population as to our immediate origin.

Late in the evening we detrained at Longpré-les-Saints-Cœurs, a small town on the main line between Amiens and Abbeville. We were well treated. No billets had been found for us, but Captain Tween rose to the occasion; his excellent French was often invaluable to us.

And now we heard that we were to leave the Somme altogether for an unknown destination in the north. After a most enjoyable Sunday at Longpré we entrained about midnight, and, after some nine hours' travelling, during which we passed along the coast through Etaples, Boulogne and Calais, we arrived at the detraining station—Arques—a short distance from St. Omer. We had thus been in France a year all but two days before we set eyes on any of the well-known ground on the older British front! After hot breakfast in a field adjoining the station we marched to the village of Blaringhem, where we remained in billets for nearly a week. What a difference between typical Somme villages and those in the north country here! Blaringhem was for the most part just an area of scattered houses. The battalion was thus widely spread, but the billets were much better than the average Somme ones.

The authorities were not slow in getting reinforcements up to us. On Sunday, July 23rd, during our short stay at Longpré, six officers had joined us. These were Second-Lieuts. A. C. Pochin (returned to duty at his own special request, although not too well recovered from his wound of July 1st), J. E. Astle, F. Hancock, A. J. Southcott, D. H. V. Dray, and L. H. Carson. While our train was halted at St. Omer on our northward journey a divisional staff officer pushed a Coldstream Guards C.S.M. into the C.O.'s carriage, and introduced him as "a new subaltern for you." William Skeat was just the man we wanted at the moment. He had gone to France with the original Expeditionary Force, and though he had seen service on every possible occasion, had never been wounded. His "word of command" was magnificent, and became a well-known institution in the brigade.

Our strength and casualty reports were still far from ready for despatch, and we decided that the only possible way to get a correct return out, and at the same time find out as much as possible about our casualties, would be by holding a battalion roll call. This was done at once, and the five to six hours so used were well spent, for useful information as to each individual casualty was obtained in almost every case, and we were able to communicate it both to the base and the relations of the man concerned.

No other physical and mental rest can quite equal that of the first two or three days following a hard battle, spent in pleasant country in the sunshine. To lie on one's back in the shadow of a hedge and breathe

the clean air, and be worried by no one and by nothing—who could desire more?

We were not left at Blaringhem too long—a week, I think. After two days' march, the second of which was very long and tiring, we arrived at the Mont des Cats, and went into billets there. Those readers who do not already know this hill will have no difficulty in finding it when visiting the northern battlefields, for as soon as one leaves Cassel on the eastward journey it is the next, and only, dominating feature in the landscape. Here the billets were more scattered than ever.

Major J. Crookenden, D.S.O., the Buffs, a regular soldier fresh home from the Cameroons' expedition, took us over the day before we left Blaringhem, and remained in temporary command till September 18th. While at the Mont des Cats we were inspected by General Maxse. There wasn't a very big muster, but it was quite a smart turn-out. As usual he cursed me heartily!

We were never long in one place these days. I forget what corps the Division was in while we were at the Mont des Cats, but we were moved from it to the II. Anzac Corps as a temporary measure. This Corps was holding the line in front of Armentières, and its other two divisions were Anzac. This transfer necessitated a southerly march by us. On Saturday, August 5th, we marched from Mont des Cats to Estaires. General Higginson, to avoid the heat of the day, started all these marches at dawn. Remember that our troops were scattered in outlying farms averaging three miles from the Brigade starting point, and you will at once see that breakfasts had to be served soon after midnight. For the first two hours of these early morning marches no one was in a particularly good humour! But the policy was sound, and we had very few march casualties in consequence. During our stay at Mont des Cats two more officers had joined us, viz., Second-Lieuts. E. H. Brown and S. R. Bonney.

Estaires was a jolly little town, and we enjoyed two days there. Billets were very much above the average. The men had much wanted baths. Many newly-arrived Anzac troops were here; they were eager for news of the Somme fighting, and still more eager to secure souvenirs. Some of our men had a superfluity of the latter, and through the agency of one of our worthiest traders, by name Goldberg, obtained good prices for them.

Early on Monday morning, August 7th, we marched eastwards to Erquinghem, the westerly suburb of Armentières. Part of the 18th Division was already in the line S.E. of that town, and we were moved up in close support. The whole battalion lived in a large disused factory on the canal bank. I believe it was an old dye works, for there were many large and multi-coloured vats. So many men were told off to each vat. Really quite a comfortable place, with excellent swimming facilities at our very door. After the Somme battle we found this area extremely quiet, and though divisional headquarters a few miles back received some attention from enemy artillery, we ourselves sustained but one slight casualty. Lindsay, the M.O.'s orderly, was sleeping full sprawl in the garden one sunny afternoon while our A.A. guns were busy peppering a Boche 'plane. A tiny portion of shell case disturbed Lindsay's slumber. His face was bandaged for a few days; he had to be inoculated against tetanus, and reported a casualty.

Huge drafts from the 8th Essex Cyclist Battalion joined us at Erquinghem. We were glad to have them—some 250 to 300 in all—for they were seasoned

Territorials of good physique, and for the most part Essex men. And they, too, were glad to get a chance of doing something in the real fighting lines; two years on lonely seawalls in time of war is not an inspiring job for any able-bodied man. Their arrival brought us about up to strength.

After a few days it was decided that the 53rd Brigade was not required at Erquinghem; it could be spared for training. Early on Saturday, August 12th, we set out for a large tented camp just south of Bailleul. This camp was very pleasantly placed in a large grass field at the foot of the Mont de Lille. The whole brigade was concentrated here with Brigade H.Q. in the town. Our training was now hustled on with pace. The visit of His Majesty the King on the Monday following our arrival did us all good. There was nothing unusual in the training carried out in this area. We were at it from 7 a.m. onwards till 1 p.m. Then after luncheon the officers usually had some staff tour or other to attend. The close defence of the village of Neuve Eglise—four miles away—provided us with a subject for much work and discussion. Officers still continued to arrive. Second-Lieuts. F. W. Goddard, J. J. Willoughby and H. C. H. Hawksworth reported at the Bailleul camp.

Conferences at Brigade H.Q. were frequent during this period. Early on we were led to believe that we might be required for an attack in the Ypres area, but towards the end of our second week our destination was fixed as being much further south. On August 25th we left Bailleul by train, at some time in the dead of night detrained at a wayside station between St. Pol and Arras, and marched thence to a small smelly village known as Chelers. Here we were warned we were to spend a fortnight in intense training ere we moved once more into real battle.

CHAPTER XV.

Preparing for Thiepval.

The day after we arrived at Chelers there was a jocular rumour current that our next big job would be Thiepval. We knew that many unsuccessful attempts had been made on this stronghold, but had been too far north to know the details either of what had happened or what was pending.

At Chelers we were in the Third Army training area. A mile west of the village the manœuvre area proper was reached. This was of considerable size, and its boundary lines were marked with huge red flags. Inside the flags troops could perform any evolutions their commanders wished; outside the flags it was a case of "Beware of the crops." The training area was certainly good, and we were given heaps to do. My memories of Chelers consist chiefly of a rapidly recurring cycle made up as follows :—Conference on the training ground, morning manœuvre, brigade conference on the ground, afternoon field work (usually a repetition of the morning manœuvre), a long and final conference, march home, tea, orderly room. Most of us found Chelers a little tiring and trying—all "spare time" was filled in at "wiring-drill." We had been at war some time before this most efficient method of wiring was established. Any morning or afternoon, when there was no training on area, platoons were kept busy at building (and afterwards taking down!) wire entanglements.

With the 10th Essex in France.

On our brigade field days the 10th Essex was always trained as an assaulting battalion. We knew quite well it was our turn to toe the line along with the 8th Suffolk Regiment this time, and we meant to put everything we had into making it a success. On one tremendous day, when General Maxse was present, we did a brigade attack under an imaginary barrage. This was the first time we had trained to attack under a creeping barrage, which was represented in the practice by a line of non-combatants carrying blue signal flags walking fifty to sixty yards ahead of the first line troops. After conference and luncheon we repeated the show in the afternoon. A final conference took us straight into a tremendous thunderstorm. General Higginson finished what he wanted to say, and then we made the best of it! Truly it was the heaviest thunderstorm we experienced in 1916—every man jack of us was wet through to the skin long before he was half-way home! We marched away from this area on the 8th of September. After three days' trek the Battalion arrived at Acheux, and went into a hut camp in Acheux Wood, some seven miles west of Thiepval. This was a very pleasant beech wood, and so long as the weather remained fair was an enjoyable spot. Rain, however, quickly turned the approaches from the main road to the camp into quagmires. On the whole this first stay at Acheux Wood was dry.

Training was continued during this time on the ground west of Lealvillers. This area was not large enough for Brigade days—we were not sorry. The chief excitement about this training was that on our march to and from the training ground we often met parties of Boche prisoners being marched to work. This arrangement was quite novel at the time, and we were all very satisfied to have "Eyes left" from these parties, ordered by the Boche n.c.o. in charge.

Day by day we expected to be moved up, and our first orders were for a move to Bouzincourt on Saturday afternoon, September 16th. These orders, however, were postponed, and it was early on Sunday, the 17th, that we set out. Bouzincourt was much fuller of troops than it had been in the old days. I was lucky enough to get hold of the room I had had in August, '15. We were called to Brigade H.Q. during the afternoon, and reconnaissances of the Thiepval Wood area were ordered for Monday; our troops were to be moved there on Monday night to relieve troops of another division then in the line. Early on Monday morning these orders were all cancelled, and in the afternoon we marched back to Forceville—a wet march so far as I remember.

During our short stay at Bouzincourt, however, certain awards for the July fighting had come through. Major Tween received the D.S.O., C.S.M. Mercer the D.C.M., Sergeant Jaggs and five others the M.M. These were our first awards for the Somme offensive; they bucked everyone up.

Forceville was about one mile south of Acheux. On arrival there we shook down in an extremely muddy hut camp. Recent rain and occupation had turned the ground between the huts into a swampy condition, but we were quite happy to know that we were not to be used prematurely; we wanted a good fight straight-away on arriving in the line. After eight weeks' rest and training we weren't keen on having our freshness and prowess worn away by holding trenches for a considerable time before being called on to attack.

This 18th day of September, 1916, was a real red-letter day for the Battalion. Lieut.-Colonel C. W. Frizell, M.C., came to take command of us that evening at Forceville. He was just the man the Battalion wanted. His war experience, his military genius, and

Brigadier-General
C. W. Frizell.
D.S.O., M.C.

Sergts. Bush, Brooks,
and Bishork.

"Round the old Camp-fire"
In the Trenches,
Somewhere in France.

his tact were everything officers and men could require of their commander. Frizell went to the war with the 1st R. Berkshire Regiment in the original Expeditionary Force as the Battalion Machine Gun Officer. At Mons in 1914 he had sat between his two guns; he did the same on the Aisne and at Ypres. Here he was wounded. Returning early in 1915, he served successively as company commander, adjutant, second in command. At Loos he was in command of his battalion when it attacked a certain well-known Fosse. Prior to coming to us, Colonel Frizell had for some six weeks been in command of a battalion of the Wiltshire Regiment. Here was the man we wanted, and he wasted no time in getting to work.

The Forceville camp was really too bad. Closer acquaintance had revealed that many roofs leaked and the presence at night of numbers of large rats. With everyone's approval, therefore, we moved on the 20th to our old camp in Acheux Wood. Here for a few days we enjoyed the use of a camp capable of holding two battalions. We spread ourselves. Training went on every morning, but we weren't overdosed with parades. Colonel Frizell had been out too long not to know the danger of over-training.

We did not receive many " other rank " reinforcements during September, but one day a large batch of officers turned up. This included Captains L. J. Beirne (a grey-haired Boer War veteran), and W. Robinson, and the following subalterns : H. Yeates, L. Coulshaw, V. S. Beevor, F. Lussignea, M. A. Levy, and L. F. Cooke. We were thus much over strength in officers, but it was decreed that only three officers a company should be allowed into the next engagement. A certain nucleus of n.c.o.'s was also to be left out.

On Friday evening, the 22nd of September, General

Higginson held a large and long conference at his headquarters at Forceville. In addition to the usual attendance of C.O.'s and adjutants, all company commanders of the four battalions were required to attend. The General's small room would only just hold us.

Here we learnt of the pending operation. The 18th Division would assault and capture the stronghold of Thiepval. Almost three months had passed since, on July 1st, the first of a series of unsuccessful attacks had been launched on this buttress immediately south of the Ancre. I believe every one of these attempts had been made from the west (Thiepval Wood). Our attack was to come from the south (Authuille Wood), the assaulting troops straddling that formidable spur, the Leipzig Redoubt, in their advance on the village. So far as the 53rd Infantry Brigade was concerned, the 8th Suffolk were to take the right, the 10th Essex the left; the 8th Norfolk were for mopping up and carrying; the 6th R. Berkshire Regiment reserve. Artillery support, greater than we had before, was to be forthcoming; six to eight tanks were to help us. Indeed, nothing which could help us and could be arranged was to be omitted. The conference was one of the most useful conceivable. Every company commander came away with a clear idea as to the general plan of things.

Early next morning the then Brigade-Major—Captain C. H. Hoare—was to be seen in the fields between Forceville and Lealvillers marking out a representation of the trenches we were to attack. Sappers spitlocked and notice-boarded the main features as quickly as possible, and towards the close of the afternoon we were able to carry out a full-dressed rehearsal.

Three objectives were given us: The first was Schwaben trench, the line along the south side of

With the 10th Essex in France. 151

Thiepval; the second, the line of the northern edge of the village; the third, the north side of Schwaben Redoubt. This gave us a good 1½ miles to do altogether.

We did one trial run over our training course. Signal flags were again used to denote the barrage, and the teaching of "keeping up close to the barrage" was the chief lesson of the day. We marched back to camp very confident; indeed, I heard several men make bloodthirsty anticipatory remarks to the various parties of Hun prisoners we met.

On Sunday afternoon, September 24th, the Battalion marched to dug-outs at Crucifix Corner, a well-known spot just east of the Ancre at Aveluy. The Colonel took the company commanders on ahead so that they could study the ground to be stormed from a suitable O.P. (Conniston post, it was called). We had a good view from here. The brick portions of Thiepval we had seen in August, 1915, were now no more, and except for the blackened stumps of a well-known line of apple trees on the south side of the village, Thiepval was devoid of all specific landmarks. Early on the morning of the 25th reconnaissance of our line of approach and our assembly trenches was carried out. The remainder of the day was spent in conferences and fitting out for battle. There were two brigade and two battalion conferences that day. Colonel Frizell was splendidly clear with his instructions. As zero hour was not early we were allowed to spend another night in peace.

We had a great thrill on the evening of the 25th—we saw our first tanks! They lumbered along by Crucifix Corner, while every officer and man stood on the bank alongside the road, interestedly watching, perchance cheering. These went up Blighty Valley to "lie up" in concealed positions till zero next day.

CHAPTER XVI.

THE STORMING OF THIEPVAL.

Thiepval was a household word in England long before September 26th, 1916. The papers had been full of it; everyone was wondering when it would fall, and to whom. Many pages could be written as to the importance of the position to the enemy, and his desire to retain it. I will content myself with quoting one passage from our Divisional Commander's message of the 25th September:—

"Great importance has been attached to Thiepval by the Germans, who have issued frequent orders to all concerned to hold it ' at all costs.' They have even boasted in writing that it is impregnable. The 180th Regiment of Wurttemburgers have withstood attacks on Thiepval for two years, but the 18th Division will take it to-morrow."

For the first time in compiling this chronicle I have assistance from records. We started our approach march at 5.15 a.m., "*A*" Company (right assaulting company), under Captain L. J. Beirne, leading the way. Next came "*D*" Company (left assaulting), under Captain G. J. Thompson; third, "*B*" Company, with Lieutenant F. W. Goddard in temporary command; last, "*C*," under the imperturbable Hunt. Our route was by way of Authuille Wood, Wood Post, and Pip Street—the last-named thoroughfare being a main communication trench. The morning was fine and bright, with but little mist for September. I never saw the battalion more cheerful, more confident, or more intent. Where Pip Street crossed the old German front line (O.G.1.) General Higginson stood to say a cheery word to every man as he passed. He was on his way back from his last reconnaissance before battle. Need I enlarge on the moral effect of his cheery "Good morning"?

One of our most classic incidents occurred in this march up Pip Street. It was just the remark of one of those wonderful "B" Company men from Stratford (by Bow). Somewhere just beyond O.G.1. he saw a somewhat decayed leg sticking up from the side of the trench, covered, to some extent, anyhow, by what had obviously been a green silk sock; the good quality of this article was still obvious. With a loud "Lor', Bill! What a toff!" this worthy from Stratford, E., passed on to his battle position. This was one of that class of priceless remarks peculiar to the British race in times of stress.

Forming-up was complete by about 8.30 a.m., and Colonel Frizell then went round all companies in their battle positions. Everything was perfectly correct. A fairly quiet morning ensued. Our guns, which had pounded Thiepval and Schwaben for days past, kept up a steady fire. The men's dinners were early, for zero had been fixed for 12.35 p.m. At that time to the second (a great deal of effort had been put into the synchronisation of watches beforehand) a heavy barrage came down some 60 yards ahead of our front line. This was the signal we were waiting for; the infantry moved forward. The attack went well from the start. At 12.48 p.m. the first objective was captured; the second fell at 1.13 p.m. The latter step meant that our leading troops had passed through the village, and that our Norfolk moppers were busy at work clearing Huns from the multitude of dug-outs in Thiepval. Our "B" and "C" Companies were in the thick of this, too, for they both followed close on the assaulting lines. The Suffolks on our right had done equally well, but on the extreme left of the village the 54th Brigade was finding the Hun strongholds very formidable, and our troops were harassed by machine-gun fire from the extreme N.W. of the village.

An hour's halt on the second objective formed part of the plan. This was very necessary; the troops wanted breath and reorganisation. We had already sustained a number of casualties—seven among twelve officers being out of action. In this assault Second-Lieuts. L. F. Cooke, S. R. Bonney, and A. C. Pochin were killed, and Second-Lieut. C. H. Walker mortally wounded; Captain L. J. Beirne, Lieutenant F. W. Goddard, and Second-Lieut. H. S. Richards wounded. Among W.O.'s and N.C.O.'s the casualties, too, were heavy—C.S.M.'s F. Mercer, M.C., D.C.M., F. Bush, M.M., and C. O. Parker were killed. Those left carried on in the true spirit, and at the end of the hour's halt made a bold attempt to push forward and capture Schwaben Redoubt. A gallant start was brought to a halt by enfilade machine-gun fire from the N.W. of Thiepval, and our line halted and dug in some 100 yards in advance of the second objective. No further advance was made on the 26th September.

I have recounted the assault on Thiepval very briefly in the above paragraphs, and made it clear that we did not make good our third and final objective. At Brigade H.Q. anxiety prevailed, and a further barrage and assault were ordered for the evening. These, however, were later cancelled. Subsequently we heard that General Maxse had said something like this : " If you take and hold your first objective you do well; if you take and hold your second objective you do just about as much as is humanly possible; and higher command sets a third objective in case of possible breakdown of the enemy's morale."

At Thiepval the enemy's morale did by no means go. The capture of the village itself was a good day's work when you remember how long it had resisted all attempts. Let us just see what had been done besides:—The British line had been advanced a thousand yards (a long distance in those days); nearly 800 prisoners had been captured by the 18th Division; and, perhaps most important of all, we had given the Huns' morale a very nasty jar indeed. The 10th Essex casualties that night amounted to 8 officers and 170 other ranks.

I have by me some brief notes in pencil, compiled immediately after our relief from the line by various N.C.O.'s and men. Some extracts from them are of special interest for various reasons.

Sergeant Purkiss, of "*B*" Company, wrote: "Every man went over in the best of spirits and smoking the usual cigarette, behind the best barrage I have ever seen. The great point of interest all through the advance was the Tanks. To see these cumbersome, elephantine Dreadnoughts ploughing their way up on a flank was too ludicrous, and every man turned round and split his sides with laughter. . . . The greater number of Boche either surrendered or fled, but one section displayed great bravery in defending the village. This was the 180th Minenwerfer Battery. . . . but the appearance of a Tank coming up the 'High Street' put the wind up them, and you can guess the rest. On resuming the advance the Germans on the right flank, quite 800 strong, formed up en masse, but our L.G. Sergeant (Sergeant Spurling) opened fire and cut them down like corn."

(Though perhaps this packet of Germans did not exceed 300, it looked very formidable, and all observers reported a counter-attack forming up on the right side of Thiepval. Possibly these troops did get out of their dug-outs and trenches with the intention of counter-attacking, but they gave up hope almost at once, and marched down by way of Nab Valley as prisoners. It was the densest mass of prisoners I ever saw come in.)

". . . . A special point of interest which inspired all the boys was the act of our company commander, Lieutenant Goddard, who, although wounded, continued to carry on, improving the position of his company before going to the rear."

Corporal Barrett and Private Cooksey, both of "*B*" Company, also recorded the excellent work done by Goddard. Other companies seemed to lack men with a bent for journalism, for I have no original reports from any other companies in my possession.

The night 26th-27th was fairly quiet. The Hun put up his usual post-assault firework display, and pounded away erratically with his artillery throughout the night.

At 6 a.m., 27th, General Higginson was up in the village, and accompanied Colonels Frizell and Hill (O.C. 8th Suffolk) round their respective front lines. Consolidation had been carried out satisfactorily, and now final reorganisation and distribution of troops was completed.

We held on tight to our gains throughout the 27th. Indeed, we had several bombing fights with the Hun in Martin's Lane and Bulgar Trench; in these we were helped by our Stokes' mortars. The Hun increased his artillery activity during that day, and towards evening commenced to play on and around the dug-out Battalion H.Q. in the village. This dug-out was only some 300 yards from our front line, was large, and of course well known to the Hun, and now carried a wireless aerial! This, I am sure, the Huns could see from Schwaben. From the point of view of personal comfort we wished wireless had never been discovered.

On the 28th September the advance was continued, but we were considered too weak to assault again, so a fresh battalion, the 7th Queen's, was sent through us. We continued to act as garrison of Thiepval till the morning of the 29th, when we were relieved by the 6th Royal Berks Regiment. Second-Lieut. A. Carpenter, who had done excellent work as Intelligence Officer during the battle, was wounded in this relief.

After spending the remainder of the day in and around O.G.1., we marched back in the early night to billets at Forceville. We were glad our commanders were pleased with us; we were delighted to hear that the name of our Division was in everyone's mouth from the C.-in-C., who called personally at Divisional H.Q. to congratulate General Maxse, to the traffic control man in Bouzincourt, who, on finding we belonged to the 18th Division, said, "Well, you ain't supposed to go along this road in that direction, but seeing as 'ow you took Teepval, you shall"; but on the night of the 29th September we wanted but two things in the world, viz., a good hot meal and undisturbed slumber. When we arrived at Forceville we found both.

Saturday, 30th September, we washed ourselves and had a battalion roll-call. Colonel Frizell addressed the men; in return they cheered spontaneously. On October 1st General Higginson addressed us. Sometimes now I think war is well worth while when it means hearing a man such as Higginson say to an assembled battalion: " Colonel Frizell, officers, warrant officers, non-commissioned officers, and men of the 10th Service Battalion the Essex Regiment, I desire to thank you. . . . ." I can write no more of what the Brigade Commander said that day; such speeches are the sacred property of those entitled to be so addressed. There can be no such incidents as these in peace time.

On October 2nd an empty goods train (after a great deal of persuasion) conveyed us to a rest area.

CHAPTER XVII.

OCTOBER, 1916.

40 HOMMES. 8 CHEVAUX EN LONG.
"*Free Tickets to the Battlefields.*"

Our journey from Belle Eglise—a well-known British siding made for the 1916 Somme offensive—to Candas, some 10½ miles distant, was long and tedious. A returning supply train was once more destined to remove us from the forward area, and once again we sat in fields around the siding and waited and waited. The autumn evenings and early nights were cool now, and we were glad of our great-coats. Ten weeks had passed since we had squatted at "Edgehill," waiting for a train to remove us to a rest area; we had fought but one battle since that time. What changes had come over the old battalion during that period! Twenty-four officer and 516 other rank reinforcements had been absorbed, and 9 officers and 195 other ranks had become casualties. Truly, the "Original Tenth" had about come to an end! This may have been the case in personnel, but not in spirit, and our "esprit de battalion," carefully nurtured from the earliest days at Shorncliffe, was now a very real and worthy possession. Happily, too, some of our originals were patched up and rejoining. Captain C. M. Ridley turned up at Forceville, and took over "A" Company. A little later Neild, who had been vegetating since Christmas, 1915, as Brigade Intelligence Officer, rejoined, and became Ridley's second-in-command.

Eventually, somewhere after 10 p.m. we were allowed into our compartments—they were of the hommes-chevaux type. Another long wait, but the train did get out before midnight, and just before dawn we were detrained in another field near Candas. A jolly little march of 8 to 9 miles followed. Early morning marches after protracted train journeys are to be placed among the most trying episodes of the war. Montigny-les-Jongleurs, our destination, was reached just after 8 a.m. We had breakfast and went to bed. I seemed to have hardly got to sleep before I was awakened by an orderly, who informed me that the General and the Staff Captain were in the mess! I went straight down in my pyjamas. They had just called in to see if we were comfortable, and to get news of our train journey! General Higginson was certainly a little over-zealous occasionally. But I had saved the Colonel being disturbed, so went back to bed full of self-righteousness.

Montigny-les-Jongleurs was a poky and somewhat

smelly little place. Its name was the only beautiful thing about it. We rested about a fortnight. A small draft or two came along, and received the usual kind of welcome; the band, which had dwindled down to about 8 performers during the summer offensive, was re-formed, and practised ardently; there were the usual inter-company football matches. For those who liked exploring, there was the small town of Auxi-le-Chateau, on the Authie, some four miles away, and some glorious beech woods and ravines around Bernâtre.

Our rest was not unduly prolonged. On October 13th we set out to march to Albert. Three days only were spent in this, and after halting a night at Montrelet, and another at Herissart, we arrived in Albert on the afternoon of the 15th. We quite enjoyed these two days' trek on our very own—the other battalions had been moved up by 'bus.

An operation was threatening. South of the Ancre we had captured the whole of what may be called the Hessian system, bar one trench—Regina. The troops already forward wanted one more brigade to bring them up to the requisite battle thickness; the 53rd Brigade was selected. General Maxse, however, had had enough of "loaning us"—Delville Wood could not be forgotten in three months—and he consequently arranged with higher command that the "18th Division, less all its troops except 53rd Brigade group," should go into the battle.

We marched up because we were to be in reserve this time—it was our turn. The weather was now breaking up, however, and the condition of the battlefield beyond Pozières and Courcelette terribly heavy, to say the least of it. On the 17th September we took over the front line for two days so that the assaulting troops could dry themselves once more. They relieved us on the 19th, but again the attack was postponed on account of the condition of the ground. It was now decided to go on holding the line by 48-hour shifts, either shift to be ready to make the attack on the first possible day. We struck it the first morning of our second shift in, and over we went, with the 8th Norfolk Regiment on our left, Canadians on our right.

Regina Trench was just a minor operation—an advance of 250 yards, and the capture of a single trench. I have already indicated, however, that it was an important operation, and the fact that in it we ourselves captured over a hundred Germans, reveals the importance attached to Regina Trench by our enemy.

Only two companies were used to attack—"B" and "C." Very few casualties were suffered in the actual assault. In holding the line for the next 48 hours, however, we had a bad time from enemy guns, which, from their positions in Loupart Wood, had our new line in enfilade. During these two days 6 officers were wounded; 18 men killed, 96 wounded. Lieutenant J. A. B. Thompson ("C" Company) and Second-Lieut. V. S. Beevor ("B" Company) were subsequently awarded the Military Cross for gallant leadership in this fight. On relief on the evening of the 23rd we went down to Albert—7 miles away.

The conditions of existence during this autumn campaign of 1916 were very hard and trying. Our base, Albert, was 7 miles away, and between this town (very overcrowded indeed) and the line there was no decent dry accommodation. The condition of the front line area was naturally very bad, for it received alternating showers of rain and high explosive without interruption. The tracks up, too, had not yet been properly organised and laid. More often than not, therefore, we arrived already wet, after a 7-mile march, to hold a very wet and muddy trench. On relief we had to get back to Albert. Some power kindly put 3 or 4 'buses on to ply between Ovillers and Albert during our relief, and these did help our worst cases of fatigue and feet greatly. Remember, too, that for the most part it was physically impossible for anyone to lie down in the line—drowning in mud would have been the result! Even Albert itself was dreadfully muddy at this time; in the gutter outside our billets in the Rue d'Aveluy it was quite 9 inches deep.

Operations were to be continued, and we were told that possibly we should be required to advance on Miraumont in a few days' time. This job would involve the crossing of the Ancre and its marshes, and, in view of the weather, sounded, to say the least of it, ambitious. Indeed, rain so delayed operations that on the 29th October the 53rd Brigade had to relieve the other troops of the Division now in the line, who had been waiting to continue our advance of the 21st.

In the first instance we were in support positions in and about Rifle Dump. Rain fell heavily during our stay here, and every form of shelter the individual man erected for himself in Zollern Trench fell in. On the afternoon of the 31st October we went up in very little packets (twos and three) to relieve the 6th Royal Berks Regiment in Regina Trench. The portion we took over was that straddling a well-known long valley leading down to Miraumont—Death Valley, it was named subsequently. Battalion H.Q. moved up to Hessian Trench, and from here the whole of our front line could be surveyed. We suffered one casualty from enemy artillery during the relief. Captain C. M. Ridley, better known perhaps as "dear old Riddles," was killed shortly after he had arrived in the front line. A very enthusiastic soldier and greatly missed.

We buried him near the Battalion H.Q. in Zollern Trench we had just left.

The next two or three days were uneventful. The ration of rain was somewhat reduced and we kept ourselves warm baling out the mud. "D" Company on the left of Death Valley was in a particularly muddy stretch, whilst "A" Company on the right was in chalk and therefore relatively dry. "B" and "C" Companies in support positions had nothing specific to complain of; they had to content themselves with one variety or other of the general grouse.

I believe we were kept in the line until November 3rd. In addition to Ridley's death I remember only two other incidents worthy of recording. On either the 1st or 2nd of November as I reached "C" Company H.Q. I met a stretcher. On it was our falsetto singer—Shelton. He was smiling very brightly and smoking a cigarette. I asked him what had happened, and he told me that in clearing out his position in the trench he had picked up a buried German bomb. The pick had pulled the string, but Shelton had no idea that anything had happened until the explosion came and his leg was shattered. I left him smiling; he died very shortly afterwards from shock, and those who were back where he died saw the same smile to the end, I'm sure. There were many Sheltons in the 10th Essex.

General Higginson, on one of his early morning visits to the line, stood with me on the top of our Battalion H.Q. at Hessian Trench. Out from Death Valley two men came rolling heavily, evidently bound for Battalion H.Q. I knew them at once. They were two of our very best signallers and had been out for hours during the early morning (it was now about 7 a.m.) patching up the lines with the forward companies. "Was there a rum ration last night?" asked the General. "Yes, sir," I replied. "I believe those men are drunk," he said. I explained that I did not, my reasons being knowledge of their work during the past six hours and of the method of rum issue in the Battalion. They were sent for the doctor's immediate examination, and he found them suffering from intense fatigue only. I was glad, told the Colonel, and forgot all about the incident until some five weeks later General Higginson wrote to know what the doctor had determined. Any casual reader may now realise the degree of discipline maintained in the 53rd Infantry Brigade.

It seemed a longer trek than ever back to Albert this time, and it was well past midnight before we all fetched up. Everyone was dead beat and there were some cases of trench foot. One man, carrying a Lewis gun, was found leaning against an old lamp-post fast asleep!

Next day we had to march back to Warloy, as our Corps had no right to the billets we were in at Albert. Truly the infantry in those days had no place whereon to lay their head.

CHAPTER XVIII.

NOVEMBER AND DECEMBER, 1916.

When we set out for Warloy we thought we had seen the last of the mud and slush of the Pozières-Courcelette area for several weeks. Another push was in sight, however, and for this we marched up again. One noteworthy event occurred during our brief rest. The Divisional Commander pinned ribbons on the breasts of various officers and men who had been awarded decorations for gallant conduct and good leadership in July or September. At first it was hoped to hold a brigade parade but the weather made this inadvisable. In the end the ceremony took place in the quaint and small village concert room. The recipients marched to the platform one by one; the onlookers had seats in the gallery. Of the Essex Captains, W. G. P. Hunt and G. J. Thompson received M.C.'s for their work at Thiepval.

A night at Albert, and then on the 11th we moved to the support line around Rifle Dump. Once again the 6th R. Berks Regiment was in the line in front of us. We knew that an attack was to take place further north. This came off at dawn on the 13th. We took no active part in this operation, in which Beaumont Hamel, Beaucourt, and St. Pierre Divion fell to the Naval and 51st Divisions. Before dawn we had come into battle formation on the right of the Royal Berkshires, so that in the event of the enemy completely breaking before the attack north of the Ancre, we might swoop down on Miraumont. The heavy fog rather messed up all ideas of exploiting, and our operations on the 13th were confined to active patrolling in and around some old gun-pits in front of Regina Trench. Captain Hunt, Lieutenant J. A. B. Thompson, and Sergeant Culver were the leaders of these, and did extremely well. An encounter took place on the steps of a Hun dug-out, and the Hun came off worst; a very nice pickelhaube was brought back; it belonged to a Hun marine.

The 55th Brigade relieved us on the night 13th-14th, for this brigade was due for a fight, and we went down to Tara Hill. Here we spent the remainder of the night under tarpaulin bivouac sheets on the hillside. About midday on the 14th General Maxse came along and collected the officers round him, to tell them of the operations of the 13th. He really interested us much more when he opened up on the recent amendment to a paragraph in K.R. which deals with the shaving of the upper lip, and one or two "young officers" looked supremely uncomfortable. His remark, too, that the 53rd Brigade had probably done with active operations for the year 1916 did not leave us cold, and later in the day we had further cause to rejoice—accommodation was found for us in Albert. Here we stayed till Sunday, the 19th. The period was uneventful except for enemy shelling. As we lay in bed one morning violent explosions occurred at regular intervals. No whizz or hiss preceded, but a very considerable racket followed them. A good many of us were lying on the floor in that bedroom, and we argued hotly as to whether "they" were "his" or "ours." We felt so far off from the Hun in Albert then that we couldn't believe a shell could arrive from "him" with such a velocity that no warning whizz would be heard, and the majority favoured the idea that some new Naval gun of ours was in action in the château grounds near by. After breakfast the padre and doctor went for a stroll to inspect this wonderful new piece, and found a new series of huge craters instead. What an expense and trouble the Hun had had for nothing, for not one casualty had been inflicted by his Long Lizzie on her first appearance. Marmont Bridge was missed by a few feet only, and this shell nearly collected our Q.M. Stores, but actually only dug up a certain portion of main road. Sergeant J. G. Culver received his commission (into the battalion, too) while we were at Albert this time.

We did not set out on our march back for the Christmas vacation without being startled several times with warning orders for further activities; indeed, when we turned in on the 18th we actually had orders for forward movement next day. Somewhere after midnight these were cancelled, and shortly afterwards orders for the trek back came in. We knew we were due for the Abbeville area; our billeting officer, Hancock, was already there, and we were out to make the most of the holiday.

The march back took nine days. Of course it needn't have done so had we been wanted at Abbeville desperately. As it was we were marched to fit in with available housing, and our course was consequently somewhat zigzagged. The whole trek was quite enjoyable, and so far as I remember we got wet once only. This was on the last day but one, and I remember it well as being the only time I "had a row" with a French civilian. This gentleman was Maire of the village which was our destination that day. We arrived wet through. The billeting officer reported the Maire an obstructionist, and billets were

Standing: —, Hughes, Burrows, Purkis, Chaplin, Drake, Gentry, Stammers, Harris, —, Smy, Smythe, Walker, Gascoine, Cox, Cole, Lovett, —, Hendrie, Cole, —, Fisher, Willett, Allison, —, Harrington.
Sitting: Hall, Silver, Smith, Pitt, Mann, Brown, Boyce, Juller, Brown, Treasure, —, Harvey, O'Brien, Sutliffe, Birch, Starling.
Front Row: Major Lewis, C S.M. Jaggs, Col. Frizell, R.Q.M.S Burrell, Capt. Chell.

N.C.O.'s GROUP, XMAS, 1916.

not ready for the men to march straight into as they
arrived. Well—billets weren't too bad by the evening, and the Maire and I parted on reasonable terms
of affection.

Lamotte Buleux—destined to be our home in the
rest area for the next five weeks—was a good clean
village lying about one mile west of Crecy Forest.
The inhabitants had not been disturbed by many
British soldiers at that date, and were glad to have us
with them. Life at Lamotte was tranquil and quite
undisturbed by war, and the weeks slipped by very
quickly. Some new officers and some small drafts of
men arrived. Of the former I remember the arrival
of Second-Lieuts. J. G. Wood and E. W. Daniel; they
turned up in an old fly from Abbeville—surely a
unique way to join a battalion on active service!
Hardaker and Haile, too, joined at this time. Our
training was not too severe, but our football was
strenuous. Leave had opened a day or two before
we left Albert, and we rejoiced, for at this time there
were a goodly number of "old originals," who had
never had leave. They went away in big batches
now, and were all "worked off" before we returned
to the line.

Our stay at Lamotte is memorable chiefly on
account of the Christmas we spent there. We knew
fully a month ahead that unless the very unexpected
happened, we should be there in settled residence
over the festival. Colonel Frizell sent Major Tween
and the padre to Paris to shop, and certainly the pork
that was missed in 1915 was made up for by the turkeys of 1916. Every Company had an excellent
banquet, and there was no shortage of good beer.
The Colonel visited the men's messes in turn to drink
their healths in accordance with time-honoured
custom. This ceremony went with great éclat, but

those of the Headquarters who were in such positions in the "C" Company mess that they had to drink the port substitute "C" Company provided rued the day the next few hours.

Tween and the padre were responsible also for the officers' dinner in the evening. This was a splendid affair for active service, and for once we messed as a battalion. A good dinner and a good noise, and we went to our billets wishing that we hadn't to get up early next morning for our photos to be taken.

A day or two later we moved, but only to another village in the same area—Millencourt by name. This move was made for training reasons. Near Millencourt was a Brigade area in which the German line before and in Miraumont was dug out in full scale replica. Here for a fortnight we practised storming Hill 130 (south of Petit Miraumont), crossing the Ancre, and storming Miraumont itself. It was at the conclusion of one of these field days that General Maxse introduced our new Divisional Commander, Major-General R. P. Lee, C.B., to us. General Maxse left a few days later to take up the command of the XVIII. Corps.

Early in January we commenced our forward march. This time no nine days were spent on trek; after four days' marching we reached Martinsart Wood. Our halts on the way up were at Beaumetz, Gezaincourt, and Herissart. The cold weather of early 1917 was beginning, and after the comforts that had been inflicted on us in the Abbeville area, we found our wooden shacks in Martinsart Wood distinctly cool at night.

In November, 1916, the scheme for the steady removal of N.C.O.'s to cadet schools in England commenced, and for a considerable time we were expected to send away two a week. This was a great drain on our resources, but we were able to conform with the wishes of higher authority in this matter for many months, for our N.C.O.'s were full of the right stuff. We hated losing them at the time, but now are very bucked to think that the battalion was the early training ground of so many successful officers.

CHAPTER XIX.

January and February, 1917.

We wore more clothes by night than we did by day during our stay in Martinsart Wood. The wooden huts in which we lived were of an old pattern, and somewhat worn and draughty. Preparing for turning in was quite a performance! Finally every possible garment was heaped " on top " in the hope that we would manage to sleep unfrozen through the night. What a thawing out there had to be every morning! Water supply was none too easy, and even the quick-flowing Ancre was nearly frozen across. On the flooded marshes by Aveluy some of our Canadian friends indulged in hockey on the ice.

These days in Martinsart Wood were quite enjoyable. Our work was mainly on roads and trenches. In every case the ground was frozen so thoroughly that a day's work could hardly be seen at all, and there was no desire to slack, for hard work meant relative warmth. Tactically we were in reserve behind the 54th Infantry Brigade, who were holding the line at the time, but both sides were relatively quiet, and in consequence we had an undisturbed 12 days in the wood. When the 53rd Brigade took over the line (Desire Trench, south of Grandcourt and Miraumont) on about the 27th January we marched up to an encampment of Nissen huts (the first we had met), named Warwick Huts, on the roadside just E. of Authuille

Wood. Here we spent a quiet six days; the weather was still very cold. Brigade H.Q. was just a bit up the road in a dug-out in O.G.1. Tobogganing on tin trays was the chief pastime of the officers' servants at this time.

On the evening of February 2nd we went into the line. Our front line was Desire Trench from Sixteen Road to Stump Road; Battalion H.Q. were in Zollern Redoubt. The ground was still frozen hard and covered with a slight layer of dry snow. The whole battle area looked incomparably better in its arctic garb than it had looked in the days of wet November —white dry snow now; squelching mud then. And the snow covered up many horrible sights, too. We took over from the 6th R. Berkshire Regiment, with "C" Company on the right and "D" Company on the left. The line continued to be quiet. Communication trenches to the front line were non-existent, so visits had to be made at night only. Happily we were favoured by a moon. "C" Company went in prepared to raid Folly Trench, and this operation was successfully executed on the night February 4th-5th.

Desire Trench cut Sixteen Road at its junction with Grandcourt Road. The former road ran northwards to Miraumont; the latter north-westwards to Grandcourt. Some 250 yards north of Desire Trench Folly Trench ran across, linking the two roads, and was the most advanced German position on our front. The enemy had strong posts each end of it, the one near Sixteen Road being much the stronger. We set out to snaffle both posts. Second-Lieut. A. Carpenter was in charge of the right raiding party; Second-Lieut. A. D. Whiting of the one on the left. Our supporting artillery put down a barrage to cover the raid throughout. Owing to the extremely cold weather, and, it was said, faulty ammunition, a great many shells burst short, and we suffered several casualties from our own artillery fire. These included Second-Lieut. A. Carpenter, who was so badly wounded that he did not again rejoin the battalion during the war. A good leader in battle and always cheery, but he simply couldn't whisper even if patrolling the enemy's wire. Our main raiding party caught and killed no one. They had no leader when they bumped the Hun wire, and were a bit bewildered with fire from behind. On the left, however, Whiting's party got in, took one Hun prisoner for identification purposes, scattered the rest and came home. In quiet times such identifications were most useful to the Intelligence Branch.

Early in the morning of the 8th February we captured Folly Trench, and joined up with the Naval Division south of Grandcourt, a village from which the Hun withdrew the day before. The evacuation of this village was the very first step in the Hun withdrawal of 1917. Second-Lieut. A. D. Whiting was wounded in this action. Two days later we were relieved by the 12th Middlesex Regiment, and marched down to Martinsart. Here we stayed for some five days, and the frost held up to our last day here. We lived in Gloucester Huts, and were not at all badly off. On the 15th February the concentration for the impending operation necessitated our marching to St. Pierre Divion. We were not wanted to fill any tactical rôle at this place, but our accommodation in Gloucester Huts was wanted for one night for another battalion. In these days concentration of troops was very much a game of draughts, at the stage in which the majority of the pieces are kings. At St. Pierre Divion we occupied a series of elaborate Hun dugouts—certainly the finest and largest we had been in up to that time. The operation now about to take place was an attack on the enemy positions south of

Miraumont. He had one sound line of defence here covering the Ancre crossings. The main trench of this line was known as S. Miraumont Trench. If I were writing a narrative of the 53rd Infantry Brigade I should need to say a good deal about this battle, but as we formed the Brigade reserve and were not used in the fight (this was the first time since the Somme battle had opened), I will summarise the operation as shortly as possible.

The attack was launched at 5.45 a.m., 17th February, 1917. The 2nd Division was attacking on the right of the 18th Division, and of our Division, the 54th Brigade attacked on the right, the 53rd Brigade on the left. The 8th Suffolk Regiment and the 6th R. Berks Regiment were given the main 53rd Brigade attack. We marched into "close-up" positions—Grandcourt and Hessian Trenches—with Battalion H.Q. at Zollern Redoubt. The thaw had started as we marched up to our posts on the early morning of the 17th. The Hun knew the attack was coming, and gave our assaulting troops a bad time whilst they were forming up.

But he did not stop the attack, and most of our objectives were gained. We played no part as a battalion till the morning of the 19th, when we moved up very early and relieved the two battalions then in the line. The relief, which was complete at 6.15 a.m., went extremely well, and our band, acting as a carrying party, marched up close behind our men, bearing food containers filled with tea. An hour later these bandsmen came back along Sixteen Road, their food containers empty. It was a fairly risky thing to attempt, but they went at it without hesitating and got through.

The line we held faced north-east, and was close up against the Miraumont Bluff. The trench line was

M

not continuous. "*B*" Company on the right straddled Sixteen Road, and "*C*" Company held the left down to the Ancre, east of Grandcourt. Nothing of real interest happened during the time we were in the line. "*B*" Company H.Q. and Battalion H.Q. were each shelled at intervals. Fortunately the enemy had left substantial dug-outs behind.

On the morning of either 21st or 22nd February we were relieved by the 8th Norfolk Regiment, and went back to the Zollern area. From here we moved the same night to Warwick Huts. Captain T. M. Banks rejoined at this time; Second-Lieut. G. C. Stanford was invalided home—he had gallantly stuck out the period of active operations under the most trying conditions; Lieutenant R. H. Binney joined.

We stayed at Warwick Huts for the remainder of February. During these last days of the month the enemy withdrew from Miraumont and Pys. We were kept *au fait* with the situation and prepared for the next attack. Officers and N.C.O.'s were kept busy with conferences and reconnaissances.

Salvage commenced to come very much to the fore at this time, and with the coming of the thaw there was a great increase of recovered treasure. Colonels, even Generals, would be met with every assortment of old iron on their backs trying to look as if their dearest aim in life was to become an old clo' merchant. And woe betide a company commander if General Higginson should happen to find a clip of ammunition lying about unnoticed. One hesitates to calculate the number of these unconsidered trifles that he must have amassed in his pockets in the course of a morning's walk.

CHAPTER XX.

THE CAPTURE OF IRLES.

The last week of February, 1917, was full of excitement for us; the enemy withdrew to what was then a considerable depth on our front. The 55th Infantry Brigade was in the line at the time, and had the privilege of reaping the fruits of the battle of the 17th February. Petit Miraumont was occupied without a fight, and junction effected east of that village with troops on the north side of the Ancre; Pys was captured on the 25th February by the 7th Buffs, and it was hoped that the enemy would yield Irles—which on our front was the one remaining outpost position to the Loupart Line—without further resistance. We quite expected further retirement here, for, north of the Ancre, Gommecourt had been given up. The plan during the last week of February was for the 53rd Infantry Brigade to be prepared to assault the Loupart Line—the enemy's next main line of defence —so soon as the 55th Infantry Brigade had made good Irles.

By the 1st of March, however, it was clear that the Hun was not prepared at present to withdraw from Irles. He boasted of "withdrawal according to programme"; on the night 3rd-4th March the 53rd Infantry Brigade took over the line with a view to reducing the length of the intervals between the moves in that programme. The 8th Suffolk Regiment took over the line, which ran roughly north and south, between Miraumont and Irles. At this time the enemy held not only the village, but a very good trench line (Resurrection Trench) to the west of it. Our position was one of close support; three companies were in the Miraumont quarries—where a number of huge dug-outs had been left by the Boche—while the fourth company and Battalion H.Q. were in Petit Miraumont. Except for bouts of enemy shelling from his positions in and behind Loupart Wood, we had a reasonably peaceful time till the night 6th-7th March, when we took over a portion of Resurrection Trench from the Suffolks—a portion captured by them the night before. The 8th Norfolk Regiment was now in position on our right, and we were almost ready for action; not quite, however, for some enemy still remained in the most northern part of Resurrection Trench. This packet held the highest portion of the line, but their position was somewhat isolated, for to their north the ground sloped down rapidly to the railway valley.

This little band of Huns was a gallant one, however, and on the 8th March gave our "*B*" Company a very trying day. In the dawn our left bomb stop was rushed; it was assailed from the trench and from above ground. So far as I know we lost no prisoners, but a running fight ensued throughout the day, and at dusk we were quite 100 yards too far south in Resurrection Trench. The attack on Irles was more or less fixed for dawn on the 10th, and it was therefore imperative if we were to form up in Resurrection Trench that the enemy should be cleared out of it before dawn on the 9th. Beevor took a patrol of "*B*" Company up the line of the railway as far as possible, and then made for the Hun strong point from a north-westerly direction. Wood, meantime, "stood to" with two strong sections of "C" Company by the bomb stop in the trench. It must have been about 2 a.m., 9th March, when Beevor's patrol was spotted by the Huns. An interchange of bombs and rifle shots started at once. Wood had waited patiently for this, and led his sections over the top in a northerly direction along the line of the trench. In a very few minutes we had all the ground we wanted for "forming up," and a useful identification, too.

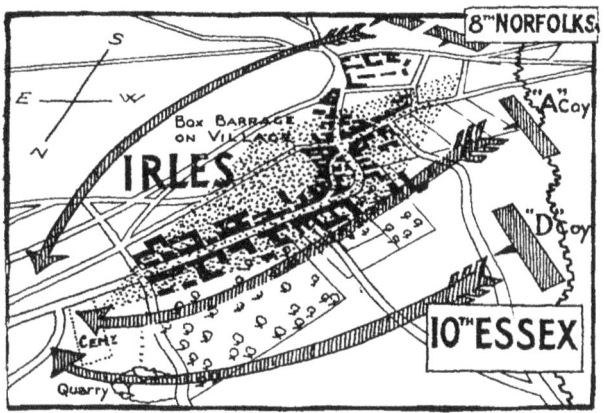

The village of Irles lay on a spur, which juts out in a south-westerly direction from the Loupart Wood ridge. The centre of the village was some 1,500 yards from the Loupart Line, and the main road through the village ran N.E.-S.W. The highest point in Irles is the cemetery at its N.E. end, and the greater portion of the houses stood under the south side of the spur.

Roughly, the 53rd Infantry Brigade plan of attack was for the 8th Norfolk Regiment to make good a trench position to the S.E. of Irles, while the 10th Essex, nearly 1,000 yards to the north of the Norfolks, advanced due east, and made good the N.E. part of the village. The low S.W. part of the village was to be left alone, so far as infantry was concerned; a box barrage was arranged to deal with this from zero to zero and 90 minutes, and patrols were detailed for clearing up anything this barrage left behind.

In 1916 attacks had always been shoulder to shoulder, and adjacent troops advancing in the same direction; indeed, tactics generally seemed to be an attempt at a human demonstration of the truths of the second book of geometry (rectangles and parallelograms). Now our commanders were realising the existence of a third dimension, and the consideration of tactical features both reduced the number of troops to be used and lessened the casualties.

Our actual assault was carried out by two companies and one platoon. "*A*" Company (Captain W. C. Neild) was on the right; "*D*" Company (Captain T. M. Banks) on the left; one platoon from "*B*" Company was lent to "*D*" for its extreme left strong point; while the remainder of "*B*" Company (Major A. S. Tween, D.S.O.) "rounded off" the line from "*D's*" left to the line of Albert-Arras railway and established touch with the 62nd Division. "*C*" Company (Captain W. G. P. Hunt, M.C.) was in reserve in Resurrection Trench.

Forming up took place between 2 a.m. and 4.30 a.m. on the 10th, and was not subjected to enemy interference. There was, however, an interesting incident in connection with the process. Snow had fallen lightly in the evening, and the ground was so white that there was a fear that the approach march over the top would be detected. So white mantles were served out to the assaulting companies, and they presented an extraordinary sight clad apparently in nightgowns but with the appurtenances of warfare beneath, detracting somewhat from the sylph-like lines of waist and corsage. The snow melted before dawn, and they discarded their robes de nuit before they actually went over.

At zero hour, 5.15 a.m., the attack was launched under a perfect barrage—we had never been treated to a better. The light was bad and the mist heavy. From the orchard-flanked N.W. side of Irles, against which our troops were advancing, came a considerable volume of enemy machine-gun fire, and we suffered some casualties, but our troops carried on straight to their objectives. They were, of course, helped by the mist, but the leadership was the chief asset. The fight was sharp and short, for at 5.45 a.m. we had a message back from Banks by runner to Resurrection Trench :—" To Adjutant-Ambassador (the then code name of the Battalion) : 'Road and Quarry gained and held. Casualties believed few.'—O.C. "D" Company, 5.35 a.m." This represented an advance of 800 yards. The battalion did a very useful 20 minutes' work between 5.15 a.m. and 5.35 a.m. on March 10th, 1917. The last "strong village" outpost to the Loupart line was wrested from the enemy; some 60 Huns were killed, 2 officers and 56 other ranks taken prisoners; and 6 enemy machine guns and one granatenwerfer captured. During the first fifteen minutes we met with considerable resistance, but action of leaders like Culver—who, with a handful of men, boldly rushed a most venomous machine-gun—and men like Sergeant Sanders, Corporal Evans and Privates Surridge and Argent, who performed similar acts, promptly settled all matters of dispute. Second-Lieut. L. Coulshaw was lucky on this day. His revolver saved his life, for while hanging in the holster on his belt it was hit in three distinct places by enemy machine-gun bullets, which knocked him over and killed his observer at his side but left him unscathed.

From our objectives patrols were pushed out towards the Loupart line. They advanced a very considerable distance, and found from the fire they drew that this line was still strongly held. On the left Second-Lieuts. Beevor and Carson patrolled across the railway line to make touch with the 62nd Division. They found one post, heard of another, and pushed on towards it. During this attempt to cross very exposed ground (the enemy looked right down this valley from Achiet), Beevor was shot through the heart by an enemy sniper. This bad luck was a severe loss to us, for Beevor was a first-class leader.

During the three or four hours immediately following our attack there was very little artillery fire from the enemy, for the simple reason that their F.O.O. had been captured in our first rush. His wire, too, had been cut by our fire, and back at the batteries his friends could not see what had happened. When they did see, however, they pounded our positions with considerable venom.

Early on the morning of the 11th March we were relieved by the 6th Royal Berkshire Regiment. Rain was falling heavily at this time, and our first resting-place—Boom Ravine and the trenches thereabout—not at all comfortable. On the morning of the 11th I saw an incident which well illustrates the foul luck of some men in war. While walking round about noon to make enquiries after the general health, etc., of all and sundry, I heard an explosion in a trench in which some of "*B*" Company men were resting. What had happened? A good soldier, who the morning before had been in the assault on Irles cemetery, had, in endeavouring to improve his "kip," picked into the handle of a buried German bomb. We had the M.O. on the spot in five minutes or less, but the poor boy was mutilated beyond the powers of human repair, and died very shortly afterwards.

Next night we were relieved by the 54th Infantry Brigade, who came in to storm the Loupart Line—that terribly strong line we had been studying for quite three weeks—but the Hun meantime having thought better of it, decided to quit, and his withdrawal synchronised with the incoming of the 54th Brigade. Irles had taught him a lesson, viz., his programme of withdrawal must conform with the arrangements of the stronger side. The 54th Brigade went treking on for days—right up to St. Leger, indeed. We, meantime, went back to Wellington Huts, near Aveluy, and "bucked" to our hearts' content. Two new subalterns joined—Compton and Ord—and I armed them with maps and a copy of the account of the battle, and bade them go up and study these on the ground as a tactical exercise. Irles was our first engagement to which one might be permitted to prefix the adjective "classical," and we all would do honour to the commander who formulated the plan. Neild, Culver, Coulshaw and Banks got their M.C.'s for gallant leadership in this fight.

CHAPTER XXI.

A Tale of Many Journeys.

We remained at Wellington Huts till the 54th Infantry Brigade had completed its share of the task of pursuing the retreating enemy. These days were full of satisfaction to us, for we had seen a fair whack of the heavy Somme fighting which forced this retirement on the Hun. How delightful it was to mark off a large area of regained France on our large battle map each morning and evening, and how cheerily all ranks followed the advance of the string we used to indicate the front line! Moreover, we saw bodies of cavalry move forward—ever a cheering sight for infantry. Last, but not least, we played football on ground where, in 1915 and 1916, we had not dared to show any portion of our anatomies.

Then came the news that the Division had completed its Somme tasks, and was to be moved once more to a location a considerable distance away. It must have been about the 18th March when we started our travels. The first day we marched to Warloy; our next move was to Rainneville. We had nearly arrived at this village when a motor cyclist despatch rider overtook us with the information that the village was out of bounds on account of measles. A long halt was made in the fields, while the M.O. went forward to reconnoitre. I do not remember the details of the reconnaissance, but the result was satisfactory to most of us—the measles had been localised, and we took over approved billets. We stayed at Rainneville a day or two, and as this village is near and on a main road to Amiens, sundry pleasure trips were arranged.

It was a strange coincidence that led us out of the Somme area by the same road over which we had marched to our baptism of fire on August Bank Holiday, 1915. And we could look back with pride on a year and a half of endurance and achievement that had changed us from a battalion of greenhorns into veterans who needed the fingers of both hands to count their victories. And the pride was swelled by the satisfaction of having chased the Hun from off this corner of the French fields which we felt was so peculiarly our own.

Providence mercifully concealed the future, when a still stranger coincidence was to bring us in 1918 along the same old Molliens-Beaucourt Road, with the Hun once more ensconced in his old lairs and the end of the weary war, which now seemed close at hand, to all appearances postponed indefinitely. However, that belongs to the later narrative.

The next move deserves recording, for in making it we were used as an experiment. G.H.Q. had collected various 'buses and "converted lorries" into three large parks—one north, one central, one south—for the rapid movement of fair-sized bodies of infantry to any distant spots at which troops might be required. And now the details of such moves remained to be worked out. The 'bus park in the south was given the job of moving the 53rd and 54th Brigades from a point about 6 miles north of Amiens, on the Doullens-Amiens road, to a series of points 6 to 8 miles south-west of Amiens. The number to move was roughly 5,000; each active service 'bus was allowed to carry 30 passengers only. Here, then, we had no mean transport and traffic problem.

We set out from our village about 9 a.m., and were

at our rendezvous by noon. Here we waited till about 3 p.m. Then a tremendous column of 'buses moved forward through Amiens. After "debussing" we marched to Pissy. A long day, but a useful one, for we never found authority getting quite such a mass of troops together at one embussing point again; nor did we ever again wait quite so long for the move to begin, or march so far after debussing. 'Bus moves were quite common to us during the remainder of the war, and though never as comfortable as a Sunday trip to Hampton Court in June, were preferable to several days' heavy marching.

Pissy was a delightful spot; Battalion H.Q. was never housed better. Each officer had a suite of rooms in the château, and, indeed, the good Comptesse did everything possible to make us comfortable and happy. Unfortunately, we were billed to stay only about ten hours, and the belated order received during the night there to put our watches forward one hour for summer time deprived us of one of these. We were up and marching away ere the civilian portion of the château was astir.

Our march was to Bacouel, where we entrained. The 31-hour railway journey that ensued was easily a record one for us, and we arrived at our destination over twenty-four hours late. One or two breakdowns with the much overtaxed rolling stock used for these " strategic trains," and the whole of the 53rd Brigade was left out all night somewhere between Abbeville and Etaples. A good many standing orders on railway moves were broken on that journey—e.g., our cooks got their travelling kitchens going on the flat open trucks as the train crawled along. Then, when another halt came, men rushed along and issued hot tea; others did the same with bread and jam. At one stage a sudden spurt left one of our men behind.

He jumped on the next train, and next evening caught us up at St. Omer, when the engine of the second train came up to the brake van of ours!

In the darkness of the night of the second day we detrained at Berguette, and marched on to Ham-en-Artois, a clean, well-built village some 7 miles west of Bethune. Here we spent nearly three weeks, and the Division was still in G.H.Q. reserve in this area at the commencement of the Arras battle. So when the snow fell on Easter Monday we were not sorry to be "out of it" for once in a way. No "big" training was carried out during the Ham rest; there was no suitable ground. It was pre-eminently the platoon commanders' busy time, and they busied themselves in more ways than one. Some of them undertook the task, led by our gallant padre, of mastering the mutinous mule. But Colonel Frizell's surreptitious assistance to the riding-class with a sly dig of a walking-cane induced more terrors into the hearts of the cavaliers than many a salvo of shells.

Simon Ord (aged about 50) was one of the industrious "young" platoon commanders at this time. Few who have witnessed it will forget the ceremoniousness of his salute. And when on one occasion the General passed by his platoon drawn up by the side of the road, Ord was so occupied with the salute that he disappeared into a four-foot ditch of water. But the salute remained intact. "A zealous young officer that," said General Higginson.

While the battalion was at Ham, Major J. L. Lewis, our second-in-command, left us for a course at Aldershot, and owing to subsequent indisposition did not return to us. Major Tween took his place, and Skeat succeeded to the command of "B" Company.

This was the time when the famous "Firm in the Strand called Twining" tale more nearly endangered the internal harmony of the 10th Essex than any other event in their history. The point of the tale lay in the fact that it had no point; hence many feuds of blood and perils of lynching. Tommy Thomas who introduced it was lucky to survive alive.

Our first move after Ham was to Bethune, where we spent two days. This was our only visit to this well-known town during the war; indeed, throughout our sojourn in France we were only once in the First Army area. The Fosses and coal-mining villages which played so large a part in the history of the British Army in France have absolutely nothing to say of us! From Bethune we marched to Houchin, where we spent quite a comfortable week. At this time the 53rd Brigade was I. Corps reserve, and in the case of enemy attack would have had the task of manning the " village line " between Bullay-Grenay and Loos. While making reconnaissances here we had our only glimpse of the Loos battlefield.

Then came the time for further real action for the 18th Division, and away we marched to Tangry—a very long march indeed. Concentration was quickly effected, and by the use of "tactical trains"—trains which moved the dismounted personnel while the transport moved by "march route"—we were all in the Arras area by May 1st. The 53rd Infantry Brigade spent two nights in bonâ fide bivouac on the ground between the old front lines at Beaurains. We had only our waterproof sheets and greatcoats, but the weather was dry and very hot, and there was really nothing to grouse about. We were neither bombed nor shelled here. Officers rode forward and reconnoitred the front line before Heninel, and the approaches thereto, and on May 2nd we moved forward to the valley between Neuville Vitasse and Wancourt, and as Brigade in Divisional reserve awaited the coming battle.

CHAPTER XXII.

Round About Arras—May and June, 1917.

The battle of May 3rd, 1917, in which considerable British forces were engaged, was not one of the brightest features of the war. Two brigades of the 18th Division have many reasons for remembering that day with rue, though many fine acts were performed ; but as the 53rd Infantry Brigade was in Divisional reserve for this fight, a long description of the engagement would be out of place here. Briefly, the attack was unsuccessful along the whole of Allenby's Third Army front. Objectives were only reached in a few cases, and in these they were not held. The 18th Division attacked in the neighbourhood of Cherisy, and this village, which was one of its objectives, was captured, but subsequently lost again to the skilful and determined counter-attacks of the enemy. And at the end of a disastrous day the position everywhere was more or less " as you were."

For the 3rd of May action we took up " close-at-hand " positions in the Hindenburg Line between Neuville Vitasse and Heninel on May 2nd. The weather was fine and gloriously hot, and we continued to enjoy our bivouac existence and to amuse ourselves by a wonder-filled inspection of the marvels which Hindenburg had wrought in his famous line. Trenches through which one could drive a horse and cart and belts of wire hundreds of yards thick we had not dreamt of in our wildest fancies. But here they materialised before our incredulous eyes.

Zero hour on the 3rd May was about an hour before dawn, and we had a most wonderful view, firstly of our own bombardment, and secondly of the mutual bombardments, interspersed with the enemy's multi-coloured light signals. The Hun knew of the coming attack, and during the night gas-shelled the battery area in which our troops were scattered. "*A*" and "*D*" Companies had to wear gas masks for quite a considerable period.

We did not move on May 3rd, but when on the evening of the 4th the 53rd Brigade relieved the depleted 54th and 55th Brigades we moved into positions of support between Heninel and the front line. These positions consisted chiefly of trenches scarcely begun, German gun positions and a system of German practice trenches which went by the name of "The Rookery," and we therefore had to put our backs into the matter of completing them as a last line of defence E. of the Cojeul River. A large number of British dead who had been lying where they fell in the capture of this (Wancourt) ridge the week before were buried by us. On the whole we had four days of comparative calm whilst in support. There were no communication trenches, and some movement over the top by day was therefore imperative. This usually drew a small ration of enemy artillery fire. C.Q.M.S. Mann, of "*D*" Company, fell a victim to one such sharp salvo. He had come up from the transport lines to pay his daily visit to his company commander, and was just starting out on the return journey to his relatively safe billet when he was killed. The padre buried him that night in the light of the struggling moonbeams during the eerie pauses of shell-fire, while a small knot of comrades, officers and men, paid a last tribute to a faithful soul who answered the first call to arms in 1914.

After four days we took over the left portion of the Brigade front from the 6th R. Berks. Regiment. This sector was quite interesting ; sentries in the front line had plenty to watch, and our patrols and snipers busied themselves mightily. Except for a few sharp bursts of artillery fire each day we were more or less left alone by the Hun.

After two days here we " side-stepped " to support positions about a mile further south, as a considerable re-arrangement of the front was ordered. This brought us into that portion of the main Hindenburg Line lying between Heninel and Fontaine, and here we found the wonderful tunnel still existing and quite habitable. There was a non-stop run along this tunnel of over a mile. When it did stop, it stopped, so far as we were concerned, because the Boche held the further portion of it, and rival sentry posts fronted each other dramatically in the darkness underground. It was curious to share dug-outs thus with the enemy, and later our insular dislike for such close neighbourship got the upper hand, and the tunnel was blown in between the rival tenants. Compartments ran off on either side at regular intervals, and provided a good deal of accommodation. Exits were numerous, and ventilation quite good. During May, 1917, between two and three thousand troops lived in this tunnel, and Capt. H. Ramsbotham, M.C., then staff captain of the 53rd Infantry Brigade, instituted a young officer as " Town Major of the Hindenburg Tunnel." Second-Lieut. W. B. Drake was, I believe, the first on whom this honour fell, and though he found his job a long and tiring one, his fame as such still endures.

Two days in support were followed by two days in the line. We now looked down on Fontaine, but the enemy's front line was some little distance away. About this time higher authority informed us that there were signs of a further enemy withdrawal, and a plan of action in the case of such a retirement was elaborated. Patrols had to be more active, and these were out by day and night. Some of "A" Company's patrols, under Lieutenant R. H. Binney, Corporal Meager and Corporal Goy, did excellent work. They went daringly into the midst of supposed enemy advanced posts in Pug Lane by day, and found various Huns asleep in " cubby-holes " under a bank. These cubby-holes were screened in at their entrance, just as ours were, with waterproof sheets. The sheets were lifted, and the poor surprised Huns dealt with effectively on the principle of the periwinkle. Corporal Goy was killed by a shell the day following this daring exploit.

We had a longish spell in the forward sector, as the 54th and 55th Brigades had considerable refitting to do, but we went back to the divisional reserve area towards the end of the month. This was on high ground south of Boyelles, and here, in bivouacs, we had an excellent time. Part of our work consisted of making a more permanent camp on the site of our bivouacs. This and training round Mercatel filled up our mornings, and then down in the valley of the Cojeul we indulged in cricket and football simultaneously in the evenings. All battalions and brigade and divisional headquarters ran good teams, so we were never hard up for a match. Lieutenant E. B. P. Davis rejoined, and Captain H. Innocent, of the 8th Cyclist Battalion, reported for duty whilst we were at "S.17, Central." Next we moved to bivouacs in the river valley just west of Henin, and from these positions carried on digging work in the front line area by night. The brigades in the line were steadily advancing their front line by peaceful penetration at night, and we found a good deal of the labour necessary for the successful conduct of these operations.

About this time Colonel Frizell heard of the award of his D.S.O. for his good services with the Battalion, and celebrated the event characteristically by a " drop of leave." Tween took over, with Banks 2nd i/c and Forbes as Adjutant, assiduous in the location of the " Strrombos Horrrns " (a new method of pneumatic gas alarms).

The time for a rest for the Division was fast approaching, and it was hoped that the Battalion would not be required in the front line again, but for two or three days before the final divisional relief we were required to hold the front before Chérisy. It was just after leaving our headquarters in the sandpits on the actual day of our relief that our much beloved Brigade-Major, Captain P. R. Meautys, M.C., was killed. He had done barely ten weeks' service as Brigade-Major at the time, but his energy and his sprightly and cheery ways had made him a well-known and deservedly popular figure. General Higginson also had a narrow escape in Foster Avenue, when a shell burst on the parapet above him and hurled him to the bottom of a dug-out shaft with his runner on top of him. He walked on afterwards unperturbed, but at Battalion H.Q. we knew that something unusual had happened, for he accepted the offer of a drink—a thing he invariably refused from battalions in the line even on the thirstiest of days. This was the one exception, and it took the form of a cup of tea !

A long south-westerly march brought us to Souastre, a village which in 1916 was a " close-up " billet village. Now nearly 20 miles away, it seemed quite out of the war, and we lent many civilians a hand in clearing sandbags and other obstacles from their windows and gardens. I often wondered if these same civilians did not curse us for our optimism when the Germans approached their village again in 1918!

At Souastre a good deal of training was done, for we were told to prepare for the really great offensive of the year. In the evenings we went on with our cricket. Our fortnight at Souastre was a very enjoyable one.

The move northwards, which we knew was imminent, was made during the first few days of July. This train journey was a reasonably good one, and the long coast detour was dispensed with. We detrained at the station on the south side of Cassel Hill, and marched to billets near the Belgian Frontier just east of Steenvoorde.

And at this stage I must pass on the recording of the doings of the 10th Battalion the Essex Regiment to another, for as early as the third week in May I had left Battalion H.Q. for one of those periods of vegetation at Brigade H.Q., which on closer inspection and acquaintance revealed themselves as times of very hard work. My ever-faithful Beeson accompanied me.

R. A. C.

CHAPTER XXIII.

Preparations for Passchendaele.

The previous chapters have traced the story of the 10th Essex through its long period of early training and maturity, to the costly harvest time of the Somme. Then we have seen it rapidly devouring the successive drafts which flowed in to fill its depleted ranks, and repeatedly rebuilding itself by a sad and tedious process around the tattered fibres which remained after Delville Wood, Thiepval and the Miraumont fighting. After which a long period of comparatively peaceful times followed. Arras left us largely unscathed, and a benign influence in higher quarters saw that we were spared from serious fighting for all the early summer of 1917. The most serious casualty of these middle times of 1917 was Chell, who left us for the bedizened glories of the Staff, where he was to add still further laurels to his record and reputation. It was a true instinct of the Colonel which elevated him to the higher spheres, but the Battalion was the poorer for the loss of his boundless energy and his intense self-sacrificing devotion to its interests. Apart from the disappearance of Chell, there were few changes in personnel after Irles, with the result that by the time the Battalion reached northern climes they were as bonnie and well-knit a body of men as one would wish to see. Under the skilful pilotage of Colonel Frizell, the rugged, sterling material that had never failed through the trying times of the winter was blossoming forth into a real "Shiny Tenth" again, and it was a spruce and debonair band that invaded the hearths and the hearts of the frontier folk.

Capt R·A·CHELL·D·S·O·M·C

We were fit as fighting cocks. The weather was glorious. We could look back on a year of real solid achievement with pride in our hearts, and not a few of us with something extra on the tunic above them. And the ample, well-built dwellings of Flanders gave an additional sense of fortune's favours after the mud-plastered walls of Picardy which had been our homes when such a thing as a rest occurred down on the Somme.

Yet behind all this bliss there was an uncomfortable feeling of being fattened up for the dinner table. We knew we weren't up on the Belgian border simply for reasons of health, and soon it became clearly evident that some hefty new operation was in the wind.

In the first place several strange new things were launched upon us. The Yukon pack was one of them. Struggling unfortunates could be seen bearing one, two, or three ammunition boxes (80lbs. apiece) upon their backs by means of devices which reminded one of the happy fancies of a Heath Robinson, and defaulters were in keen demand to demonstrate the kinship of Thomas Atkins to the patient, grunting camel. And the hump developed all right! The watchword of the moment was "fitness." In the early morning whole companies of perspiring men would hare through the glades of Bellewarde Wood headed by enthusiastic company commanders, with a strong rearguard of subalterns (rather eager for the post) to whip in the straggling tail of crocks, faint, but still (when an officer was looking) pursuing. In fact, the ambition of the almighty brass-hat appeared at the moment to be to convert us into a unit of super-railway-porters, ardent to transport the heaviest loads at lightning speed—and no tips!

But they were jolly times. The camel-man found his consolation in quantities of Belgian beer which was excellently plentiful and could be absorbed by the gallon without any impression even on the youngest of soldiers. Others found comfortable havens in the hospitable homesteads, which dotted the country, or the attractions which Steenvoorde itself exercised irresistibly for the gallants of the Regiment. It is recorded that two officers of a certain company were heard to remark in the mess one lunch-time that they were tired of people, and were going for solitary walks in the woods to commune with Nature. But, unknown to each other, Nature took the simultaneous form of the goddess Felicitine at the local ribbon shop, and to their mutual surprise they found each other partaking of coffee and cakes at the hands of the same young lady in Steenvoorde an hour or two later. And neither seemed over-joyed at the other's company.

The Battalion was curiously composed at this time. We seemed to consist of two classes—schoolboys and greyheads. George Prout, the blue-eyed mascot of " D " Company, was one of the former category. He joined us for Thiepval at the age of 17, and looking about 14. In the course of training at home it had been carefully drilled into him that no good soldier ever touched his water bottle without permission from an officer. But the rule was hardly honoured by strict observance in France. Imagine the surprise of his platoon commander when, at the end of a perfect day of heavy fighting on September 26th, he was asked by this diminutive soldier: " Please, sir, can I have a drink now ?" A worthy example to hold up to generations of warriors yet unborn ! But it must be confessed that Prout soon got over his precocious regard for discipline, and at a later stage in his career, when his C.O. was pinning the Military Medal ribbon on his tunic in front of a battalion parade, he was heard to say, in tones thoroughly audible to the whole assembly : " Gor' blimey, what the blankety blank 'ave they given me this for ?"

At the other end of the scale were such as Corporal Lister. One hesitates to compute his age, but he numbered many years. He had a command of five languages, none of them bad. He had sacrificed a good post in civilian life when his age would have exempted him from service, and in his faithful way he performed many excellent services, not the least being the provision of good fare for the commanding officer —an important item for the well-being of the Battalion. Memory associates him vividly with a "mixed boot competition" at the Battalion sports about this time. While he was patiently and honestly ransacking the boot pile, some evilly-disposed person had thrown his pair of boots to the furthest end of the field, and words cannot describe the perfect picture of bewilderment which poor, bootless Lister presented in a despairing search for his lost footwear.

Sports, concerts, champagne dinners in Steenvoorde and in billets, rides to Mont des Cats, convivial evenings at Cassel and Pop., made these into days of halcyon happiness. But there was always a spectre of serious business stalking in the background. Corps Commander Jacobs turned up one day and told us what a fine lot of fellows we were—a sure sign of impending offensiveness. And a "workmen's 'bus" at unearthly hours of the morning used to take up contingents of sleepy soldiers to the neighbourhood of Dickebusch, whence a wearisome trudge across the flat to Zillebeke Lake and Yeomanry Post reminded us that such a thing as war still existed.

The 55th Brigade were in the line throughout the majority of this time, and it was more dangerous than Hellfire Corner to relate to one of their number the sort of times that we were having at Steenvoorde. The old rhyme:
> "The 53rd are in the line,
> And the 54th behind them;
> But if you want the 55th,
> You'll blame well have to find 'em"

lost some of its force about this period. One officer

of the Surreys, in bitterness of heart, expressed amazement one day at seeing us still in France. He said that they had seen so little of us for so long that it was substantially rumoured that the rest of the Division had concluded a separate peace!

However, our suspension of hostilities was not destined to last much longer, and there were stern days ahead. As the end of the month approached, the well-known signs of thorough unpleasantness began to get about, and our friends of the A.S.C. would come round mysteriously with rumours of ominous moves to be whispered in one's private ear.

July 28th was spent in returning pianos and making farewells to the maidens of the fancy shops of Steenvoorde, to Marie "Au Tilleul Mazereeuw Quaghebeere" (which, being interpreted, means the village pub.), and to the many hospitable acquaintances we had made. And on the 29th of July the Battalion was once more on the pavé high-road, with silenced band and full battle kit, "partant pour la guerre."

CHAPTER XXIV.

Ypres III.

If the war had lasted a few years longer it is possible that a mastery of the art of concealment might have been numbered among the achievements of the British Army. But the natural Briton has no love for skulking, and Britain in khaki shrank instinctively from concealing its movements from the enemy as something that foreigners might practice, but which was entirely beneath the dignity of a true-born son of Albion. "Here I am, and I don't care who knows it," seemed to be Tommy's attitude as he walked over the top in preference to using the communication trench, or as he cooked his bacon over copiously smoking trench fires, and accurately located his dugout for the keen-eyed observers over the way. We might scan the German lines for days together and scarcely sight a single Hun. But the watchful Boche F.O.O. must needs have been bewildered by the variety of targets which presented themselves to his gaze on our side of the fateful strip. We learnt our lesson more fully by the end of 1918. But in 1917 it had not yet come home, and the roads of the Salient about this time were sights to rival Epsom on a Derby day. The whole of the British Army seemed to have taken a mind to perambulate towards the front, and there was no fear of feeling that we were engaged in a lone-hand enterprise.

There is something electrical and unique about the final stages of preparation—the X and Y days of military parlance—before the fatal dice is thrown. In general, too, there is an exhilaration in the air. But before July 31 this was not so noticeable as usual. It seemed a tough job at the best, and the dice was loaded very largely against us. So that it was with a little extra grimness that the 10th Essex wound its way among the multitudes crowding on to the stage before the curtain rang up on the next act of the great drama. We spent one night in bivouac in the staging area near Reninghelst. July 30th found us camped around the outskirts of Dickebusch, and thence, amid pitch darkness, illuminated only by the flickering of the guns, the companies marched silently out to play their varied roles in the battle of the morrow.

"C" Company, under Hunt, was assigned to the Suffolks; "B" Company, under Innocent, to the Berkshires, and both were to be engaged in the task of mopping-up as the Brigade went forward through Glencorse Wood and Nonne Boschen to Polygon Wood beyond.

To "A" and "D" Companies, under the joint command of Neild, was given the more inglorious, but no less severe, job of getting up ammunition and supplies to the forward troops after success had been gained.

As dawn approached the guns beat up in diabolical crescendo into that curious illusion of silence which comes to the baffled human ear in the frenzy of the zero hour, and with the first faint flush of white in the sky the 30th Division in front of us were away and over the top in excellent style. They met with little opposition until, after labouring up the steep slopes of Sanctuary Wood they reached the Ypres-Menin road, behind which the Boche had skilfully withdrawn his main resistance. Then things began to go wrong.

The 53rd Brigade was due to follow up the leading Division until the line of Glencorse Wood had been made good ; and success having been reported from the front, it shook itself free from its subterranean lairs around "the Ritz area," and marched confidently forward in artillery formation, in readiness to pass through the leading troops. But no sooner had the Berks and Suffolks crossed the Ypres-Menin road and topped the crest of the hill, than they were met with murderous fire from the unsuspected concrete fortresses which had, so far as the infantryman could judge, completely eluded the intelligence of the General Staff up to this moment. Hardly a soldier of the other Division was to be found ; in some mysterious fashion they had melted away or been diverted to the flank into Chateau Wood. And so the 53rd had to take on the uncompleted task themselves.

Colonels Hill and Clay promptly deployed their battalions and fought their way forward, but it was a hopeless business, for the barrage had gone on beyond retrieve. And, after many desperate endeavours, the line came to a halt around Surbiton Villas and the Jargon trenches.

In this muddled fighting "B" and "C" Companies played useful parts. Innocent got his company out and extended the left of the line, and Linford did some valuable work in assisting to cover up a vulnerable flank.

As necessarily happens when plans go radically wrong, the situation throughout the remainder of the day was thoroughly obscure, and darkness fell without the edge of Glencorse Wood being reached.

Meantime "A" and "D" Companies had performed minor prodigies as super-porters. Passing repeatedly through the very heavily barraged areas of Sanctuary Wood and the Ypres-Menin road, they carried forward ammunition and supplies to the troops in front with remarkable steadiness; and though casualties were numerous, it was extraordinary that they were not heavier. Compton, Thomas and others were several times hit by flying fragments of shell without being seriously wounded, and Hawksworth, of " A " Company, and Rogers, of " D," to mention two only of many indefatigable fellows, distinguished themselves by their stout-hearted efforts.

The heaviest loss of the day for us was Willie Hunt—imperturbable in battle, and lovable as a man. He was severely hit by a 5.9 on the Menin Road, and died in hospital some little time later, to the great sorrow of the Battalion. Second-Lieut. Thompson, of " B " Company, was another sad loss. He had not been with us long, but was popular with officers and men. And, for myself, I remember linked with the sorrow of Hunt's death the loss of Private Carter, another original " D " Company man, commonly known as " Tiny," for he stood 6ft. 3in. Single-minded as they make them, faithful to the core, one reckons such true comrades among the goodly number of gallant souls that shall surely meet again to hear the Great Captain's " Well done."

July 31st for many was a nightmare day. It could not be called a picnic up in front ; it was a desperate time for the gunners ; and I fancy the Higher Command further back would not willingly live through such hours again. And, speaking personally, a humble company commander shared something of these haunting experiences ; for he was left in echelon for the one and only time. And those long hours of suspense, waiting for news of the boys in front, and feeling the pull to be with them, with rumour alternating between success and failure as the trickling stream of walking wounded made their painful way towards the hopes of Blighty, and while good old Simon Ord, joint quartermaster and transport officer, waited anxiously with his stalwarts of the Transport Section and their pack-train which was never needed, have left an indelible impression on his mind.

The Battalion got together again late that evening in Railway Dug-outs, where, tunnelled into the embankment of a railway track, an incommodious shelter could be found against the continual attentions of the German shells; and the evening of August 1st saw us straggling back like a French relief to Micmac Camp.

Rain had set in firmly on the 31st, and added to the lugubriousness of everything. But it was some consolation to be out of the bitter forward areas, though we knew that there were stiff times still to come.

And as darkness fell again, and the rain slashed down upon the rounded roofs of the Nissen huts, we pitied the poor fellows still up there, and turned over in the blankets to bury the uncomfortable memories of the opening scene of the third battle of Ypres in sleep such as only the battle-weary soldier-man can know.

CHAPTER XXV.

Strenuousness at Stirling Castle and Rest at Rubrouck.

We remained only a day or two in Micmac Camp, and then moved on to Dickebusch Huts, where in sylvan seclusion a good deal of comparative comfort was found, even though quarters were rather cramped. Here we browsed for some days, not too curious of what the immediate future held in store, but hoping that the fates might give us back the blissful rest of Steenvoorde. I was sore stricken with trench fever at the time, and recollections in consequence are not particularly lively. But one or two mental pictures linger.

One is a clear-cut cameo of David Randell conducting an early morning Communion service in the tiny hut which housed the Battalion canteen. A painter's brush might have been well employed to depict that little group of kneeling officers and men among the odd and varied stores of fruit tins, cigarette packets, eggs, and writing paper which went to make up the Battalion shop. And incongruous as the surroundings were, the service lost nothing in sincerity on account of them. One came to learn in France that the temples of man are but the trappings of true religion.

Another memory is a pyjamed alarm, when " *A* " Company's cookhouse, under the immortal

Baxter, took fire late one night; but, lest it be thought that ours was a battalion of sybarites, it should be explained that to officers alone did pyjamas apply. The possession of a valise, even when the 35lbs. limit is strictly enforced, permitted such luxuries. But the portmanteau of the " other ranks " is the pack upon the back (unless one of the cooker's staff could be cajoled to carry an extra sandbag), and so the daytime greyback had to serve a double purpose as a " robe de nuit." The practice has the advantage of saving the washing bill, but even in times of dear soap and expensive laundries it is not to be recommended

On August 10th sudden orders came to hand to get forward to relieve the 55th Brigade, who had had heavy losses in the fighting for Inverness Copse, and the Battalion moved up to the Chateau Segard area. The relief of the Queen's in the woods of Stirling Castle was the height of everything that is unpleasant. A dark night in a noisy wood, with the Boche shelling heavily at frequent intervals, and guides who did not know one place from another—and atop of it all, a muddy shell-churned surface, and rain falling—such conditions are best left to the imagination; but it requires a vivid one indeed to do them justice, unless a bitter experience of Flanders already supplies the lurid colouring.

We took over somehow, and had managed to cover the front before the morning, but the operation was something of a miracle, which would not have been performed at all but for the action of the 55th Brigade-Major, Captain Runge, who, when he found the guides were failing, led the Battalion up himself.

During a week's tenure of office in that salubrious spot there was no actual contact fighting, but it must be counted among the hardest spells of garrison duty that fell to the Battalion. The first night was a marvel of ignorance and uncertainty. For the most part there were no troops to relieve, for they had been so badly mauled in their recent attack. A gap of about 500 yards across the Ypres-Menin road was discovered by " D " Company, and there was nothing to prevent Jerry walking through it and down into Ypres save for any stray gunners that he might have encountered in the battery positions below in the valley. Lussignea was sent across with a platoon to heal the breach, and I remember my solicitude for him out in the blue there; but this proved to be somewhat unmerited, for later I found that, having posted his forces, he had discovered a providential concrete pill-box nine feet thick, and a still more providential bottle of something; and, thus entrenched, was prepared to stay in position until the conclusion of the next war. His location was converted into Company H.Q. without delay.

A good many casualties were suffered in the course of the relief. Battalion H.Q. caught it rather severely, and the signallers had a hectic time that night and the next day trying to establish communication. Pinder Davis, only freshly returned from his spell of absence after being hit in Delville Wood, got a piece of shell in his hand near Dormy House, and the Tenth Essex lost his stout-hearted services permanently. He had graduated in arduousness, and when he recovered again the astral spheres claimed him for companion. Coulshaw also got a nasty hit in the neck, and an intermittent stream of Blighty ones trickled continually to the rear.

A minor operation was planned for the morning of August 12th. The Suffolks, in conjunction with the Norfolks and Berkshires, were undertaking dirty work on the left, and the Tenth Essex, of course, could not be omitted. " B " Company, which was in support at Crab Crawl, was summoned to aid the Berks, and Skeat, emulating the exploits of a famous King of France, marched his company across the wilderness to the top of the hill, and then, being told the show was off, marched them down again. The operation sounds a simple one. In reality it was something of a masterpiece of leadership and direction-finding in the dark, even at the best of times ; and at this particular time the shell-fire of the past and of the awesome present did not leave much to be desired in the way of frightfulness. In point of fact, a complete battalion managed to lose its way entirely that night, and its failure to turn up on the tape-line kept everyone on tenterhooks until the attack was abandoned at the very last moment before dawn, with tragic consequences for "*D*" Company, as shall be told.

There was an obstinate German pill-box at the corner of Inverness Copse, opposite Clapham Junction, which was a very thorn in the side of any further advance to the east, and the fiat went forth that "*D*" Company was to take this stronghold while the fireworks were in progress on the left. It was a one-officer job, and Compton volunteered. I was reluctant to accept his offer, for the poor boy had just suffered a desperate sorrow a few days before, when, learning that his brother's Division was in the neighbourhood, he went over to pay him a visit, and found that he had met a gallant death two days before. Such are the indelible bitternesses of war. But Compton was insistent on the job, and as all the remaining officers were wounded or ailing, there was nothing for it but to take his offer. Number 15 platoon was lined out on either side of Jasper Trench, which ran towards the objective, and all was ready save that nothing could be heard of the Suffolks. Zero was 4.20 a.m., and the watch-hand crept on past four o'clock with still no news, and our anxiety was intense, when at 4.10 a panting runner arrived with the message that the infantry attack would not take place, though there was no time to stop the barrage. A couple of runners went out at once to warn Compton, and he was able to get his men into shelter, and then our guns opened out. Either with set purpose, or on the spur of a gallant impulse, Compton shouted to

COMPTON'S GALLANT FORLORN HOPE.

those around him to have a go for the pill-box, and the small handful dashed forward on their lone-hand undertaking. The odds were dead against them. They had a hundred and fifty yards of flat to cover, and our shells had misjudged, and were landing beyond the leading German posts. So, with no other attacks to take their attention, and immune from shells, the enemy machine-gunners could concentrate on the little band, and they played sad havoc in their ranks. Compton and his platoon-sergeant—Sergeant Chilcott —fell together when they had covered half the distance, and the others were rapidly hit. But, amazing to say, one man actually reached the pill-box, and, finding himself alone, and unable to get at the garrison inside, he tumbled into a shell-hole, and remained there all day until darkness fell, when he made his way back to the Company. One cannot help feeling that Rex Compton was out to avenge his brother. Had he succeeded he might have gained a V.C. As it was, the failure left us mourning a very brave and likeable comrade and the followers who went with him, faithful unto death.

The remainder of the spell was not very eventful, but exceedingly unpleasant. Noteworthy was the devotion of our little M.O., Captain Belanger, who performed prodigies in the rescue of our own and of the Queen's wounded from between the lines. And Openshaw and his satellites of " *A* " Company did some excellent patrol work on the right.

On the evening of August 16th another Division came in, and we handed over our scattered posts into their keeping, and stumbled down the penitential slopes and through the strangely hushed ruins of Zillebeke—an abiding memory of slaughtered horseflesh —back across the shell-torn wastes to Café Belge, where bivouacs for the night awaited us.

That was not a very restful spot, however, for some prodigious railway guns, which were reputed to be knocking the stuffing out of Roulers, contrived to perform a similar operation with the aural apparatus of anyone who claimed their neighbourship ; and it was with more than a Hallelujah Chorus that the Battalion embussed on the Dickebusch Road, and bade a last farewell to that particular corner of beautiful Belgium.

Patient season ticket-holders on the Great Eastern Railway have known something of what can be done by immortal man in emulating the sardine, but never has any train pulled out of Liverpool Street so full as the lorries which bore the Essex and the Berks down the long Cassel Road into the green country and the blessed promise of rest. For some reason the transport accommodation was particularly insufficient on this occasion, but there were no candidates for a further sojourn in the Salient, and the old story of " Quarante Hommes," packs and everything, was repeated in the still scantier superficial area of the 3-ton lorry—with everyone supremely happy, none the less. For a good long rest was promised, in a real good spot, so rumour said, and so, indeed, it proved to be.

Rubrouck, around which the 53rd Brigade was centred, is a pleasant little village in the midst of the flat country between Cassel and St. Omer. It boasts of nothing to distinguish it except a rather Moorishly inclined style of church, and the accommodation is so meagre that by the time Rammers—the Staff Captain—had billeted himself and his batman, there was practically nothing left for anyone else. And so the battalions were spread abroad among the homesteads, as sheep without a shepherd. And this, if you can enlist the post-prandial confidences of a company officer, or the still more trenchant ones of the merry men of his command, you will learn to be an eminently desirable state of affairs. You see, even in the most blissful days of " rest," there is a spectre that stalks the haunts of officer or private. It is known as " Programme of Work." And as the time of commencement of parade has to be baldly stated in black and white, it is difficult to argue with facts when the C.O.'s billet overlooks the training ground. But where a couple of miles doth mercifully intervene there are many ways of conjugating the verb " to rest " more literally than the military dictionary allows

—many possibilities of exercises in picketing all possible means of approach and of corporate slumbers behind a haystack. And even an indefatigable Brigadier could not reduce the odds against his visit to less than 16 to 1 when companies were scattered broadcast over many square miles.

Sergeant Brown, five wound stripes and all, pitched his all-important canteen beneath the greenwood tree, and did a respectable trade, despite the competition of the licensed victuallers. Forbes and Sergeant Scholey conspired in the erection of an excellent latrinelike-looking orderly room. The R.S.M. —our one and only Lawrence—amused his leisure by grim watch over a recaptured deserter, and by bloodthirsty assurances that he was not going to escape again, repeated many a time and oft; and quite needlessly, as the event proved, for our little mascot soon evaded the majesty of the law when liberty made its call, and the R.S.M. was sleeping.

Towards the end of September things began to get a move on once more, and the Brigade marched forward to Road Camp, a well-organised area of hutments at St. Jan Ter Biezen, a few miles to the west of Poperinghe.

There had been some changes among the disposition of the officers about this period. Tween was at home on the senior officer's course, and his absence brought me to H.Q. with a step in rank. Innocent, too, achieved his majority, and was commanding " C " Company. Neild was still with " A." The unique and ubiquitous Bill Skeat captained " B," with inimitable vociferation, and at " D " Company H.Q. Openshaw had hoisted the sign of the Long Panatella. In general, the Battalion had undergone a bit of a reconstitution. But the process had diminished none of its efficiency, as later events went to prove.

The move forward brought us once more under the familiar leadership of General Maxse, now in command of the XVIIIth Corps, to which the 18th Division was allotted. There was a peculiar satisfaction in encountering " the Black Man " again, and I think

"*Gentlemen, what I wahn't is........*"

GENERAL SIR IVOR MAXSE, K.C.B., C.V.O., D.S.O.

that all who had served with him in earlier days felt happy to know that he was to be the presiding genius to watch o'er the fate of poor Tommy from the pinnacles of the Corps Chateau.

Maxse was not a commander who attained position by rigid orthodoxy and impeccable respectability. The winds of controversy have blown in alternating gusts around his reputation as they have about those of all public men of strong individuality. But among the mass of men who came beneath his military sway he had the all-important capacity of inspiring confidence, and that means very much to an army in the day of battle. The familiar clenched fist, and his, " Gentlemen, what I wahnt is . . . " got right there with his hearers at many a pregnant address, and it is almost superfluous to say that, getting there, meant that he usually got what he wanted.

Well, what Sir Ivor Maxse wanted on this occasion was a square mile or so of tumbled Flemish mud, and a rubble-heap of broken trees and bricks, once the peaceful unassuming village of Poelcapelle.

As in the case of Thiepval, there had already been a number of attempts against its stubborn defence, and the British battle-line had been carried on by bloody effort halfway through the village, but could get no further. So the big men scratched their heads and bethought themselves with solemn mien; and once again they said: "We'll try the A.T.N." And once again the old Division found itself confronted with the proposition of a real tough nut.

CHAPTER XXVI.

The Epic of Poelcapelle.

There are some pages in the history of the 10th Essex over which it is hard to restrain the pen and difficult to write in modest language. The achievements of the Great War have been so many that their very number tends to obscure their greatness. A single day's work of a couple of battalions can hardly hope to figure large in history when the field of glory was so wide. Yet it is perhaps no exaggeration to say that many exploits that were compassed by a brief 24 hours may rank alongside some of the year-long wars of the past, both for valour displayed, for obstacles overcome, and for sacrifices made. And the final capture of Poelcapelle and the taking of Meunier House by the 8th Norfolks and the 10th Essex on October 22, 1917, claims a place among such exploits.

For a week or two before that date the Division had been nosing round the Poelcapelle area. On October 10th an attack was attempted under atrocious weather conditions by the 55th Brigade, to which the Berkshires were temporarily attached, but very little headway was made. The Essex and the Norfolks relieved them, and a short holding period followed, which was highly uncomfortable, but not particularly costly. One loss we suffered, however, which could ill be spared. Forbes, the stalwart Adjutant, was wounded in a curious way by the hazard of an air-bomb dropped from out of the sky on a particularly serene and tranquil morning as he was taking the air outside Bulow Farm, the pill-box which served as Battalion H.Q.

A humorous incident was provided within the same pill-box on another occasion during the tour, when a sudden spasm of gas-shelling caught the majority of officers asleep, and frantic efforts to wake up and adjust gas-masks simultaneously resulted in the Colonel nearly choking himself with mal-adjustment, the fiery-minded Doctor Belanger becoming apoplectic with rage at the usurpation of some of his functions by the Assistant-Adjutant, and Padre Randell getting his right foot firmly and inextricably wedged into his left boot.

After a few days' acquaintance with the area the Battalion moved back again to camp, and with a brief respite and the usual thorough overhauling and instruction, the stage was ready set for the drama of the 22nd.

On the 20th we moved out from Tunnelling Camp and took the train to the line. Methods of transit and the consideration of the men had vastly improved since the days when we first came out, and the railway now took us as far forward as the original July 31st front trenches. So the usual long tramp up was dispensed with and there was but a short distance to go to the intermediate bivouacs. These were in Cane Trench, the old German support line, where a motley collection of battered concrete and dilapidated hurdle shelters furnished us with lodging for the night. The place was much waterlogged and knocked about, and being under the German observation into the bargain, it could not rank as a first-class health resort. And the Hun had evidently sighted activity there, for he gave the locality a liberal sprinkling of gas shells throughout the night, and "*B*" Company in particular suffered a number of casualties. Besides those who were evacuated, numbers of others were affected by the gas, and, to their honour, went through the rigours of the attack of the 22nd undaunted by the disability, although a great many had to be sent into hospital subsequently.

Battalion H.Q. was fortunate enough to secure a lodging for the night with Colonel Segram, of the Gunners, in an enormous concrete blockhouse, which reared itself like a super-Dreadnought among its lesser brethren.

During the following day we were heartened by a visit from General Maxse himself, looking more worried than his wont, but firm in the conviction that his old and trusted Essex were going to crack the nut. And it doubled one's determination to learn once more of his trust and confidence on the eve of setting out upon our perilous enterprise.

Late on the evening of the 21st October the forward march began. It was a Calvary way up those miles and miles of duck-boards which spanned the scarred wilderness of re-conquered ground. The whole area was sown with batteries belching out at sudden intervals, and the Hun was shelling them continually with heavy, nerve-shattering stuff. And down in the hollow he dumped his gas shells, and overhead the shrapnel searched the roads and tracks, so that the slow, painful march of the heavily-encumbered Battalion, strung out in single file over nearly a mile in length, was an agonising experience. And it was down the same snaky paths that the wounded had to make their precarious way before they could reach a haven of safety; in very truth, a Way of the Cross after a battle such as this one.

The assembly, on the whole, was a lucky one, for

there was a lull in the shelling at the critical moment of approach. Joe Culver had got the tapes out successfully in the twilight, and the Battalion formed up on these and dug itself in to wait for the morning. And it was that waiting part, under heavy bursts of Boche shells and knee-deep in shallow, watery shell-slits, that was the most trying business of all.

Battalion H.Q. was located in an old Boche pill-box on the Langemark Road, just outside the remains of the first houses of Poelcapelle. The scene here when we arrived was a ghastly one. A shell had just burst outside in the middle of a knot of waiting men, and some of the survivors—and what survived of them —were inside having their blood staunched and their grievous wounds attended to. Poor, mangled things! who can describe the agony and the dreadfulness of it all?

This H.Q. we shared with the Norfolks, who went over with us, and the scene within it made an arresting picture.

Imagine a place not much larger than the average sitting-room, but low-roofed and windowless. And into this some sixty human beings crowded—colonels, adjutants, artillery and liaison officers, signallers, runners, stretcher-bearers and doctors, with all their paraphernalia—pigeons, buzzers, medical stores, a wireless installation in one corner, a Primus stove going in another, and all lit by two or three spluttering, inefficient candles. And round about, and on top, shells were bursting almost continuously. A sentry was killed by one before our eyes as he stood sheltering in the doorway at my elbow, and the frequent force of near-by shells exploding would blow the candles out repeatedly.

This was the nerve-centre of the battle on our front, and round it all day pulsated the news and messages fraught with so much importance. Runners brought in word of the capture of the main objectives as they were taken, running the gauntlet of the shells and arriving breathless with the tidings; while the 'phone confirmed their information from the rear by messages from pigeons released from the forward line and arriving back at their dove-cots far behind, whence their news was again rapidly transmitted forward. And here the C.O.'s and the Adjutants, poring over their maps upon the improvised table, formulated their plans and dispatched their orders to the forward commands as the situation fluctuated from moment to moment, like admirals in a conning-tower amid a sea of mud.

The night of waiting was perhaps the worst the 10th Essex ever experienced. The assembly positions lay in a projecting tongue of land, hemmed in on two sides by the enemy, and subjected to the heaviest concentration of fire from half a circle of enemy guns, feverishly expectant of attack. A dump on fire in the rear partially betrayed the assembly, and heavy rain after midnight completed the hardships of the waiting hours, but could not daunt the courage of the men; and when zero hour came, the line, much thinned by casualties suffered during the night, went resolutely forward to the attack with undiminished determination.

The attack was launched at 5.35 a.m., and soon afterwards the news came back that the Norfolks had got the Brewery. Two hours later our fellows made a second leap from the line gained by the Norfolks, and " even the ranks of Tuscany could scarce forbear to cheer." There was the usual inter-battalion rivalry between the Essex and the Norfolks, but one and all of the other Battalion paid tribute that day to the magnificent way in which our boys went through, soaked to the skin, weighed down by heavy equipment labouring and struggling through the awful mud, with faces set towards their goal. Officers and men were exhausted before they had covered half the distance, but they floundered on somehow, and triumphantly reached the eminence of Meunier House and the ruins of Noble's Farm, alongside the Westroosebeke Road.

Bill Skeat performed prodigies on the left. Never were his stentorian tones heard to better advantage. Urging men on by name, directing the movements of his platoons by word of mouth, ordering and carrying out attacks on isolated machine-gun posts, all at the top of his voice ; his company assert that the barrage was eclipsed, and that if he had gone through the detail of piling arms they might have imagined themselves upon a barrack square instead of in an inferno of mud and explosive. Neild and Binney led their companies through in the centre with equal gallantry, though there was little left of " C " by the time the Meunier mound was scaled.

" D " Company, on the extreme right, had a curious operation to perform. While the main attack was in progress they were ordered to lie doggo, and then, by means of dummy figures on poles, Maxse's famous " Chinese Army," was made to draw the enemy fire. When the attention and the ammunition of the enemy in this quarter had been distracted, they were to sweep round in an enveloping movement and join hands with the other companies. This little scheme proved successful, for scant opposition was met when the time came for " D " to go forward. Openshaw, indeed, full confident of the prowess of his stout fellows, mounted to the roof of Gloster House, and there, like an enthusiastic race-goer on the grand stand at Epsom, was surveying the advance through his binoculars. when a piece of shrapnel hit him in the seat of the breeches, and he had to retire from the conflict.

The process of consolidation was a heartbreaking one, for water poured into every hole that was dug, and it was all the men could do to keep their rifle-bolts working, so clogged had they become in the course of the advance through the atrocious mud-fields. Going round the line was an unenviable task, and one was nearly beat before completing half of it. On "*D*" Company's front I discovered that an intrepid corporal and a couple of men, not content with what had been gained, had patrolled out some distance ahead on their own account into a heap of ruins known as Tracas Farm. It was a good bit of work, for our own guns were still shelling the place intermittently, and it was something of a marvel that the patrol managed to escape them. And as the point was a commanding one, it was a valuable position to hold; so, when our guns could be persuaded to lengthen their range, "*D*" Company pushed forward and added Tracas Farm to the day's bag. Corporal Bowley got the D.C.M. for his pluck and initiative on this occasion, and the Battalion earned a special paragraph in the Commander-in-Chief's communique.

A remarkable incident took place near the same spot a little later in the day. Sergeant Dupree and the C.S.M. of "*D*" Company, in adventurous mood, decided to investigate another pill box which lay out in front of our positions. So the couple of them set out. But, as their rifles had been rendered useless by the mud, all that they carried with them was a Very pistol—not too wise a weapon for two men wandering about in No Man's Land. In some way the pair of them became separated, and Dupree, forging on ahead, under the idea that the pill-box was un-

POELCAPELLE, MEUNIER HOUSE, HOUTHULST FOREST,
and a few square miles of Flanders mud.

BULOW FARM.
A typical Concrete Pill-box.

occupied, stumbled on a couple of Germans manning a machine-gun. Pointing the flare pistol at the machine-gunners, he made them put their hands up, and was about to disarm them and march them back as prisoners, when a score of their companions came tumbling out of the pill-box and made a dash for Dupree. A rough and tumble ensued, in which the sergeant managed to give a good account of himself. He discharged his pistol into the middle of his assailants, kicked the machine-gun into a shell-hole, and then set about defending himself with his fists. But he was outnumbered, and although the Germans could not shoot at him for fear of hitting one of their own men, a rifle butt on the head put an end to his resistance, and he was dragged into the pill-box, but not before he had left his mark on more than one of his opponents. The German officer inside could speak English, and told Dupree that if a further attack was made he was going to surrender. Whereupon Dupree did his best to persuade him to come over with him right away and save further trouble. The German seemed inclined to fall in with the idea, but after some cogitation finally decided to wait till dusk, when his orders bade him withdraw. So throughout the day our sergeant stood under guard, with his back to the wall, within the cramped interior of the pill-box, arguing with his captors, watching their nervous anxiety at any signs of movement in the British lines, hoping against hope for the advance which did not come. And when darkness fell, and his comrades were stumbling down the duck-boards to shelter and rest, Dupree was marched eastward into captivity in Germany.

It is invidious to single out a few individuals for mention when so many fine actions were performed, but records are not easily available, and if only a few are mentioned it is not because their deeds were preeminent. Full many a gallant act has gone unnoticed amid the hurly-burly of war, and any such chronicle as this must needs be incomplete. Among the little-noticed exploits on October 22nd was the plodding, plucky message-carrying of the Battalion and Company runners. The work by itself was a severe test of physical endurance, and the heavy shelling of the areas through which these errands led demanded lion-hearted courage. The stretcher-bearers similarly did wonderful unobtrusive work under our unrivalled Philipe Belanger—a perfect marvel of devotion and self-sacrifice on the field of battle. Not only did he clear our own wounded, but the majority of the Norfolks' also ; and the number of men who owe their lives to the tireless efforts of our little French-Canadian from McGill University, both on the 22nd and at other times during his service with the Brigade, is legion.

The afternoon after the attack was fairly quiet, but Jerry was taking stock of our new positions, and in the evening the S.O.S. went up to herald a strong counter-attack advancing up the Westroosebeke Road. Happily it could be seen in preparation for some time, and Hight, though many of his rifles were out of action and his men were dog-tired, did splendid work in repelling the menace. Davey, one of his Lewis-gunners, when the mud so clogged his gun as to put it out of action, performed the feat of stripping the gun, cleaning it, and putting it together again, as cool as a cucumber, while the enemy were nearing the position. And that gun contributed in no small measure to the subsequent defeat of the attack.

By this time scarcely a man in the Battalion was capable of anything further, so the necessity for relief was strongly represented to Brigade, and the Middlesex and Royal Fusiliers hastened in to the rescue.

" D " Company had a bad time from the Boche guns on their way out, and if it had not been for the leadership of Nicol, who, when severely wounded in the head and face, saw every man clear of the danger area before he would permit any attention to be given to his wounds, the toll would have been a good deal heavier.

So the very night after we had trekked up, the wearied, muddied remnants trudged down to the former half-way house in Cane Trench, dead dog-tired, but triumphant in duty done and victory won.

Though Meunier House cost the Essex 250 casualties, with Lieut. E. H. Brown killed and a number of officers wounded, the real victory of the 22nd was wrested less from flesh and blood than from the pitiless ordeal of shellfire and from that inexorable opponent, General Mud, ensconced in his own home country, Flanders. Mud impeded the assembly, soaked and chilled the men during their long wait, trapped every step in the assault, clogged rifles and Lewis guns, and cut off all but the slowest and most laborious communications. But, do its worst, it failed to quench the unconquerable spirit of British soldiers—of Essex and Norfolk men.

CHAPTER XXVII.

A Month's Hard Labour at Houthulst Forest.

It was a very tired Battalion that took the train back to Tunnelling Camp on October 24th, and the gaps in the ranks put a veto on cheerfulness, though there was a sense of satisfaction in knowing that we had done a job and done it well. Quite a shower of congratulations from the great ones of the Earth tumbled in by message or in person, and a goodly number of decorations followed in due course.

From Tunnelling Camp the Battalion moved in pouring rain, past that picturesque spot on the outskirts of Poperinghe, which rejoiced in the name of " Delousement Station," to Poll Hill, not far from Houtkerque. At this stage the Colonel deemed the time to be ripe for a month's leave, and a very just judgment it proved; for the next month turned out to be the quintessence of beastliness. But, remembering that he had been in France almost continuously since 1914, no one could begrudge the thoroughly merited respite, and, Tween being still at Aldershot, the reins of command fell into the hands of the present writer. It was not an enviable task. The men had got it firmly in their heads that a rest was due to them, and rumours were rife of a move to the sunnier climes of Italy. So that, when orders for the line came in, the Battalion, for the only time in recollection, began to get a real grouse going. The first spell in was a severe test of discipline with such ideas current, but the old spirit stood firm, and once the companies were in the thick of things the minor grumbles were forgotten, and successive spells of the most rigorous hardships only seemed to restore and intensify the usual bonhomie ; and at the end of a month's "hard labour, without the option" the 10th Essex emerged in as cheerful a frame of mind as it had known since the days of Steenvoorde.

The first unpleasant experiences were attributable to the nasty habits of the enemy who, with that entire lack of consideration which characterised him, now developed a special form of annoyance known as H. Vic. (High Velocity guns), whose range ran back to 5 or 6 or even more miles behind the front line and whose playful pyrotechnics were arranged at such times when all good citizens of the rearward areas had fondly reckoned upon repose. To be shelled is never pleasant, to be shelled in the open with ordinary 5.9's less so still, but if you are asleep in pyjamas in a Nissen hut and a stream of rushing missiles comes out of the harmless blue from goodness knows where, with a rush like an express train passing through a wayside station, and an emphasis at the end like the same express mistaking a terminus for a non-stop signal, you tend to become disheartened if not a little demoralised.

It took some time for the Army to accustom itself to these high velocity efforts. They became a recognised feature of the 1918 campaign, but at this time prudence had not suggested to the Staff that it was inadvisable to site an unprotected camp within easy range of their vagaries. And Coldstream Camp, on the hillside above Boesinghe, consequently became a spot that a medical adviser would hesitate to recommend to patients with weak hearts. One day an unfortunate shell landed in the middle of a hut occupied by Colonel Snepp, of the Norfolks, and the result was like a pack of enormous cards being thrown skyhigh into the air. Unhappily Colonel Snepp was seriously wounded, but the other occupants had phenomenal escapes. Within the Essex camp there were similar escapes. The Orderly Room was riddled through and through with fragments. And many members of the officers' messes spent considerable periods face downward on the floor like devout Mussulmen at prayer, while the men, with less ceremony, betook themselves to the open shell-holes when the evil times were upon them. Eventually we were forced to evacuate the camp and take up quarters in the Canal Bank, whence the Guards had most gallantly crossed the Canal and conquered the heights on July 31st.

From here to the front line in the fringes of Houthulst Forest was a matter of nearly five miles as the crow flies. But no crow, even after the most Bacchanalian orgies, has ever flown in such erratic courses as those followed by the duckboard tracks that wobbled to and fro across the muddy wastes of shell-hole-studded Flanders; and so the mileage that a human flat-foot had to cover to come to grips with his mortal foe were subject to the addition of quite an appreciable distance discount.

Our dispositions at this time were something unique in the way of tactics, and they gave General Higginson some anxious thought, I know. The Canal formed the frontier of civilisation. Way back in the problematical distance behind the Divisional H.Q. fleshpots at Elverdinghe lurked the resting Brigade of the Division. Along the Canal Bank the Norfolks and Essex, suffering a trifle from the housing problem, managed to make themselves comfortable without the aid of a Municipal Loan. And then from there, like three long antennæ, ran the odd six miles of duckboards, known as Clarges Street, Hunter Street, and Railway Street, spanning the evil Steenbeek near Widjendrift, where "A" Company and Innocent led a miserable mustard-gassed existence, and the still more unhealthy Broembeek, near which Byerley and his mud-sodden Company existed even less hygienically. And at the extremities of the antennæ, out in the wild and woolly Forest, the gallant Berkshires and Suffolks confronted the enemy, miles from the first solid reinforcements, and almost weeks away from real support if anything went seriously wrong. But self-reliance is a primary martial virtue ; and a second one is consideration for the men. Higginson always trusted his battalions with a faith that they can fairly boast to have justified ; and he never forgot the comfort of his henchmen where it was possible to study it. Hence these dispositions.

For three or four days the Brigade remained in this formation, and then on November 7th the Essex relieved the Berkshires in the left front sector.

Reliefs, of course, in this open kind of fighting were always by night, but usually a start would be made from way back while it was still daylight. And as the heavily-laden files trudged slowly eastward the light would fade until dusk enveloped them and the Battalion was completely swallowed up by the darkness and the Great Unknown of the forward areas. Nervy work, this tramp up, at least for commanders. One used to wonder if the men ever worried about it as we did. For, conceal it as one might, there was always the haunting fear of an enemy barrage descending on your hapless command, and then, slaughter infinite.

So, in memory, one plods up over the interminable boards, holding one's breath, as it were, for the sudden dull burst of thuds in the distance which herald the dreaded flight of shells, past our own batteries, grouped with muzzles almost touching the track, and whose playful humour it was to open a rapid strafe just as the P.B.I. got in front of them, on to the deserted areas beyond. Then Clarges Street suddenly merges into a swamp, and one or two men are in it up to their necks and very nearly drowned. And a Company gets adrift from the boards and wanders in a circle for half-an-hour before they are again recovered.

And thus with solemn weary progress we come to Louvois Farm, where misty figures in rifle and bandolier loom up and lead the companies to their respective places.

Then the C.O. and his faithful runner are left to wander off down the splintered road to the pill-box in the ruins, where waits a hearty welcome from the C.O. in occupation. Usually a whisky stands ready on the table, for there is a niceness of etiquette about these ceremonies, and one arrives thirsty. Then there are all sorts of details of the sector to discuss:—Enemy posts discovered, work in hand, stores, transport, signals, etc., etc. The careful study of maps and discussion of points will take an hour or two, and then over the 'phone, or perhaps, by runner, comes a cryptic message "Neild 11.45," which tells that "*A*" Company is in place, and O.K.; and that bit of responsibility is lifted. And one by one the companies report their relief complete until the pre-arranged code-word can be wired back to the Brigadier that the Battalion has taken over. The out-going C.O. glances outside:

"Think it's pretty quiet now and I'll have a shot at it. So long, and good luck."

"Thanks, and a safe passage down,"—so the captains and the kings depart, and the world is left to darkness, and to us—with Jerry over the way for boon companion.

Momentarily there is an infinite loneliness. Brigade H.Q. seems upon another continent, Division as distant as the Falkland Isles, and Blighty situated in some other planetary system. But jobs soon spring to hand, and we forget all about the isolation in the pressing cares of the moment.

The discomforts of the Line would require a chapter to themselves for an adequate description. Suffice it to say that some who remember them take comfort to themselves from the fact that the nether regions,

"*What was you, Bill . . .*"

at all events, are reputed to be dry—though there is an uncomfortable rumour about a mud lake down there.

The men had no shelter, nowhere dry to sit or lie, no breastworks, no wire in front of them, no warmth, nor possibility of motion except at night. How they stuck it is a perpetual marvel. I think this was the time when one sentry in conversation with another in an inundated shell-hole asked his mate:

"What was you, Bill, before you joined the Army?"

"'Appy," replied Bill, laconically.

A few utterly inadequate and highly insanitary pill-boxes at Panama House, Colombo House and the Cinq Chemins gave a little more specious comfort to the staffs of Company H.Q., but with conditions such as one fancies obtain within the igloos of the Esquimaux. Binney thought he might improve one of these shelters by digging out the floor. But the discovery of a decomposing Teuton changed his mind, and the principles of "laisser faire" were found to be of sounder application.

Ajax House, which served as Battalion H.Q., was something of a 12-foot square palace compared to the remaining accommodation, but there was little spare space, even when the usual retinue of H.Q. was reduced to a rigorous minimum; and standing like a war memorial in full view of the enemy, it was not a spot around which one slumbered in deck-chairs on the verandah.

By day we hibernated. At night activities began. The first night was particularly active when Byerley discovered that the Second-in-Command had mixed up the ration of whale-oil with the rum jars and that Neild had got a double portion of the essence of existence, while "D" Company's cruse overflowed with oil and not a tot of rum had reached them. Arthur Byerley nearly gave up the war altogether that night.

Besides the arrangements for getting rations up the duck-boards, there was the problem of getting them out to the men in their isolated shell-holes, working parties to be found, wire to be carried up, liaison to be established, and a policy of active patrolling to be maintained. So that the hum of activity when dusk obscured us from the vigilant German watchers at Marechal Farm and Chateau Cortvriendt was like a beehive when the sun comes out.

At first the supplies were all humped up by parties of men from the rear battalions, but as we became more settled into our new positions, Ord adventured up with mules ; and in the dead of night it was curious to hear their soft-treading feet along the deserted roads where it was death to pass in hours of daylight. Nor was it a pleasant job for the transport men ; and all honour to them, for though theirs was often an envied life, they never flinched when duty led them into danger, encumbered with animals that could not be stowed into a shell-hole, as was the habit of the human animal when shells oppressed him sore.

One night we nearly lost our next day's nourishment, for a confident soul at the head of the train was only stopped in the nick of time by a French outpost when he had passed the last of the British posts and was like to deliver the Essex rum and rissoles to a German commander at Renard Farm.

Throughout this period identifications of the troops opposing us were badly wanted, and frequent patrols were the order of the night. The French, our next-door neighbours, were lucky to secure one without effort. For one pitch-dark night a bulky German sergeant-major presented himself at the door of one of the French pill-boxes with a guttural enquiry for " Herr Hauptmann." He was seized, and his grief on discovery of his whereabouts dissolved him into tears, for in his pocket was found a leave-warrant to Hanover, which he was bringing to his company commander for signature when he lost his way in the blackness of the night and the unrecognisable wastes of the forest.

It is a curious thing, however, that the 10th Essex, with all the fame they won in full-fledged battle, never excelled in the quieter pastimes of raids and cutting-out. On this occasion, indeed, the Hun was more than usually wary and conditions of weather and ground did not help patrolling. Several attempts on small posts were made, but invariably to find them unoccupied, and it is sad to relate that the only identification secured was one of ours, by an enterprising party of visitors from over the way.

On the night of the 8th I had just visited an isolated post and had gone on into the wood which separated the two portions of the Battalion front, when a burst of bombing told of something amiss. While the C.O.'s inspection of the post was in progress it seems that there must have been a score of the enemy lying within a few yards, and when the visit was concluded they deemed the time to be opportune for rushing it and overpowering the four occupants. It was a blow to our pride to lose four men like this, but perhaps with pardonable egoism it may be counted fortunate that the raiders did not make their rush ten minutes earlier, or their bag might have included a very scantily armed senior officer and his runner, and this narrative would have needed another author.

Weather conditions precluded long spells in the Line at this time, and a four-day period usually brought us all not very far away from the limits of physical endurance. Then came a brief breathing-space back at De Wippe Camp, where the joys of a bath and a change of underclothing could be indulged in, a day or two on the Canal Bank, and then " once more into the breach."

We were largely a Battalion of locums at this time. The Colonel was on leave, Hardaker also enjoyed the sweets of Blighty, and Norman steadfastly substituted him. Culver too was away, and Willoughby took his place as Intelligence Officer. Innocent propped up an inexperienced C.O. with his usual resource and cheerfulness until, poor fellow, he tried to share the same piece of mud with a 4.2 in flight and was badly blown up. He was a pitiful spectacle to behold, with blackened face and blood-stained tunic, and we were much alarmed for him until, with head and neck swathed in field dressings, he hobbled out on the arm of a stretcher-bearer to make his way down to the rear. Then with a parting pun, he assured us that it was more bandage than badinage! And we recognised the old Innocent through his disfigurements, and knew that he would soon be all right again.

Father Neild, staunchest of fellows, came to H.Q. after Innocent's departure, and left his Company to Hawksworth. Linford was running "B," Binney captained "C" Company, and the only old-hand Company Commander was the veteran Arthur Byerley.

Yet with all this inexperience the Battalion played up wonderfully, and its three punishing spells of Line duty left it in good form and with a weathering that was to stand in good stead in the harder tests that came in the spring.

At the end of the month the 53rd Brigade ceded place with profound satisfaction to the 54th Brigade, and the frost-covered duck-boards saw many hurried feet on the night of the relief as we turned our backs on Houthulst Forest for the last time.

Truly these Jacob's ladders seemed to climb to Paradise that night. Too often, alas! for many a British soldier in Flanders they have seemed to lead to hell on earth. Yet, who knows, there may have been angels along them guarding his feet, and many a brave fellow has trod them to the Heaven which surely awaits all faithful duty done.

CHAPTER XXVIII.

Christmas, 1917.

The close of 1917 found the 10th Essex a somewhat weary Battalion. Passchendaele activities had not only depleted it in numbers, but had emptied it of buoyancy and native optimism. But let it be remembered that the weariness was born not of the definite actions in which we had been engaged. From July to the middle of December life had been lived in indescribable conditions. There was not a glimmering of beauty, except that which came forth from the men—their majestic patience and silent submission to the bloody task. Nature was torn into appalling ugliness. A landscape, once fair and fertile, was now a pressing pain upon the senses. The destruction, the waste, the mud, and now the cold thrown in—one almost dreads the memory of them! Quaint humour was dying down. There was a hollowness, like a leaden weight in the heart. Experience is age, and here was experience for a thousand years. And yet, paradoxical as it may sound, we were just children. And it was just the child-like character that carried us through. There was always a to-morrow, better surely than to-day. And the children's festival par excellence was now at hand.

What Christmas meant to the men in the mud cannot exactly be described. It brought forgetfulness of wretchedness, and it crowded life once more with happy memories and anticipations. And now the question on everyone's lips was : " Shall we be lucky enough to be out of the line over Christmas?" The uncertainty did not delay nor in any way impede the preparations. Major Banks, now second-in-command again, took over the work to such an effect that it was rumoured that the inhabitants of St. Omer were short of provisions for many days. Turkeys, geese, fowls, and pigs in ample quantities were bought. The beer came from Wormhout ; the quantity put into operation the whole of the Battalion transport ; the quality guaranteed sobriety. The whole Christmas fare was lavishly arranged, and the only anxiety that remained was our location over Christmas.

Unexpectedly the Division was ordered to hand over its positions in the mud to the 57th Division on December 19th, and we went back to Hopfland for a week's rest.

Hopfland is about two miles N.E. of Herzeele, and consists of a few scattered farms, in which the companies were billeted at some distance from each other. The versatile and imaginative Ord was charged with the transport of the good fare from its distant sources of supply, and under his supervision the groaning wagons brought their welcome loads into haven. All the preparations, down to an extensive levy on the crockery of the countryside, were successfully completed, and even the climate collaborated in producing a really Christmas atmosphere by a deep fall of snow.

Christmas Day opened with services in "B" Company barn. Arthur Byerley had trained a choir of carol-singers for this event, and the pride of place of the choristers of Westminster or of the Southern

Syncopated Orchestra—one hardly knows which—was momentarily in peril. Dinner came next, and this proved a feast of feasts. Heaps upon heaps of food upon the plates, a wealth of menu variety which would have made Joseph Lyons or Mr. Lockhart green with envy, quart after quart of the light amber ale of the country—very light—and a general oblivion to the things of yesterday and of the morrow, combined to make it an unforgettable feed, and the gratitude of the participants is a treasure that abides in the memory.

In the evening the officers dined together at Battalion H.Q., and this was the occasion of a humorous incident which became classic in the annals of the Battalion.

Prior to the great day the Colonel had shown a master's interest in the things to eat and drink. And among the special items of his care was a case of port and liqueur brandy, some sixty years of age, which had been supplicated from a fond uncle, and was earmarked for the Christmas dinner. Captain Neild, in the absence at the Senior Officers' School of Major Tween and Major Banks, was acting second-in-command, and was commissioned to see to the perfecting of arrangements for this Belshazzar's feast. Piano, band, and singers were all complete, and items elaborately detailed on a choicely-printed programme. The varied dishes were specially cooked by Martha and Elizabeth, the daughters of the house. There was nothing left to be desired.

All went well. Skeat's voice grew shriller and shriller: Neild exercised a detective eye on wants; the Colonel fondled the last button of his tunic with affection, and beamed good humour around him. Toasts were drunk and speeches made, and at the appropriate moment the band struck up the King. Then the age-long brandy was called for. Corporal Tozer, in stentorian tones, passed on the order to his henchmen. Pause, and subdued conversation. But no brandy was forthcoming. So Neild expostulated with the mess corporal over the delay. The Colonel was visibly agitated; Corporal Tozer dashed about in fury, and loudly swore at the cellarer. Impatience had reached its height. "Corporal Tozer, where is the brandy?" With a tear in his throat the harassed Tozer made reply, "Please, sir, the waiter says 'e put it in that there corner afore the dinner." Everyone now looked to the corner, but no brandy was discoverable anywhere.

The playing of the band had by this time become strangely fantastic. Their heavy midday meal was obviously not conducive to artistic renderings, and they were thanked for their services, and informed that no more instrumental music would be required that evening. Arthur sang as few men can sing in a drawing-room. Tommy essayed at a song and fainted into the piano. Lucy rendered, "I fear no foe," to a traditionally high-pitched key, and Skeat produced his one and only, "Tall Bobbies and short Bobbies." The Colonel drew forth rolling laughter in the sketch of a conducting officer in Delville Wood—"Please, sir, where's Germans." And in this way a happy Christmas came to an end. But there was no brandy!

So next day a full Court of Inquiry was solemnly convened to inquire into its disappearance. Neild was Inquisitor-General, but the confusion of evidence was sufficient to baffle a Lord Chief Justice, since memories of the night before had become strangely obliterated. After protracted sittings, however, the testimony of the ladies of the household that "Le petit Gingaire was dronk, dronk, dronk, and was trying to kiss we," and the discovery of a case of emptied brandy bottles broadcasted in tell-tale fashion in the orchard, circumstantially convicted the said little Ginger, who had hitherto led a respected life as servant to the Padre. And he was dismissed with ignominy from the mess. No doubt he subsequently philosophised that a crowded hour of glorious life more than compensated for the return to duty, for few men, one imagines, can tell of the consumption of several quarts of sixty-year-old brandy within the brief and lurid space of a single Christmas evening.

CHAPTER XXIX.

EMILE CAMP, ROUSBRUGGE AND SOUTHWARDS TO THE OISE.

The period immediately following the Christmas rest was not, after all, what was anticipated. With Hopfland left behind, a return to the line, with occasional diversions in the way of attacks on a local scale, seemed to be a virtual certainty. But when the Battalion reached Boesinghe it became known that the 53rd Brigade would not be required for line duty, but instead was to provide the brawn and the sinews for the works of fortification in which our sapper chieftain gloried.

The battalions were accordingly settled into reasonably comfortable camps near Elverdinghe, and thence the working companies would sally forth for their daily and nightly flounderings along the duckboards up to the forward areas, where the products of Essen found an ever-ready market. Here there were many tasks to be performed. One of them was inspired by a pious desire of those in authority to tidy things up a bit, and much time and effort were spent in striving to coax the erring Broembeek from its marshy vagaries once more into the routine flow of a single channel. It was a labour of Hercules, but the comfort of Divisional H.Q. inculcated optimism in such matters. And if the mighty had desired the

North Sea baled dry, the 18th Division would have attempted it.

Back in camp a number of diversions served to keep the spectre of monotony from the door. At this period of the Great War a nameless genius hit upon the idea that, when not fighting, the troops would be excellently employed cleaning up the devastated areas, levelling them out, digging them up, and sowing the fruitful grain or cauliflower. " Every man to his own allotment " was the slogan, based, one presumes, on the theory that if the U boats sank every ship upon the ocean, the Army at least would have a cabbage or two to fall back upon. And so the Battalion was ordered to reclaim two acres in the neighbourhood of the camp, and under the leadership of Neild, the agricultural element from the fruit-farms of Tiptree, or the plough-lands of Newport and Braintree, were enabled to display their prowess before their City-bred brethren. The flaw in the scheme was that one reaped not where one had sown. And it demanded a larger share of altruism than is normal to the present development of human nature to work in perspiration for the fruits which would fall to other Divisions at some other date. No doubt the harvests of Emile Camp were garnered by men of our own nationality, but on the Somme the scheme came to irretrievable ship-wreck when the labours of the early spring were inherited by our brothers Boche in the course of their advance to Weltmacht and Niedergang.

Simultaneously another idea became fertile in the minds of the powers who made our destiny. In the line there was an excitement, which bred a certain forgetfulness. Outside the mind woke to the consciousness of things. And to deck out the drabness, and to obliterate the interminableness of the war, concert parties and cinemas received strong encouragement. Within the 53rd Brigade the famous Zero troupe were born. Captain Pocock, of the Machine Gunners, piloted the project, and with the able aid of our Norman, of Corporal Ellis, of the Essex band, " Phyllis," the female impersonator of many wiles and much wardrobe, and Tich, of the Berkshires, a most creditable show was produced, which became a household institution and a steady source of cheerfulness throughout the remainder of the history of the Brigade.

At the same time, another item of entertainment was provided by the exhilarating sight of Elverdinghe Chateau on fire. Fighting units experienced a subtle inward joy when luxurious, substantially-quartered Divisional H.Q. were put to sudden discomforts. But the joy was of little duration, for " Old Bill " Cutbill, scenting a place of refuge at Emile Camp, commandeered our best huts, and the greater discomfort again fell on the patient backs of the P.B.I.

So the time passed by with no closer acquaintance with the realities of fighting than the nightly working parties to the Broembeek, and the thrice nightly visits of the Boche bombing machines overhead.

Then came rumours of a move to the southward. Already there were mutterings of the gathering of Germany's hosts across the way, and through the calm which succeeded the din and reverberation of the Passchendaele battle there seemed to echo the tramp of the Hunnish hordes from Russia massing for the great world-battle, which was to decide the fate of generations.

On January 29, 1918, the 18th Division was withdrawn from the Houthulst Forest sector, and the Battalion marched out on a glorious frosty morning to Rousbrugge, in Belgium, where, in common with the whole of the British Army, it was subjected to a radical process of reorganisation from a four-battalion to a three-battalion Brigade. Halt was made here for ten convivial but sorrowful days. They were happy days because the Battalion was settled in a delightful area, with an attractively pretty town within five minutes' walk of the camp ; sorrowful, however, because it was here that the original 53rd Brigade came under the pruning knife of the Adjutant-General, and the process involved the disappearance of three fighting units of the first water.

From the days of the formation of the 53rd Brigade at Colchester in 1914 until January, 1918, its composition had been unchanged, and 8th Norfolks, 8th Suffolks, 6th Royal Berks and 10th Essex, under the training of such Brigadiers as Hickie and Macandrew, and the leadership of General Higginson, had compiled a record for unfailing victory which was a byword in the Army. Now, alas ! three of these stalwart units were doomed to disbandment, and the 10th Essex alone continued to exist. The Norfolks, under the ægis of Colonel Ferguson and the Berney-Ficklings, always a Battalion of smartness and display, and withal, as we came to learn in the partnership of many a hard-fought action, one of the truest soldierly mettle ; the old sturdy Suffolks, slow on the uptake but sure as they make 'em, and invariably with some individual and peculiar way of doing things ; and our particular brethren-in-arms, the 6th Berks, with whom our only source of rivalry was their never-failing gallantry ; all three of these trusty comrade-units were dispersed, and their places were taken by the 7th Royal West Kents, from the 55th Brigade ; and the 8th Royal Berkshires, from the 1st Division. Very excellently did our new-found friends supply the places of the original units, as the history of the 1918 fighting shows. But it was with real sorrow that the 10th Essex parted with their staunch companions of the Somme, of Arras and of Ypres, despite the signal honour of being left as the sole original custodians of the rich traditions of the Brigade, and the pride of receiving the title of "The Old Guard" from their well-loved commander, General Higginson.

The few days at Rousbrugge were crowded with farewell dinners, sports, football matches, and all the proud, sad ceremonial of military adieux. And then the Battalion entrained for the extreme right flank of the British line, and went into quarters at Bethancourt, south of St. Quentin. This was but a pretence at a village, for the Huns had razed it to the ground in the course of the 1917 retreat; but Major Tween, with rare genius for comfort, established every man in a happy corner, and we lived here in Arcadian bliss for a fortnight.

Speculation was rife as to what the future held, but there were many assurances that the sector which enshrined our immediate destiny was a quiet one, and with these comforting prospects the Battalion moved forward to Remigny on February 25th, and in the dusk of the same day into Ly-Fontaine. The promises of quietude were dispelled early, for the entry into Ly-Fontaine was heralded by a brisk shelling of the village and entry roads, intermingled with gas. Entering a completely new area under such conditions is a distinctly unpleasing experience, especially in the dark; and two incidents that occurred at this time are worthy of record.

The Battalion moved into Ly-Fontaine by companies with an interval between them on the road, and behind each company came a limbered wagon carrying the rations for the following day. During a salvo from the enemy guns which landed uncomfortably near, two powerful mules—Pearman's greys—which were drawing the limber behind H.Q. Company, bolted, and but for the presence of mind and tenacious courage of Captain Forbes, the company immediately behind must have suffered casualties from the stampeding animals. Forbes hung on to the two mules like grim death, until he and they were down grovelling on the road together. And it was characteristic of the man that when he was extricated he moved away quietly in the dark as though he had done nothing unusual. But severe bruises next day told their own tale.

Another incident was Arthur Byerley riding into Ly-Fontaine in the thick of raining shells to ascertain conditions there for the Colonel, and reporting on his return, " Not very bad, sir!"

Such little happenings as these are among the trivialities of wartime life, but the memory of such simple acts of heroism performed without ostentation or further thought among the occurrences of the everyday will remain an inspiration to those who have witnessed them—an abiding witness to the nobility of soul inherent in human nature.

CHAPTER XXX.

Waiting Hours. March, 1918.

After the inhospitable welcome of the first entry into Ly-Fontaine, the unspeakable Hun gave no further cause for complaint, and the Battalion settled into the most peaceful spell in the line in its history. But the peace was superficial, for underneath there was massive disquiet, as we were soon to discover. For over three weeks the weather was exceptionally brilliant and warm, and the war itself, on this, the extreme right of the British line, was absurdly simple and holiday-like. To prove this, all that one has to do is to point to the casualty list of the Battalion for the period—one man wounded in the nose ; and that man was lying on his back on the fire-step of a trench watching an aeroplane fight, when a spent bullet from one of the machines dropped inconsiderately upon his upturned face. Enemy shelling was the very minimum, and hardly ever was the shelling repeated on the same object. To the unwary it seemed quite purposeless and fantastic. Past experience had been familiar only with shelling on a definite object, and that discomfortingly repeated. But here otherwise. We grew bold and happy ; so bold that officers had their valises in the line, and men had their periodic baths in the Brasserie of Moy in the actual front line positions, though the Oise Canal ensured a certain security from unannounced intruders in the bathroom. So happy were we all that we literally groused when we had to hand over our positions in the front line and take over support positions.

When in support there was more than ample work to do, and many an arm ached with digging defences against the looming probability of an enemy attack. In the line alertness alternated with delightful spells of laziness and the mind was lulled into a false sense of security. But a few hundred yards to the rear one came within the range of the mental activities of G.H.Q., equipped with all the far-seeing, long-distance hearing antennæ of the Intelligence Service, and the result was aggravating discomfort and disquietude. Full-blooded Generals from Army H.Q. would swoop down on us with strange informality in hours of darkness, ask mysterious questions, and then disappear. Companies would practice marching out into positions of battle in the defensive line until they were fed up with this imaginary warfare. In the line there was none of this bewildering business. All was so quiet; the enemy so harmless, if not friendly; so why all these touches of "Qui Vive"? The untutored mind said, "The Boche is chucking up the war, for he's blowing up his ammunition dumps." From the front line huge fires were seen nightly in the enemy country. Our own guns were too quiet to create these fireworks, and our night-bombing 'planes were not so active here as we were accustomed to know them, so that superficially everything pointed to a state of desperation in the mind of our adversary.

It was only by a gradual process that the light of truth began to filter through the unwonted happenings across the way, and the man in khaki came to realise that he was in for the severest ordeal that Britain's

With the 10th Essex in France. 253

Army had encountered since the dark days of 1914, when the gates to the Channel were barred by the heroism of his early predecessors. The Boche, in spite of all his little tricks, was intending a gigantic attack. He resorted to every artful ruse to assure us otherwise, and we, for our part, rigorously started to lecture and train every man into preparedness for the hundred and one things that might happen when the storm of battle broke.

There came a strange seriousness and tension into every face. From ease and quiet we were turned into a state of mind crowded with expectation. Everyone felt the incubus and divined the little game of Boche bluff. It was the playfulness of the cat before eating its victim.

In the past, training was virtually confined to one thing only—to go over the top, to attack. And now we sought to learn the unfamiliar—to stand our ground, to await the enemy and to hold on when there was nothing left except the will that said "Hold on."

On our right was the 58th Division, and on the left the 14th Division. The line held by the 5th Army was a record in length, and it seemed incredible that it could be successfully held. The extent of line held by the Battalion was over two miles, and the same length approximately was held by others. The C.O.'s tour of the line was arduous in the extreme. From Battalion H.Q. he would make a start at 4.30 in the morning, and it was after 11 before he had completed his inspection. Long stretches of the line were unmanned; it could not be otherwise. Machine-guns and gunners were of the utmost importance in a line so thinly held.

General Higginson was everlastingly in the front systems, assisting battalions in fixing and arranging machine-gun posts. This great Apostle of Duty laboured day and night, and he was held in awe as he was met making his tour into the line for the third time in a day.

At Ly-Fontaine the Battalion spent seven days, then it took over the front line from the Berks. Seven days was our spell there facing Alaincourt, then we sidestepped and took over the Moy sector from the R.W. Kents. In this way we spent seven days in support and fourteen days in the front line. On the night of the 19th-20th March the Essex were relieved by the 7th Royal West Kents, and passed into Brigade support in the battle zone. And here we were, with the Berks and Kents widespread across the four-mile line in front, when the impending crash came.

Before that never-to-be-forgotten day events came which spoke of big things. Opposite St. Quentin very heavy gas casualties were reported. This, it was felt, was a feeler, and further careful precautions were taken. Every conceivable thing was done to be absolutely ready, and the Battalion stood as fully prepared for all eventualities as it was possible for its officers and the Brigade Commander to make it. But there could not fail to be misgivings about that long, long line in front, so thinly held. And it was well known that there was not a single man behind us except the reserve Brigade of the Division, and the crocks and the Chinese of the Labour Battalions.

On the 20th March Ly-Fontaine was subjected to a whole day's shelling. There were two six-inch howitzers within a few yards of Battalion H.Q., and we consoled ourselves that these were the object of the enemy shelling. There was a considerable change in the landscape when the shelling stopped, and we could view the world once again. And beyond the disappearance of the cosy and well-structured Battalion H.Q. latrine there were no casualties. But the incident left a further uneasiness in the mind, which was not allayed by the revelations of the pilot and observer of a Boche 'plane brought down in Ly-Fontaine that very morning, who admitted under examination that the great attack would be launched at 4.15 next morning.

Major A·S·TWEEN·D·S·O

Colonel Frizell had gone home on leave earlier in the month, and Major Tween was in command of the Battalion. The strain placed on him during this period cannot readily be appreciated by those who have not known the responsibilities of command, but those who were there know what patience, skill and courage he displayed in those anxious and testing days. Courage here has a different sense from that which he displayed later. Here it refers to the way he changed the view-point of the whole Battalion from attack to defence as the present necessity. On the night of the 20th every little detail was seen to by him in event of attack. Everything was made as clear as daylight. Every officer and man knew what to do, where to be. Everyone rested early. Officers changed into their worst uniforms, packed up their valises, and lay down to an early evening's rest. Intuition, plus information, left one in no doubt that the morning would test us to the uttermost.

CHAPTER XXXI.

The Flood-Gates Open.

Every tragedy has as many view points as there are actors in and witnesses of it. This is true of every simple event. It makes as many different appeals as there are persons to look on. How far this is true of the most critical event in the history of the British Army will be obvious to every fighter when reading any narrative of it. No man alive can possibly cover every detail of a single life; but when a record is made of a Battalion's part in the event known as the March Retreat, only a simple, human generalisation can be made. To set down every detail of those eventful days would be to hazard the task, not of a chapter, but of many volumes. In looking down on the valley landscape from the mountain top, the familiar details are lost to view, and only the main features stand out in bold relief. It is this mountain view that must be attempted here in reducing into one single chapter days literally crowded with ineffacable incidents of fatigue, endurance, and daring.

At 4.15 a.m. of the 21st the enemy bombardment opened on us. To say that it was severe would be to use a mild expression. It was wild and mad. Shrieking, hissing shells, like the tearing of millions of pieces of calico, arrived in continuous unbroken streams; thunderous explosions, like thousands of earthquakes, swayed and rocked the earth. Companies hastily moved out of their shelters, through the inferno, to battle positions, and wondered how they ever got there without wholesale annihilation. The dense mist made the finding of battle positions a miracle. Every man's life was so crowded with awe and thrill, and yet dominated by duty, that those who were lamentably swept over the borderland by the racking fire disappeared without the immediate knowledge of their " pals." When a man cannot see his hand held up in front of his eyes, he cannot know precisely the happenings a few yards from him. If the earth goes up and he is lifted out of his place, he, and he alone, knows if his senses are left to him.

Byerley moved out " D " Company from shelters in Remigny, literally through active scythes, into battle position. " A " Company, at Caponne Farm, in moving into their trench from the dug-outs, suffered appalling casualties, leaving Nunn alone as officer, in charge of a mere handful of men. The Battalion was deprived of that most gallant and intrepid of officers, Hawksworth, in the very initial hour of attack. Culver was grievously wounded, and crept back to the H.Q. dug-out to destroy the papers before the Huns could find them. Here he was captured. " B " and " C " Companies suffered, but not nearly so heavily. Telephone communications were blown into the limbo of forgotten things almost with the first salvo. This withering fire continued until 10.30, and every man stuck it till he was " picked off." Runners maintained primitive communication in difficulties that can be imagined ; but there was no news. We were oppressed with a painful loneliness.

At about 11 o'clock the bombardment died away into a memory, and the sun dispelled the mist. The sight before our eyes is not given to every man to see ; familiar Ly-Fontaine was so transformed that it required an effort of will to believe that it was Ly-Fontaine. It had been blown into ribbons. The sun's appetite in taking up the mist made it possible to see all around us. On the right, between us and Vendeuil Fort, small parties of the enemy could be seen making stealthy advances. On our left, on the 14th Division front, the enemy had penetrated deeply, and left our flank swinging wildly in the air with the Hun more than a mile behind it. Immediately in front the Royal West Kents' Headquarters, under Crosthwaite, was making a herculean defence securely surrounded. The Royal Berks H.Q. was forced back to Brigade H.Q., where, in conjunction with Hedley's T.M.B., a vigorous all-day defence was made at close quarters. It was not until late that evening that "*A*" Company and Hedley's gallant contingent, after holding out all round the clock against the increasing pressure of a numerically superior enemy, extricated themselves from a position in which they were being assaulted front and rear, and where they had to fire from both parapet and parados of the trench to keep off their attackers. Unceasing rifle and Lewis gun fire was directed on the pressing enemy till 11 o'clock that night, when the 54th Brigade and cavalry covered our withdrawal through Remigny and across the Crozat Canal at Liez, to Frieres. By this time the enemy was at Montescourt, and pressing on Jussy. Our position through the collapse of the Division on our left was one of extreme peril, as the Germans were well behind us.

At Frieres we breathed, replenished our ammunition pouches, and reorganised. The 54th Brigade dug in on the west side of the canal, and fought continuously the next day (22nd), while we remained in support. Here we discovered that the 53rd Brigade consisted only of one solid, though depleted, unit, the 10th Essex. The Colonel of the Royal Berks had under his command a curiously composite handful from the T.M.B.'s, M.G.C., and his own H.Q. Company, with one or two men of the Royal West Kents, and echelon parties.

Ere long the enemy had once again penetrated the defences on the left, and forced a passage across the canal at Jussy. This necessitated our retirement to Villequier Aumont. Here the Brigade rested in the stables and outbuildings of Rouez Farm for the night. Breakfast on the following morning was partaken to the recital of many a thrilling tale, punctuated by silence. And this was our last breakfast for many days. Then followed inspection. During this process streams of French Poilus were passing through into Rouez Wood. Cheerful greetings were exchanged, and hearts swelled once more with invincibility.

Presently the crackling of rifle and machine gun fire obliterated the sound of tramping feet. A French liaison officer, feverishly gesticulating, and asking for the General, bore on us the truth that the enemy was in the wood, and only a few hundred yards away. Orders were rushed on company commanders, and in a twinkling companies filed out into the wood. There was barely time to get a line flung out along the road to Frieres when the advancing hordes were upon us. On they came rank after rank inexhaustible. And the rapid fire crackled out from our thin line like the rattle of a hail-storm on an iron roof. With their bolts working like the " Old Contemptibles," the Essex fire scorched through the grey hordes like jets of fire through withered grass. Then new lines sprang up, to be mown down again until one sickened of the slaughter. An after-Armistice visit to this Rouez battlefield proved that along the Battalion front at least three battalions of the enemy (apparently freshly thrown into the fight) were decimated and hurled crippled back by this unwavering defence. But the Battalion paid a toll, too. From a keeper's cottage, which the Hun filled with machine guns at every window, a deadly fire galled "D" Company, and Farquhar was hit mortally when exhorting his men with the light-hearted gallantry characteristic of his leadership. Binney, too, who had proved his stout-hearted fearless-

ROUEZ, MARCH 23RD, 1918.
The Keeper's Cottage.

ness on a hundred occasions, was wounded unto death, and seen fighting to the last with his captors. Many deeds of heroism were performed that must go for ever unsung. And even the admiration of the unspeakable Hun was evoked ; for when a year afterwards a pilgrimage from the 10th Essex visited the scene, they found the unusual tribute on the wooden crosses over our wonderful dead—

"EIN TAPFERER ENGLANDER."
(A brave Englishman).

It was a perilous moment when after midday the enemy broke through to a vantage point on our right. Realising the vital importance of this, Major Tween, our commanding officer, gambled on " hoofing " out the enemy by attacking with Battalion H.Q.—pioneers, signallers, runners and sanitary men. With a shout and a dash, led by Major Tween, the position was taken, but Tween himself, alas! was mortally wounded.

Small and unimportant as this attack may seem in relation to the whole, it was pregnant with consequences. Every moment gained by the 18th and 58th Divisions at their vital junction-point with the French Army was of incalculable importance in preventing that insidious wedge on which Ludendorff was pressing with all his might from biting irreparably into the grievous gap on our left. The poilus with whom we were fighting shoulder to shoulder were unfortunately short of ammunition, but French armoured cars dashed up and down in acrobatic fashion, pouring out bullets in streams, and effectively assisting in holding up the enemy. Advances on both flanks rendered once again our position one of great peril. By nightfall the Germans were well behind us, and but a narrow exit corridor remained. It was something of a miracle that any of the Battalion got out at all, and another two hours would certainly have seen them entirely surrounded. But back they got, leaving many stricken when the good fight had been fought. In one grave alone at one particularly bitterly-contested point there were buried four Englishmen, one Frenchman and four Germans.

We were ordered to fall back through the French on Caumont. The roads were so congested with every conceivable article of the paraphernalia of war, that movement on foot was becoming an experience of extreme difficulty and danger. After a few hours' rest at Caumont, we were ordered to fall back on Caillouel, through Commenchon and Bethancourt, for rest and food.

We had not been in Caillouel an hour when it was reported that the enemy were on our heels at Bethancourt. The Battalion dug in on the north-east side of the village, and in a very short time encountered the enemy. Enemy aeroplanes flew almost along the ground, and supplied the infantry with knowledge of our positions. Guns were brought to bear upon us, adding considerably to our casualties. Magnificent defence was put up here and there by isolated parties, notably one under Hight, of " B " Company, yielding only in death to overwhelming numbers.

At 3 a.m. of the 25th we were withdrawn to Crepigny, to form a line in conjunction with the French and 55th Brigade. Owing to the outflanking success of the enemy, we were forced to fall back further on Babœuf, units covering each other's withdrawal. So congested was the Noyon-Chauny Road at this stage that movement one way or the other was an impossibility. Ord's striking success in piloting the Brigade transport over tracks, by-roads, and ditches revealed the experienced map-reader and adventurer.

In the early hours of the next morning, the 26th, we were forced back across the Oise at Varennes. Here we covered the withdrawal of the 54th Brigade, who attacked and captured some prisoners. A short halt at Pontoise, and we marched back out of action into Caisnes. Here there was a rest till 4.30 p.m.; then to Nampcel for the night. Next day we moved to Autreches, and met Ord with his ample stores of prepared food and whisky from the abandoned canteens. Here, too, Colonel Frizell rolled in from " Blighty," to find a hungry, bedraggled and decimated Battalion. Facing a Battalion reduced into a respectably-sized company, calls for no eulogies. It is the moment for silence, for the silence never errs from dignity and eloquence. Hungry we were, so hungry that Byerley and Jock Richardson, a fellow-company-commander of the Berks, spying a scrap of biscuit lying in the dust of the road, made a simultaneous dash for it, and struggled for a moment to get it; then, realising what they were doing burst into laughter and agreed to share it. Weary we were—utterly exhausted. But it only needed food and a good night's rest to fit us out for the next urgency.

Not so, however, for in the unholy hours of the following morning, the 29th, we marched out through Vic to meet the lorries ordered to embuss us to the neighbourhood of Amiens, for reorganisation. On the road news arrived that the situation was developing as seriously as it possibly could. All along the route wholesale evacuation was in progress. Our destination as a result was changed. At 12 o'clock that night, after 20 hours' in jolting lorries, we debussed near Boves, and marched into Gentelles, to take up a support position.

In the thick darkness we had no idea where we were, but all was very quiet, and the whitewashed houses of the village looked comfortable and inviting. It did not take long to allot the village for billets, for we found it completely evacuated. We were the sole inhabitants, with every comfort to gladden our tired senses. There were cockerels crowing, hens cackling, and pigs snorting, alarmed at the unusual tramp of feet! Hunger had been hard to bear, but here was the reward. Next day we gorged on fowl and pig. So lavishly did we feed on these, that for long afterwards the sight of feathered fowl and bristled beast awakened the feelings of a sea voyage! With mouths full of fowl, and with cooks working at high pressure feathering and roasting more, we were moved out (March 30th) about a thousand yards east of the village, and dug another defensive line.

Instead of finding ourselves going back to Gentelles that evening to renew the interrupted feast, we were ordered to concentrate near the village of Hangard, and to take over the line from the Australians. And so followed a period unrivalled for its weariness, fatigue and intensive struggle against the enemy. The Retreat itself became a pastoral dream in comparison.

From this time to April 12th, when the Battalion brilliantly attacked the enemy at Hangard, was a period of no sleep, no rest, iron rations and fighting. We worked in close conjunction with the 5th Australian Brigade. The enemy pressure along the Villers Bretonneux, Cachy, Hangard Line, seeking to force through into Amiens, was unremitting and bloody. Men, gas, munitions, were hurled on to us on a prodigious scale. The line, however, was held with the grimness of death.

Gentelles was being slowly demolished, and when we were relieved from the line we sought the open fields around, as Gentelles was the place for sure death. Heavy casualties were reducing us into seeming impotence. In hurriedly filling a gap in our line at Bois de Hangard, Forbes was shot through the lung, but refused to be taken down till he had instructed Mulkern, O.C. "B" Company, what to do. Incidents such as these were so numerous that their record would fill a volume.

On the 12th the situation was more perilous than ever. The French were attacked and forced out of Hangard. The Battalion was moved into position of counter-attack with the French. Only verbal instructions could be given to company commanders. "D"

Company attacked on the right front, "C" Company on the left front; "B" Company moved into close support; and "A" Company remained in reserve, and supplied reinforcements.

Officers and men were on the verge of collapsing through fatigue, but there was nothing for it but to attack and retake the village. The French attacked on our right. From 7.35 p.m. to 7.50 p.m. our 18-pounders put down a shrapnel barrage on Hangard.

Companies stepped off from forming-up position at 7.35 across the exposed ground. The enemy replied with a terrific 5.9 barrage; but weary, maddened men do not care what happens to them, and, moving forward undeterred, they retook the village, consolidated their positions, and proudly handed over a number of machine guns and 60 prisoners. It was desperate, it was costly, it was successful.

The next day we were relieved, and rested the night in Boves, and from there we moved the next day to S. Fuscien, under the command of Arthur Byerley. It was a memorable march to S. Fuscien, for there were only four officers and a few score men, whose feet moved as though they were leaden feet. All the others, from the C.O. downwards, were either killed, gassed, wounded, or missing. And when next day the Corps General came round to congratulate Arthur on the brilliant success of the counter-attack, Arthur forthwith ordered a new tunic, with added chest measurements! We were proud, but we were literally done.

CHAPTER XXXII.

THE VILLERS-BRETONNEUX FIGHTING.

At the conclusion of the epic period of the Retreat, and the superhuman effort at Hangard village, which so gloriously closed the chapter, the 10th Essex was withdrawn to S. Fuscien for rest and reorganisation. And, indeed, both were badly needed. For more than a fortnight the Battalion had been engaged in continuous fighting, or within close range of alarm of action, and flesh and blood had been strained beyond the limits of human capacity. And the wastage of these strenuous days had reduced our gallant Battalion to the strength of a good-sized company, and almost completely depleted it of its leaders and of well-tried rank and file. Both Colonel Frizell and Captain Skeat suffered severely from the effects of mustard gas during the Hangard village operations, and had to be evacuated for treatment; and the loss of the Colonel at such a juncture was a heavy handicap. Byerley was the senior surviving officer, and for a brief three days reigned in regal state at Battalion Headquarters. Then Banks, who had for a similar spell been dressed in a brief authority in command of the Berkshires, returned to his old love, and, with the faithful Arthur once again as his right-hand man, the task of assimilating the drafts of beardless boys and brand-new officers which came pouring in at all times of the day and night was tackled with sleeves rolled up. The job was no sinecure, for so few experienced hands remained. But with J. C. Parke, well-known in many a doughty fight on the battlefields of sport before the war, in partnership with Peter Nunn at the helm of "*A*" Company, Mulkern with "*B*," Chaplyn as the popular Company Commander of "*C*," and Bobby Haile with "*D*," a creditable show could be made in the company commands, and the task of assimilation was simplified. But the trouble was that there was so little time to hand, for already the wave of the German advance, which had spent itself within exasperatingly little distance of Amiens, was hunching again for another desperate launch to gain the coveted city.

At this time General Higginson received his well-merited advancement to the command of the 12th Division. It was with pride that we saw the recognition of those sterling qualities which we had known so long, but there was a poignant sorrow in parting from a trusted leader, and his adieu to his "Old Guard" in the fields below S. Fuscien is a scene of memorable recollection On the evening of the 23rd April a farewell dinner in his honour was held at Brigade H.Q., and hardly had the wassail concluded, and the guests retired to bed, when the windows were shaken by the thunders of bombardment, and the heavens afire with the lightning of the guns. There could be little doubt that the battle of Villers-Bretonneux had commenced, and that we should be needed ere many suns had risen. And, sure enough, at 4 a.m. came the word to "stand by," and by 5.15 a.m. the Battalion was on the road in the grey fog of the morning, with 'planes circling inquisitively overhead, and with faces set towards the now diminishing gun roar, and the uncertainty which cloaked the issue where the battle rocked and swayed.

Lt.-Col. T. M. Banks, D.S.O., M.C. *(then 2nd Lieut.) in the trenches near La Boisselle, 1915.*

It was a hurried turn-out from comfortable billets, even for war-hardened veterans; but for a draft of eight new officers, who had arrived only the evening before, the awakening must have been particularly rude. Poor fellows; theirs was a brief and crowded hour of glory, for within three days there was only one of them who was not either wounded or killed.

The Battalion halted near Boves, in the valley of the Avre, while the situation was being unravelled, and then moved forward to the neighbourhood of Glisy, where touch was established with the 8th Division, under whose orders the Brigade was operating. Every moment we expected to be called upon for a counter-attack upon Villers-Bretonneux, into which the Boche had penetrated, but the day dragged on, and eventually it turned out that the Battalion would not be wanted that day, as the Anzacs had the situation well in hand.

So shelter for the night was found in a system of old practice trenches, and here, huddled beneath a rough hurdle roofing, and within a space so confined that it was impossible to sit upright, the new Brigade Commander, General Barker, was introduced unceremoniously to his henchmen of Essex, and fealty was sworn over a strictly teetotal cup of luke-warm cocoa.

It was difficult for a man of 6ft. 4in. in height to be impressive when he is bent in twain in the attitude of a cock-fight. But the cheeriness of our new chief, so constant a source of strength in the long days of effort ahead, showed itself at the very outset, and left no doubt that here was a worthy successor to Higginson, and that the old 53rd was in good hands.

There was little time for social amenities, for next day the Battalion was suddenly called upon for a counter-attack upon Hangard Wood, in conjunction with the famous French Moroccan Division. So, after hasty plans, nightfall brought it once more to the outskirts of Gentelles, of evil memory, and through gas-filled valleys to the forming-up line facing Hangard Wood, now completely in the possession of the enemy.

The surrounding country between the wood and Villers-Bretonneux seemed alive with interminable lines of Frenchmen, making their way to the front with wonderful cheerfulness. Among them was the famous Foreign Legion, and it was an honour to fight alongside them. But they left the wood, the hardest nut of all, to the Englishmen, and it seemed strange that only ourselves and the Queen's had been allotted to the task.

Forming-up was quiet except for shell-fire, and the temporary loss of the Queen's, though our irrepressible V.C. Brigade-Major James provided some excitement by riding out on horseback in front of the assembled troops, almost up to the German posts.

Then at 5.15 a.m., with the grey light of dawn, the guns started in stentorian tones, and up we got and at 'em. The Essex objective was through the left portion of the wood, but, alas! scarcely a shell of the French barrage fell within it, and no sooner did our khaki lines show through the mist than up rose the Boche undismayed, and clatter went his machine-guns, and our men began to fall thick and fast. Still, the lines pressed forward, and with difficulty fought their way through the dense undergrowth. It was stern, perilous work, but the raw material, as yet scarcely assimilated into the Battalion, played up as only Britishers can do, and emulated the battered veterans of the Retreat in steadiness and pluck.

Perhaps an extract from a personal narrative written just afterwards will convey an impression of the battle as well as anything:

"Went over with the third wave, and had nearly reached the wood border when ping! went something through my boot, and a sting in the big toe announced a gold stripe. Hit number one!

"Could see then that we were in for a rough passage, so pushed forward through the undergrowth to see things straight in the forward lines.

"Bullets fairly zipping round and vicious crackling from all sides from the beastly Boche concealed invisibly in the brushwood. Found that we were properly held up in one corner, and the French suddenly started a rearward movement which was spreading panic-like to our men, but managed to stem this, and we held the ground gained. Nothing for it but to dig in here, so got the men busy about this when bang! went another bullet through the fringe of my sleeve, grazing the wrist, and killing a Frenchman behind. Hit number two!

"About this time my first runner became a casualty, so I went back to headquarters for reports and control, and got another one. He, poor fellow, had a short life, for while I was trying to push through the wood to see whether any of our fellows had reached the further side, the unspeakable Hun laid a trap for us which did him in, and nearly accounted for me too. We had pushed forward with a small party of our men, until we saw some figures beckoning us on, some fifty yards ahead. So, thinking they were some of the leading companies, went on, until sudden suspicion flashed intuitively over me. Got glasses out to see. They were Boche! Opened fire on them at once, but the cunning blighters had a machine-gun close up to us on our flank, and let drive simultaneously. So, like unto the serpent which goeth upon its belly, we beat retreat, yearning for a body of the thickness of cigarette paper. Poor

Church, a faithful friend of olden days, was killed at my side by a shot through the head, and another rapid tear in my sleeve announced a third hit. The best souvenir of all, this one, for it cut tunic, shirt, and vest without breaking the skin.

"One more escape I must record, though they read like the romance of a fevered brain. Was sitting in a hastily scratched hole, planning operations with a French captain, and with one of my officers by my

BATTALION H.Q., HANGARD WOOD, APRIL 26TH, 1918.

side and a Frenchman sitting on the other side, when the Boche opened out his machine-gun, and the bullets came slick through the mound of earth in front of us, wounding my officer in the head and the Frenchman in the arm, and left me unscathed.

"All seemingly miraculous, but nevertheless true.

"Could make no further headway against the machine-guns, so failed to take all the wood, which was a great disappointment. But half of it was ours, and that we hung on to, which enabled the French to complete the victory two days later with aid of Tanks.

" Remainder of that day and night was spent with reorganisation and consolidation. Our worst plight was for officers. Only four remained, so it meant many efforts to get things straight. Guildford was acting as my adjutant, and the faithful Worcester kept us going in our 8ft. by 3ft. shell-hole Battalion H.Q. with many cans of tea, concocted marvellously on candle-grease fires. One's stomach revolted from food.

" We were promised relief that night, but it never came, so had to hang on till the following one. Not a pleasant job, for both sides had a perfectly execrable habit of putting down barrages on the slightest provocation. And the evening of the 26th was hideous, with nearly two hours of continuous strafing. Only shell-slits saved us from instantaneous disintegration.

" Relief for the weary came in the shape of the French Battalion Patriache at 2 a.m. on April 28th, and with a few more years on our lives we stumbled back through the darkness to the welcome of a quiet couch on a grassy sward within a copse."

Hangard Wood cost us dearly in officers and men. Poor, cheery little Chaplyn we never heard of again. Lawrence, of " D," was killed by my side. Mulkern severely wounded, and Haile hit through the leg. We nearly lost our stalwart J. C. Parke in his virgin fight with the 10th, for an inconsiderate C.O. sent him out through hordes of machine-guns to learn the situation, and he got caught with his runner wounded in a shell-hole, within close range of a vicious gun, and it was only by the most gallant efforts that he got back to home and beauty, and brought his runner with him.

It is difficult for any account of the battle of April 26th to do it proper justice. And perhaps this story is peculiarly inadequate, for it was one of those days of ill-chance when the vagaries of Fate put the main leaders early hors de combat, and split the fighting into the independent efforts of individuals and small groups, led as best they might be at the moment. Greenaway, new-joined the previous day, did cool and excellent work, until he was swept into the stream of casualties later on in the afternoon. C.S.M. Little and Sergeant Berry were gallant mainstays when no Essex officers were left in the Wood. On the C.O. devolved the task of pulling the scattered remnants together, which demanded his continual personal leading in the hottest quarters; and as the duty of co-ordination and control from Battalion H.Q. also rested upon him, it was necessary to run the gauntlet repeatedly across the belt of machine-gun bullets to receive and issue reports, and again plunge forward into the thickest of the combat, over heavy ground, nearly a mile each way.

It is a measure of the tension and exhaustion of the day that when late at night I managed to get down to have my toe attended to in a near-by quarry, where Captain Battin (U.S.A.), our mother-like Medical Officer, had established his Aid-Post, I fainted away for a brief moment amongst the wounded waiting huddled in the candle-light.

Hangard Wood was not an entire success as success is commonly computed, but I am not sure that the two Croix-de-Guerre which the French awarded us for that action, do not mean more than many a shower of decorations given for clockwork victory.

CHAPTER XXXIII.

BACKS TO THE WALL—MAY-JULY, 1918.

It was but a brief breathing-space that could be spared from the breathless moments of these pregnant times—scarce sufficient for the new recruits to the Battalion to get to know their new comrades, or for the hurriedly-despatched Cadet officers to realise their new-found responsibilities.

A long trek brought us into the depths of peaceful country midway between Amiens and the sea, and here, with nothing but shreds of the Battalion of a few days before, and less than the fibres of the proud unit of but a month earlier, one stooped wearily to build afresh with worn-out tools.

Then the unwearying lorry-buses took us forward over the Molliens-Beaucourt road, along which we had first marched to war in 1915, and by which we had quitted the Somme in 1917 in high hopes of victory near at hand, once more to the familiar country between Amiens and Albert. On May 6th the Battalion moved to Behencourt, where accommodation was found for a large part of it in a chateau, which had but lately lost its tenacious tenants, only persuaded to " give possession " by the arrival of high-explosive lodgers in the upper apartments. Thence we went forward to still more familiar ground, where, in the flush of the enthusiasm of 1915, the 18th Division had marched in review before the King and the Prince of Wales, and again before their patron saint, Lord Kitchener. How much had happened since then? Kitchener was sleeping beneath the waves of the Northern Seas, and many thousands of the men who had responded electric to his call had followed him on his long pilgrimage to Duty's throne. Strife and battle had come and gone around poor, battered Albert; and now the tortured town was once more beneath the agony of the guns—and the young crops where Kitchener had stood were marked ominously with fresh shell-holes.

Here we were on tenter-hooks for the next Boche attack. Nowhere along the British line was safe from the threat of Ludendorff's heavy punches. And it was credibly reported that the next one was to land in our region. So morning by morning we strained our eyes and ears through the grey dawn to catch the opening thunders of attack. And day after day those tense morning hours passed peacefully by—to our mystification and immense relief—until the blow fell elsewhere, and at last it became apparent that the German C.-in-C. had missed his sure grasp of things essential, and had had his gaze distracted to other points. From the moment of that realisation—shared perhaps by only a few, as yet—the load of care began to lift, and by a gradual process we drifted progressively into a normal routine of trench warfare.

Around the steadily crumbling ruins of Lavieville, alongside the well-known Albert-Amiens road, across the hump-back ridge of Nine Elms, down into the erstwhile peaceful billets of Buire, recalling resting-times during the long winter of 1915, but now in the hurlyburly of the front line, we took turn and turn about with our brothers of Berkshire and Kent. The urgent anxiety was lessening, but it was nevertheless a time of much strain, for the morale of an army which has gone through retreat needs the tenderest of nursing.

Near Buire the front trenches ran through the middle of an erstwhile British Casualty Clearing Station abandoned pell-mell in the helter-skelter of the Retreat. Our men were not slow to furnish themselves with anything movable that could be purloined from the deserted huts, and in their dug-outs the strangest collection—hot-water bottles and articles of the wards and sick-beds—was amassed. One man made a hobby of collecting clinical thermometers. Goodness knows why. And in the trench shelter of one of the sections the sentries off duty took it in turns to occupy an ample chair equipped with all the appurtenances of modern dentistry!

Then there were new drafts to be assimilated. Two hundred unknown men came to us one night when we were holding the front line, Emma Trench, and the task of absorbing these amid a mutual shell-strafe from both sides can be better imagined than described. Company Commanders were all new to the Battalion—Harvey, who had worked his way up from the ranks of the Battalion, was finding his feet in " A "; Bland was getting the focus of " B," and incidentally impressing his sterling personality upon that Company; Westall and Wenley controlled a difficult handful of subalterns in " C "; and Wells and May were licking " D " into shape. Loyal fellows all, and already growing into the peculiar spirit of the Battalion. But it entailed much anxious care and puckering of the brow for the Commanding Officer, and he would have been a worried man indeed were it not for the splendid support of his triumvirs, Parke, Byerley, and David Randell at Battalion H.Q., and the unstinted efforts of Simon Ord and the Quartermaster, Jordan.

A short spell of rest and refurbishing followed the anxious days of May. The Battalion was located for the time in a laburnum grove, perched on the steep sides of the valley between Contay and Warloy, for residence in those villages was no longer practicable, owing to the bombing activities of the Boche 'planes.

This brief time was notable for two events. First, David Randell, our fearless padre, proceeded home to take to himself a wife. He was given facilities for an extended leave to enjoy the new-found bliss. But his old love still claimed him, for, scorning to sport with Amaryllis in the peace of Britain while his loved flock of Essex needed his care, he cut his honeymoon to the barest few days, and returned to duty within his fourteen days! How strong a spell the comradeship of the 10th Essex could cast over its members can only be realised by those who were privileged to serve with such a uniquely-welded band of real brothers-in-arms.

The other event was the daylight robbery of a full brass band—instruments, instrumentalists, and all! This was the old 12th Middlesex band, turned adrift in the process of re-organisation earlier in the year, straying amid the Philistines of the Labour units in the interval, and now returned to the 18th Division. They were destined for the Royal Berkshires, but by dint of barefaced effrontery and the skilful manipulation of documents, we secured their diversion to the Essex ranks. Here, despite efforts at dislodgement, they remained throughout the remainder of the Battalion history, and under the baton of Bandmaster Purcell and afterwards of Sergeant Egan, they rewarded our desperate brigandage by many hours of delightful music —all the sweeter for the fact of being stolen.

At the beginning of June we took our turn in the line again in front of the historical chateau of Henencourt. Here again the original warriors of 1915 were amongst well-known haunts and landmarks. There was Bouzincourt on the northern skyline, sadly shattered now, but still recalling the days of first acquaintanceship with warfare. And down below, beneath our continued scrutiny, the familiar sticks and stones of Albert were being pounded into powder—the leaning Virgin with the Christ-child in her arms deposed at last from her lofty place of vigil over stricken France, and every building and spot recalling memories of yesteryear and of comrades no longer with us.

These were days of less strain than before. The Battalion was knitting together into an old-time smartness and dignity. Such things as waste-paper baskets in the trenches betokened a return to the more settled conditions of the past times of trench warfare, and a notice prominently displayed at the entrance to Australia Street trench, exhorted :—

" Cleanliness is next to Godliness.
If you can't go to Church,
Keep your Trenches clean."

Sergeant Brown with his faithful assistant, "Ted" (Lance-Corporal Bird) ventured up to purvey his chocolate and cigarettes during the longer spells in the line, and David nearly ruined the Canteen funds by hawking eggs to the front companies, for the appearance of the padre with his wares made his customers think that this was some new form of benevolence, and David-of-the-warm-heart could not bring himself to disillusion them by asking brutally for such a thing as payment for what he was selling.

There were sundry episodes of a more warlike character. On one night Graham and Woodhurst led an awe-inspiring horde from " C " Company, with faces blackened by burnt cork, on a raid into the enemy trenches. But the Boche was a wily customer, and held his front posts with discretion rather than valour, so that when our fearsome-looking raiders hove up upon the hostile parapet all that greeted them was the rear profile of three large Jerries streaking back to their support lines like greased smoke.

At intervals throughout this period we had the interesting experience of initiating our cousins-in-arms from across the Atlantic into the ways of modern war. Fine fellows they were, too, and as keenly interested in everything as a young boy with the inside of a watch. Their ways, though, were not always as our ways. Captain Bland, for instance, was a good deal disconcerted on one occasion when a Yankee n.c.o. approached him with : " Say, Cap'en, are you the Big Noise round here?" At another time, when a company commander was conducting a stalwart American up a rather unusually shallow trench exposed to the enemy, he was surprised to find his companion had disappeared. Retracing his steps, he found his pupil seated in the bottom of the trench with the remark : " Excuse me, Cap'en, but guess I'll wait right here and see what it looks like when it gets dark." Their amazement at the sang-froid of our boys under the shell-fire, which was so new and terrifying to them, was a revelation. But we made some excellent friends, and it is unlikely that some of them will forget their breaking-in under the auspices of the 10th Essex.

At the beginning of July Sadleir-Jackson and the 54th Brigade began to eat fire over in the Bouzincourt sector, and life became thoroughly uncomfortable for their near neighbours. It was an ill-starred effort, and its effect was to turn our quiescent sector once more into an erupting volcano. So that when the order for relief came on July 11th there was more than the usual pleasure in quitting our posts in the far-flung battle line. But we felt a little legitimate pride in marching out, for the sector was surprisingly changed since it came into our hands. Then everything was in embryo. But hard, continuous work had transmuted it from a series of uncomfortable, overlooked shell-hole positions into a formidable system of redoubts and fortifications. Trenches were everywhere joined up, wire had grown like crops of evil weeds, deep dug-outs and shelters had been constructed lavishly, and the whole thing approximated to a regular trench system such as in the days before the flood of March, 1918.

The door to the Channel was more than slammed —it was bolted, barred, and double-locked as well.

CHAPTER XXXIV.

HITTING BACK. AUGUST 8, 1918.

From July 12 until the beginning of August the battalion had a regal time in rest at Picquigny, on the Somme, a little way behind Amiens. The officers were quartered in the small town, and the remainder of the Battalion lived in a canvas camp on the top of the hill, overlooking rich expanses of country. It was a noteworthy time, both for work and play. Perhaps the latter predominated, for at last the load of apprehension was lifting, and with the news of the French victory on the National Day of France in the middle of the month, a new electricity came into the air, and we began to talk of what we would begin to do in the way of pushing the Huns about in the spring of 1919. Little did one dream, in those days, of a broken enemy and a victorious Armistice within scarcely more than three months. But the easier feeling was sufficient to justify an extensive programme of competitions and amusements. Water polo in the canal, swimming sports, Marathons, musketry contests, horse shows, band concerts, and other entertainments, tumbled one atop of the other, in worthy effort to chase the dull care of yesterday away. The most notable event of all was the ambitious race meeting, organised for the Division by our old friend, Bill Cutbill. Field-Marshal Haig himself attended this, and the neighbourship of a Cavalry Division ensured excellent sport. Here for the first time Major Wheatley's old horse, "Pello," despised and rejected for long, blossomed forth from the careful training of Ord and Joe Costigan into a real racehorse, and under the cognomen of "Rejected," commenced a career of many victories for the black, yellow, and purple of Essex.

At the end of July the rest period came to an end, and lorries took us to Querrieu, whence we marched forward to Bonnay, in the valley of the Ancre. Here, nestling under the steep escarpments, the Battalion, full of pep after the recreation of Picquigny, took over a burrowed camp from the Australians, and settled in to contemplate the next period of garrison duty in the stormy sector which the Anzacs had bequeathed to it. So we passed a few days of excessive happiness, with short hours of work and long hours of laziness in the sun, or bathing in the wooded streams below, whenever the Boche was not in irate mood and venting his spleen by shelling them.

Suddenly, with every oath of secrecy, we were told that great happenings were impending. The French had already shown at Chateau-Thierry that there was life in the old dog yet. Haig was about to demonstrate the same, and to prove that the bulldog still had some of his teeth remaining. There followed a few days of intense activity and preparation. They were days of anxiety, too, for our brethen in the 54th and 55th Brigades were suffering severely in attack and counter-attack up on the saddleback above us, and at any time our plans might have to be thrown to the winds and we should be drawn into the bitter local fighting. As it happened, however, the other Brigades were able to hold their own, and the 53rd remained the corps d'élite for the grand attack on the 8th of August.

In the afternoon of the 7th of August, the Commanding Officer addressed the companies in turn. Just anyhow they turned out and grouped round expectantly in the hollows round the camp. Wonderful fellows! Full of keenness and cheeriness while it was explained to them how they were to form the spearhead to the thrusts which were to follow, and how England next day would thrill to the tidings of their exploits. And the cheers to finish up left a lump in the throat as one thought of the rents which the morrow would tear in the ranks. Then there were the final details to attend to, a sending back of valises and spare kit to the Transport lines, and a gradual mustering of tin-hatted warriors in the gathering gloom.

And at 10 p.m., company by company moved off in sober silence into the darkness, up along the tracks of the grunting lines of tanks which were crawling forward, too, for battle in the morning.

Shell-fire was encountered as the lines of troops neared the Bray-Corbie road, and some of the companies were knocked about most unpleasantly by instantaneous-fused 5.9s. It was with a great deal of difficulty, and by dint of super-efforts by Forbes, that the Battalion was finally piloted into position of assembly in the Clermont line at 2 a.m. Hot tea and rum were then served out, and we settled to rest until the zero hour, with many mingled thoughts of what the morning light held for us.

Just before the dawn a sudden fog set in, and when the moment came to scale the parapet it was barely possible to see beyond the glowing cigarette ends of the nearest gallant fellows of the advancing line. Down into a valley, and then up the slopes on the other side brought us into the thick of the German barrage, and shells, smoke, fog, and a blazing Tank split the companies up out of all formation, and the isolated parties pressed forward as best they could.

Captains May and Daniel were hit at this stage, and "*B*" and "*D*" Companies were left without commanders. It was a case of seizing on whatever troops one could, and leading them on somehow, somewhere, so long as it was towards the dawning light. "*A*" Company became split up, and went right and left, one party under Captain Harvey and another under Lieut. Hatcher. Portions of "*B*" Company pushed well on beyond the first objective, and other portions were cut off or compelled to withdraw. So far did some of them penetrate, however, that it was not until the following day, when a further attack was launched over the same ground, that a number of wounded men of this Company were recovered from the hands of the enemy. Amongst these was C.S.M. Moyse, who put up a wonderful fight after being severely wounded, and was recommended for the highest award for his gallantry. A portion of Battalion H.Q. also went adrift, but the remainder, under the C.O. and Captain Forbes, joined forces with a group of "*D*" Company, and carried out the original programme of advance.

It was eerie work, calling for more than a little faith and confidence, to press on for kilometres into the unknown. Enemy machine guns, invisible in the fog but unpleasantly active, were still in action on every hand. Some of them we struck and silenced. Others were further away, and those had to be left to the attention of the troops we hoped were coming up on the flanks. Gradually the machine guns were outdistanced, though their clatter continued ominously until it grew fainter and fainter as we pushed on in the uncanny wastes of woolly mists.

On arrival at the line of the first objective no more of our own troops could be found, and the advance had been delayed so that the friendly barrage was already lifting forward and there was scant time for search or deliberation. "When in doubt go forward" is a good motto for the soldier man in the day of battle. So we went on. But it was now apparent that we were out on a lone-hand adventure, of which the issue was becoming increasingly more doubtful. At one point a British Tank came upon us up the Bray-Corbie road, firing 9-pounders and machine guns furiously. Poor Corporal Curl, the C.O.'s runner, a boy with the heart of a lion, was killed by this tank, and Second Lieut. Elstone was wounded by my side. But despite difficulties from friend and foe, our dwindling band of adventurers pressed steadily on, taking a few prisoners on the way, until the brickfields near the Bois des Tailles were reached, and the long three-mile advance was successfully achieved.

And, truly, it was an achievement, and we were weary. The conditions of confusion at the outset had doubled the labours of attack. A Brigade lent at the last moment by another Division to take the first objective was scattered by the fog and severely handled by the stout resistance of picked German troops in the foremost lines, so that it fell to us to complete their task as well as to perform our own. And these circumstances, and the virtual impossibility of direction finding, had stopped the advance of all the neighbouring units an hour before, and brought us into splendid but perilous isolation a mile and a half ahead of the line to which the other battalions had attained.

As the lone Essex party came on to their final objective, looming suddenly through the fog, they descended upon a couple of unsuspected and unsuspecting batteries of German field guns. The gunners, thinking that the din and hubbub of the morning had been but a repeat performance of the attack and counter-attack of previous mornings, were resting and breakfasting after serving their guns, in fond belief that "Tommee" was miles away from them, and that lines of their own men filled the intermediate distance. Their astonishment when "Tommee" invaded their gun-pits was paralytic. Two of them, more demoralised than their fellows, took their boots off and offered

AN INTERRUPTED BREAKFAST.

them to me as a ransom for their lives. But I hadn't much time to think of starting a branch of Lilley and Skinner's there, and I told them not to be verdammte Esel; and they were rounded up with the remainder of the guns' crews, several dozen strong, and sent rearwards in charge of a single wounded man. Hardly had this been done when the battery commander, a rotund Boche Major, resplendent in Iron Cross, emerged from a dug-out in the wood near by to visit his guns. His dumbfoundment to find his own men spirited away and khaki warriors in their place was pathetic. He had not long to wait before he, too, joined his own men on the rearward trek.

At 8 o'clock Captain Macdonald, of the Royal West Kents, brought up a welcome reinforcement of that regiment and got his men out to extend our left wing. Mason and Toole came up also, full of boyish enthusiasm, but, alas, with only a handful of men. And it was men above all that were wanted. In all I suppose the whole party numbered few more than eighty.

Meanwhile the sun began to penetrate the fog, and stock could be taken of the position. Patrols were sent out left and right, but failed to find any more of our men. Machine guns and an enemy battery were in action some way to the rear, and another enemy battery, in the edge of the wood 500 yards ahead, turned its guns on to our hastily-dug positions, and started a devilish shelling of them at close range over open sights. A fat Boche 'plane circled leisurely a few hundred feet overhead, peering inquisitively at the brazen band who had penetrated so barefacedly into the very heart of the German lines, and machine guns, one by one, began to dribble round, and to gall us with their fire.

There could be no blinking the fact now that the situation was desperate. Ranks were faced about for all-round defence in a resolute attempt to hold the ground gained against the hoped-for arrival of reinforcements, and the men dug in like Trojans, though they looked ready to drop with fatigue. Most disheartening of all, our own shells began to drop among our lines, and the cup of our distress was full indeed.

It seemed hopeless to remain, but it was hateful to think of retreat, and the relinquishment of ground thus won. And so, for three long hours we held grimly on, with the enemy steadily sapping round, hoping against hope for the arrival of the supports, for which imperative requests had been sent back.

At 10.15 a.m. the enemy started a comprehensive movement to cut us off entirely. Posts were faced about, and fire opened on him, but it only succeeded in slowing him down, and the process of dribbling continued, until there were but a few hundred yards left open in the narrowing circle of beleaguers.

At this moment a message came up from the Brigade Major that no reinforcements remained, and Forbes arrived back from a gauntlet-running expedition to the rear with the news that he could discover none of our troops within miles. So, with heavy hearts, we held a council of war, and decided, almost with tears, that there was nothing for it but to give the order for retreat if we would save any of the party at all. It was therefore resolved to cut our way back, or to sell our lives dearly. With great steadiness, the posts were withdrawn, and, under the covering fire of the Lewis guns, the first stages of the withdrawal began.

The Boche, in the interval, had aligned his machine guns one after the other on either side of the road along which retreat lay, and as our troops came on to the skyline, they played havoc in the ranks. Worse still, a battery of German guns, which had remained in action further back, now came into play broadside on to the road, and inflicted heavy casualties among the retreating force, without possibility of retaliation. Semblance of an orderly withdrawal had to be abandoned, and the command was given to scatter and get back as rapidly as possible to the nearest line held by our own men. And so the battered remnants straggled back, with many brave fellows, alas! left behind, wounded, missing, or killed.

Gallant old Forbes, whacked to the wide, was badly shaken and holed by the rain of shells, and, heroically unselfish, begged to be left behind. But so sterling an officer could not be allowed to sacrifice himself thus, and, limping painfully down on his C.O.'s shoulder, we floundered from shell-hole to shell-hole, under the galling accuracy of the German guns in Malard Wood, until we struggled into the foremost British posts, just as the advancing enemy came down the road.

It was a sad ending to such an exploit. Captain Harvey, Second Lieut. Wood, and Second Lieut. Cleall were missing, the last-named after many brave efforts in his maiden fight. More than half the men who had gone forward were casualties, and only a portion of the distance advanced remained to British credit. But, as the subsequent days of fighting showed, we had badly shaken the Boche.

Yet more, the 10th Essex had again proved themselves, as the Divisional Commander had admitted, the finest of fighting battalions under his command.

There were many noteworthy acts of individual bravery that day. Kington (already in possession of the M.M.) got a D.C.M. He was wounded at dawn and went through the day indefatigably in the thick of dangers and carrying a specially heavy load. His shoulder was stiff and badly torn, but he would not disclose it or give up until the evening, when he had to be ordered sternly to the rear. Two recommendations were made for the V.C., and many decorations were awarded.

But the greatest satisfaction of all was the feeling that at last the tide had turned. Some months ago Haig had told us our backs were to the wall. And the British Army had come to bay with all the glorious traditions of the past. We had stood our ground, and now, at last, we were hitting back, and victory was already flushing into dawn over the battlefields of the reddened Somme.

CHAPTER XXXV.

The "March to Berlin" Begun.

After the strenuous events of the morning of the 8th August, there was not much left, either in numbers or in sparkle, of the proud unit which had gone over the top but a few hours before. J. C. Parke came up to take over command from his exhausted C.O., and was invaluable in reorganisation, assisted by the faithful David, who had been spending a giddy day chez les Boches, endeavouring to deliver chocolate and comestibles to a non-existent Battalion H.Q., sited in confident anticipation in a spot firmly held by the German machine-guns.

The 9th August was spent in the task of collecting up individual Essex men from a score of different units to which they had joined themselves in the turmoil of the fight. On the afternoon of the 10th, the Americans of the 33rd Division attacked through the British lines in company with Tanks, and the demoralised enemy, remembering a pressing engagement to the rear, rose from their positions like one man, and disappeared from mortal ken. A few of the Essex thereupon, with characteristic promptitude, assumed the self-appointed task of moppers-up (of souvenirs), and in the process one German pack was ransacked, and found to contain, neatly packed in brown paper and addressed to Gretchen in the Vaterland, the Essex Battalion flag, which had been lost in the retirement two days before. No doubt that particular Hun had had his interest in trophies abruptly cut short!

Next day Colonel Banks, in company with Colonel Pritchard-Taylor, had an impromptu and exciting contest with the adversary on the further side of the Bois des Tailles.

The position was a curious one. The Yanks had reached their objective on the edge of the wood and were trying to dig in there (with their bayonets, poor fellows, for American "Q." had forgotten to provide shovels!) But the wood lay just below the crest of the hill, and the inexperience of our new Allies had not taught them the art of exploitation. So they were content to sit where they were. Brer Boche, on the other hand, had had the fright of his life and run like a good 'un far over the hill and down the other side. Thus the crest overlooking Bray, with all its invaluable observation, was untenanted and to be had for the asking.

When the two free-lance British Colonels came on the scene they discovered the bargain which lay patent but unadvertised; and simultaneously someone on the other side had made the like discovery. So while one Colonel ran back to assume an unconstitutional command of Uncle Sam's legions and to urge them forward, the other held the fort on the top of the hill, brandished his revolver and tried to look like fifty men. The ruse succeeded, but there were breathless moments, and the race was won for the Stars and Stripes by seconds only. Up tumbled a platoon of Doughboys, and spatter went their Lewis gun just as the Germans got their machine guns into action as well. But we were on the crest, and they were a hundred yards short. And we didn't offer any more free gifts to the Kaiser!

Then on the 11th the Brigade was relieved, and marched back to recuperate at Baizieux. Here there was a re-shuffle of commanders. Colonel Frizell had recovered from his gas-poisoning, and once more assumed command of the unit which owed so much to him. There were emotional moments when the General congratulated the Battalion on their performance on the 8th, and Colonel Banks bade farewell to his stalwarts of that fight, and watched the companies march forward to the line once more, leaving him to the command of the Berkshires.

For five days the Battalion held the front line on the thrice-familiar Albert-Amiens road. On August 16th we were relieved to Henencourt Wood, where two days were spent in refitting, and in absorbing drafts of officers and men from the Worcesters and Staffordshires.

On the 18th we moved still further back, and put in some real useful training, until battle was joined once more by the 54th and 55th Brigades in an attack on Albert. The Essex were moved forward ready to join an advance guard, in case the Hun attempted to repeat his 1917 tactics of rapid withdrawal; but instead, he offered such a stout resistance that at the end of the day Albert had only just been cleared, and a precarious footing gained on the slopes beyond.

Major Parke had meantime taken over the command, while Colonel Frizell was running the Brigade, and spent most of the day of the 22nd at Brigade H.Q. in the railway cutting south-east of Albert, watching the fluctuating tide of battle, and waiting anxiously on events.

Late that afternoon it was decided that the R.W. Kents and the Essex should attack Tara Hill next morning at dawn. This left little time for preparation, as the forming-up positions had to be reconnoitred, orders got out and conferences held, all before 11.30 p.m., when the approach march commenced. But Parke delivered the goods, and fortunately it was bright moonlight, and there was an entire absence of shelling, so the Companies reached

Major J·C·PARKE

their positions in plenty of time. "A" and "B" Companies were in attack, "C" in support, and "D" in reserve.

At 4.45 a.m. the lines advanced with traditional steadiness and gallantry, and pressing doggedly up the hill in face of stiff but somewhat scattered opposition, gained the summit by 6 a.m., and enabled the Berkshires to pass on through to the conquest of the old crater battle-grounds of La Boisselle.

Our casualties were not so heavy as on the 8th, but "A" and "D" Company Commanders were both killed—Captain Tebbutt, who had only joined the Battalion three days earlier, and Second-Lieut. Binley, who had taken over "D" Company when his Captain was wounded on the 8th, and had been running it since with conspicuous courage and success. We also lost Orfeur, a lovable boy, who had done well on the 8th. Both of the other Company Commanders—Captains Bland and Wenley—did yeoman service in the task of leadership and re-organisation, and the award of 1 D.S.O., 1 M.C., 3 D.C.M.'s and 4 M.M.'s to the Battalion is an index of the devotion of all ranks in this successful action.

It is worthy of note that in 1915 the 10th Essex helped to construct the defences of Tara Hill, which they themselves were called on to capture three years later. Such are the strange mutations of warfare.

From this time onward the motto was "Steadily Forward," and it was not until October that the Battalion re-crossed the line of the Albert trenches, which marked the high-water mark of the Boche advance; and already by that date the industry of the French peasant was ploughing into the fallow fields which had separated the hostile armies through the preparations of the summer, now yielding place to the autumn harvest of real victory.

On August 25th Colonel Frizell returned to the command of the Battalion, and by this time the German resistance had already receded several miles. Following on the heels of the Berks and Kents, we made our way through Mametz and the valleys beyond, plagued by heavy high velocity shells, but with spirits ascending as we once more trod the ground, hallowed by deathless memories of the 18th Division's achievements in July, 1916.

August 27th was a day of proud record in the annals of the 53rd Brigade, for on that day the Royal Berkshires and the Essex in combination met and defeated the German Guards in a bitter all-day struggle around Trones Wood. The Berks and Kents had assaulted in the morning, and gained their objective beyond the wood, when a counter-attack by the German II. Guards Grenadier Regiment threw the Berks back again from the confines of the wood. Sharp fighting followed, and "C" and "D" Companies of the Essex, under Wenley and Morrow, were hurried up and placed under the command of Colonel Banks, now serving beneath the dragon of Berkshire. These reinforcements steadied the situation, and then, as evening approached, they crept stealthily forward, until, with a wild burst of artillery, they dashed to the assault, carrying all before them in a magnificent bayonet charge, inflicting heavy casualties on the German Guardsmen with sheer cold steel, and capturing 70 prisoners.

Thus Trones Wood was once more captured for the Division, and the immature boys of the Berks and Essex vindicated their superiority to the flower of the German troops.

It was a curious experience for those who had fought round here in 1916 to traverse the old ground, to chance on spots that held memories of other fights and old comrades, and to battle through the forests of little, blackened wooden crosses that told of slaughter infinite in that time of heavy sacrifice and strange inexperience. Now we were campaigning with the experience of veterans at the game, some of us with secret marvelling at heart that Providence had spared us so long through the manifold perils of these long years of war. But with all the experience it was frequently a baffling task to recognise the old landmarks. Woods and villages had been wiped out of existence in a way which would seem incredible to those who have not known the devastating power of modern warfare. A brief example may serve to illustrate.

From Caterpillar Wood, an early conquest of the 10th Essex in the 1916 battle, the Battalion was ordered to take up a covering line running through Leuze Wood—euphoniously known as Lousy Wood in the vernacular of the British Army—and Major Parke went forward with two of the Company Commanders to reconnoitre. Bernafay Wood, Trones Wood, Montauban, and Guillemont were all very nicely and clearly marked on the maps, but on the ground it was difficult to distinguish where wood began or ended, or, indeed, that these were truly woods at all, except for some shattered trunks dotted here and there. And when the party reached the middle of Guillemont village, Parke was still vainly searching for it, as not one brick could be seen standing upon another. Even some gunners, whose battery was planted in the centre of it, could throw no light as to where the village was!

After the Trones Wood fight we marked time a bit while the other Brigades were exploiting into Combles and beyond. Then, on September 3rd, the Battalion, in conjunction with two Companies of the Berks, made a successful attack on the northern portion of St. Pierre Vaast Wood, which gave us possession of that important feature, and opened the way to the crossing of the Canal Du Nord two days later. Here a stranded Boche ambulance was found in perfect order, and the versatile Captain Hume, of Brigade H.Q., penetrating into No Man's Land with a tin of petrol in hand, performed the feat of starting it up and driving off, under the noses of the enemy. And for some weeks afterwards General Barker toured the

TRONES WOOD.
The 53rd Brigade Memorial.

country in his extemporised limousine, under the coat of arms of Imperial Germany!

This was an inspiring time. Prisoners came trooping in with every air of dejection. Fresh victories and advances were reported hourly. And from the captured eminence at Government Farm, there was a Pisgah view of green country beyond the ruined lands of the 1916 struggle, while far into the distance great columns of smoke told of dumps being destroyed, and heralded further enemy retirements. Truly our march to Berlin seemed to have got a fair and promising start.

Yet the Boche was still fighting with spirit. The Battalion had some sharp patrol encounters along the line of the Canal Du Nord, but managed to secure the crossings and the possession of Riverside Wood before it was relieved out of the van of the advance by its brethren of the 9th Essex on the 5th September.

CHAPTER XXXVI.

Cracking the Hindenburg Line.

After the unexpected resurrection of the British fighting man and the shattering defeats of August, the depression of the German Army was extreme. One ray of hope remained to the Boche. The lines which Hindenburg had constructed in 1916 still stood for them as their new "Watch on the Rhine," and from the most exalted Red-hat to the simple Jerry private, they pinned their faith to holding this last bulwark, and stemming the onslaught until the spring, when Dame Fortune might again reverse the hour-glass, and the sands which were running so ominously against them might trickle perchance once more in favour of the Fatherland.

So we gathered from the prisoners who had come within our well-filled net, and the thought chastened the soaring hopes which repeated victory had encouraged.

Way back in 1917 the Division had lived further north for weeks within the colossal fortifications which Hindenburg's genius had created, and had grown to know their formidable character. And here, where they fronted us, they were strengthened by the inclusion of the broad St. Quentin Canal, and the task of breaking through seemed well-nigh a superhuman one.

Thus we meditated during the 10 days' training and recuperation at Favière Wood, and it was frankly speculated whether Haig would essay the task that year, with ranks depleted, and with an Army weary with the severest strain which it had known since the days of the Old Contemptibles.

We were not left long in doubt. For a few days we rusticated in the sylvan bowers of Favière Wood, and then preparations for fighting started once more, and we were initiated into the plans for attacking the outworks of the redoubtable line. On September 16th lorry 'buses took the Battalion forward to Gurlu Wood, where two nights were spent, one of them signalised by a thunderstorm of tropical violence, which nearly washed us out entirely.

At daybreak on the 18th September the 55th Brigade and the Royal West Kents attacked the village of Ronssoy from the direction of Ste. Emilie, and the Essex moved forward in support to trenches just short of the village, where we made ourselves as comfortable as possible while awaiting events. About 3 p.m. that afternoon, after a morning of confusion in the area of fighting ahead, Major Parke, who was in command of the Battalion, received three messages simultaneously—the first to move forward, the second to stay where he was, and the third to report at once to General Wood, of the 55th, in trenches south-east of Ronssoy. It looked as if we were wanted urgently —or not wanted at all, according to which message was first read—and on reporting to the gallant General, Parke found him engaged in a personal battle with a group of German machine-guns, and rather annoyed at any interference by reinforcements. The only thing nearer the Boche than himself was one of our field guns, rather more impetuous than wise, which had planted itself with superb cheek in the morning, and which the gunners were still continuing to fire at intervals when they got the chance, just to prove that it was still in action!

We could not force our attentions on our unwilling host, but remained about handy under what shelter could be found. And during the night we reverted to General Barker's command, and returned to our morning trenches east of Ste. Emilie.

Everyone seemed to forget our existence for the next two days, and we were left blissfully in peace while the Berkshires completed the capture of Ronssoy, and added Lempire to the bag.

However, on September 20th, someone at Brigade H.Q. remembered us, and, perhaps with some idea that we might feel hurt by the seeming neglect, promptly booked us for an attack on Tombois Farm and the Knoll beyond. It was a pretty idea—at any rate, from an armchair in a rear headquarters—but the knowledge that the Knoll had defied repeated attacks in 1917, the paucity of supporting troops, and, above all, the lack of co-ordination which characterised the hurried scheme, stamped the enterprise from the outset as a hazardous one. And the forebodings, alas! proved to be justified only too well.

September 21st was an ill-starred day in the history of the 18th Division. Attack by well-nigh exhausted troops was ordered over a wide front with deep objectives. The Essex were in a particularly unfortunate position, for an eleventh-hour change of plans left them unsupported on an exposed flank, with no troops at all to mask their progress across the front of an unengaged enemy.

Major Parke was wounded after the completion of a reconnaissance late on the afternoon of the 20th, and Colonel Frizell returned at once from Brigade

H.Q., and assumed the reins. Under his command the Companies were successfully manœuvred into their difficult forming-up ground between the Berkshires' lines and the Boche, and in the first grey flush of light the attack was launched. No sooner were the lines away than a murderous fire was opened out from the uncovered flank, and, taking the lines in enfilade, the ranks were decimated before they had long left their starting point. Scattered groups struggled forward up to the farm itself, only to be mown down ruthlessly, and the attack was brought to a standstill ere many hundred yards were gained.

It was a tragic business. Perhaps the worst feature of all was the plight of the wounded. Hardaker and the Colonel worked energetically from the H.Q. at Yak Post to get the survivors reorganised and rescued, but many had fallen within a few yards of the Boche trenches, and these were beyond redemption. What their sufferings were must be left to the imagination. Poor Parrack was one. A splendid boy, with the best qualities of leadership, his leg was shattered with a bullet when he was at the head of his men within a few yards of the hostile parapet. Falling into a shell-hole, he lay there while our formidable antagonists, the Jaegers, counter-attacked across the ground, and left him for dead when they withdrew again to their own trenches. For three days he lay there, under the very noses of the enemy, while our own shells battered and pounded all round him in vicious retaliation and preparation for further attack. At last, after an experience such as few men can know in their lives, the Americans of the 27th Division attacked, and he was rescued and sent down with infinite care to the ambulances in the rear. It was impossible to save his leg, and for many months he was in hospital. But his life was saved, and he was well enough to attend the first annual gathering of officers when peace had borne her fruits, and the unit in which he had fought so gallantly, and suffered so grievously, was dispersed, every man to his own home.

The disastrous 21st left the 10th Essex a shell of its former self. Two hundred and eighty casualties, of which 67 were buried side by side in the Lempire Cemetery, was the toll paid by the Battalion on that hapless day. But our fighting in that quarter did not finish, and confused and isolated struggles for Egg Post and neighbouring enemy positions took place for several days afterwards, without much tangible result, until our friends, the Yanks, came in to continue the acid struggle around these all-important last enemy ditches.

On September 29th a combined assault by British, Australians, and Americans broke through the Hindenburg Line, and exploited on over the Bellicourt Tunnel, into the fringes of Le Catelet.

The 18th Division had gone back to the neighbourhood of Combles when it was relieved on the 25th of September, and the Essex, encamped near Priez Farm, started to take stock of itself, when the process was rudely broken into by the order for another march forward. "Rest?" our commanders seemed to say. "What hast thou to do with rest? Turn thee again." And so, with weary steps, we turned again. But this time there was not much call on our services.

On the 29th we marked time in the neighbourhood of Epéhy, while the situation was being cleared up around Guillemont Farm. On the 30th the 55th Brigade penetrated into Vendhuile, and the same night the Battalion took over a frontage round Ossus Wood, overlooking the St. Quentin Canal. It was a short spell of duty here, for on the following night the 50th Division, newly reformed from troops from the Orient, came in full of fire and go to our relief, and our tired files wended their way back to a real rest at Allonville, not far from Amiens.

It was strange to retrace our steps in peace across the country over which we had fought and advanced. Stranger still to enter Albert, which we had left in powdered ruins, with the smoke of the shells still

THE SORROWFUL HARVEST OF TOMBOIS FARM.

hanging in the air, and to find its unhappy inhabitants groping among the ruins for anything that might remain, but certainly did not do so, of their household possessions. German prisoners, in gangs, were already clearing the debris away in spots where we had last met them in hand to hand fight; a German P.O.W. camp stood in the erstwhile No Man's Land, where, in dead of night, patrols had gone forth like the serpent upon its belly. And Amiens, proud city, was covering her scars, and vending her wares at the old exorbitant rates to the gentlemen in khaki.

At Allonville, Nogi Hudson returned to the head of our brother Berkshires, and Colonel Banks came back once more to the command of the Essex. Colonel Frizell had meantime received his well-merited step to the rank of Brigadier-General in the 25th Division, and was carrying on the flaming torch into the Promised Land beyond the Hindenburg Line. Shortly afterwards Forbes took over once more, Banks being ordered off to the Staff College for a course of refreshment, in anticipation of the next spring campaign ! Not yet did we realise the magnitude of our achievements, and that the crack in the Hindenburg armour had exposed the whole rottenness of the body corporate of Imperial Germany.

CHAPTER XXXVII.

AT LONG LAST!

About the middle of October the Division was once more on the move. Tactical trains took us forward into a strange land, peopled by wan, scarified folk, who for four years had known the severity of the invaders' yoke. It was pitiful to see them stand in groups about the khaki men who brought them deliverance, dumb with over-joy, yet with all a world of gratitude expressed in their eyes; and it touched the heart to see the men doff their caps to our officers, proud and ready to do it to their liberators, where before only the jack-boot and the whip secured compliance with the German orders. Many a tale they told us which made the blood boil, and which spurred us into eagerness for future efforts to drive the Hun from the land which he had desecrated so long. Tales there were of wanton cruelty to British prisoners, of secret food smuggled through to them by the peasantry, in peril of consequences, and of the vigorous punishment which followed the discovery of such dangerous philanthropy. Tales of ill-treatment, conscription and deportation of French girls, of wholesale robbery and heavy fines for trumped-up misdemeanours. Stories of hopes raised in 1916 and 1917, when the sound of the Allied guns crept eastward in the Somme and Cambrai battles, and then of bitter disappointment and hearts grown sick when the advancing tide was stemmed, and the spring of 1918 saw it rolled back again beyond their ken.

Then they would tell us how the German boastfulness of March and April gave way to uneasiness and foreboding, how the Boche-edited papers sought to feed them with lies, while a growing muttering again to the westward and an occasional leaflet dropped from an Allied 'plane, and smuggled in secrecy from hand to hand, gave them new springs of hope, until at last they saw the Kaiser's legions in flight, and they emerged from their cellars with brimming eyes to stutter broken thanks to the stolid khaki men who brought salvation.

It was worth while—it was a thousand times worth while—to have fought and endured so long if it were for nothing more than this wonderful welcome. Our old friend, Schuhmacher, the interpreter at Brigade H.Q., had a busy time supplying the hungry mouths with food, but it was a labour of love, for his own parents were still in German hands in the region of Charleroi.

On October 23rd the 53rd Brigade debouched for attack from the railway cutting due east of Le Cateau. The assembly was a tricky one, for shells fell thick and fast in the cutting, and the ground almost immediately above was held by the leading German posts. But Hardaker and the Company Commanders worked like Trojans, and the assault was launched successfully in the moonlight at 1.20 a.m. By dawn the forward enemy lines had been overrun, and the advancing troops had swept down past a sharp resistance in the orchard below the crest into the valley of the Richemont Brook; then, crossing the stream, they pushed on victoriously up the slopes of Le Corbeau Farm, nearly three miles deep into the territory held by the enemy.

The objective assigned to the Essex, commanded in this battle by Major A. P. Churchill, was a sunken road leading from Pommereuil to Forest, and our men, triumphantly carrying all before them and capturing great numbers of prisoners, swept on until within but a few yards of their goal. Here enemy field guns at point-blank range and a determined group of machine-gunners held up the line at one point, in spite of bravely-repeated efforts to rush them, until the arrival of a Tank enabled us to overcome the resistance and the Berkshires to go on through to the neighbourhood of Bousies, which fell a prey to the 55th Brigade, operating from the northern flank.

The fight on the 23rd was noteworthy, and in some ways unique, for it was the biggest successful moonlight operation undertaken in France during the course of the war. And the surprise departure from the routine attack at dawn undoubtedly saved a large number of casualties in our ranks, and gave a sense of confidence in the capable handling of affairs by our higher commanders. It is only fair to pay a tribute to the masterly conduct of these latter-day operations by General Lee and his inspiring right-hand man, Guy Blewitt, at Divisional H.Q., and by General " Tommy " Morland at the XIIIth Corps.

Attack followed hot-foot upon the heels of attack in these hectic latter days, and on October 26th the Battalion was again advancing to the assault.

In the days between we had been spending the time in the village of Bousies and among the homesteads in the surrounding country. A curious life of improvisation it was—improvised H.Q. and communications, supplies and mails a fickle quantity, and all the time a pregnancy in the air which made this time altogether different from anything we had known before. One thing did not differ. The hostile artillery showed no abatement in zeal. Indeed, it seemed that they had abandoned all the maxims of gunnery, and were pouring the contents of their ammunition dumps through the gun-barrels as fast as they could, rather than let the dumps fall into the hands of their attackers. In the course of these fevered bombardments Battalion H.Q. suffered badly. R.S.M. Cousins was one of the victims. He had come to us in latter days, but, with an indefatigable energy and a kindliness strange to the office of R.S.M., he had endeared himself to all ranks.

Another tragic shell-burst wrought havoc among the runners and orderly-room staff. It was heartrending to see these gallant fellows—literally the bravest of the brave—wiped out thus when we were on the threshold of peace. Corporal Plume had served from the first fight of the Battalion up to this closing phase, and Stunt, Phillips and Harrison were the sort of fellows who would stand out in a bombardment like ducks in a shower of rain. They just didn't know the name of fear. They were buried together, eight of them, as they served so faithfully together, in a single grave on the outskirts of Bousies.

Carson and Haile, outstanding types of the best and most gallant of England's young leaders, were also killed in these bitter last days. We mourned them deeply, missed them sorely.

About this time it at last began to penetrate into the mind of the soldier-man that there was a possibility of this interminable war terminating, and at no very distant date; many were incredulous, and many the wagers made in the cellars of the farms of Bousies, as we awaited the next advance. Unnerving it was to feel that the chance shot might get you before the "Cease Fire" sounded, and even the coveted "Blighty one" was no longer in demand as hereto-

LT.-COL. R. FORBES, D.S.O., M.C.

THE GATEWAY TO PREUX.

Through this gate the Battalion made its way between enemy posts on either side, and forming up behind the German line, advanced victoriously to the batteries beyond.

fore. But there was no perceptible faltering, and the Brigade went over on the 26th with the steadiness of yore.

The objective assigned was a slight eminence beyond the Landrecies-Englefontaine road, which went by the name of Mont Carmel. We were now penetrating into a difficult terrain, a country intersected with hedges and sunken roads, and thickly studded with orchards and plantations, and a good deal of confused fighting took place, resulting finally in the line being carried on beyond the road, and a jumping-off ground secured for the last fight of the 10th Essex on the borders of Mormal Forest.

The battle history of the Battalion closes fittingly with an epic fight which ranks high among the records of its successes. The days succeeding the Mont Carmel action were occupied with preparations for operations on a large scale. The march of events had brought the XIIIth Corps up against the broad Forest of Mormal, one of the most difficult strategical snags which the advancing British Army had to negotiate. And a stiffening enemy resistance and our former experience of the murderous character of wood fighting made us view the forbidding fringes of the forest with apprehension.

Immediately in front of the Essex position at Petit Planty lay the open rising ground of Mont Carmel, Beyond this rise the country dipped again into a labyrinth of orchards and small fields, fringed with thick hedges running up to the northern outskirts of the village of Preux. Before the German occupation this picturesque little hamlet nestled closely up against the thickly wooded forest. But the depredations of the invader had bitten large clearings into the forest edges, in order to supply the trenches with timber. And in the middle of one of these large clearings, situated just behind the village, there stood an imposing German saw-mill. This clearing and the saw-mill formed the main goal of the Battalion. And to get there it had to pass through the maze of orchards and streams and hedges, and deploy on the cleared ground beyond.

To the 54th Brigade was assigned the task of clearing these orchards and the village of Preux, after which the Essex would push on to the further objec-

"GOODBY-EE!"
Our last sight of the German Army.

tive. But the village proved a hard nut to crack, and obstinate resistance was met on its northern outskirts, so that the Essex attack appeared to be frustrated, when Lieut.-Colonel Forbes, now in command of the Battalion, reconnoitring forward, discovered a gap of a couple of hundred yards in the enemy lines. Through this he determined to manœuvre his command, and, leading them in person through a single gate within the German posts, he performed the phenomenal feat of forming up the Battalion behind the enemy's front line, and advancing to the attack of the support lines and gun positions, while the enemy's forward posts were still in action. The manœuvre was a brilliant success, and contributed very largely to the capture of a big haul of prisoners in Preux, and the complete breakdown of any further resistance in the forest.

The last sight of the German Army which was granted to the 10th Essex was a solitary unarmed Hun proceeding at top speed down one of the long forest rides, in full cry for the Fatherland.

Six days later the Armistice was signed.

L'ENVOI.

THE LAST DAYS OF THE " OLD GUARD."

After the overthrow of the enemy rear-guards in the fringes of Mormal Forest the 55th Brigade pushed on over the field of battle to the eastern edges of the Forest, while the remainder of the Division was squeezed out by the converging advance and withdrawn to Le Cateau.

Here we were when the news of the end of the War came on the wings of the morning of November 11th. How we had talked about the wonderful moment. With what riot of imagination had we given reins to fancy in the dreary dragging hours by the candle-light in many a shell-strafed dug-out!

And yet, when the last gun fired the 10th Essex was on parade drilling with an ingrained habit as if to prepare for the next war (save the mark!), and the culminating moment of the years of effort scarcely disturbed the routine of the day.

It was not that the soldier-man was lacking in imagination. But blatant demonstration seemed out of place amidst the scenes of sacrifice and service. Perhaps, too, the iron had entered too deeply into the soul of the man in the fighting-line to allow of jubilation untinged by sadness or solemnity.

And each Armistice Day, one imagines, brings those who fought and won to the threshold of a shrine where are stored the memories of heroism and selflessness, of effort and comradeship—such comradeship as did not shrink from the sacrifice of life for the sake of friends.

After a short time at Le Cateau we moved to Premont, and then not long afterwards Genève and Ponchaux, on the borders of the battle-wilderness, where the Battalion was destined to spend several months in a quaint exiled existence.

General Lee had refused the chance of going forward to the Rhine, in the hope of securing an earlier demobilisation for the 18th Division. And so, instead of garnering the fruits of victory in Rhineland, we were set to gather in the rusty aftermath of war which abounded on the fields of combat. Miles and miles of barbed wire we must have reeled in, hundreds and hundreds of tin hats—Boche and British —were picked up, and bombs, rifles, shells, guns, aeroplanes, ammunition boxes, derelict wagons, loads of timber and every conceivable form of war material accumulated pyramid-like in monumental mounds along the sides of the roadways. The energy we expended on the new task in the first few weeks was colossal. But the machinery for getting the stuff away to Blighty was not conspicuously adequate, and gradually it began to dawn on the consciousness of the soldier-man that there was scant chance of much of the mouldering stuff we had collected ever seeing the white cliffs of old England.

It seemed a poor job at the best to be left to scavenge the dirty mess the Hun had made, and the victorious warrior came to the conclusion that someone was getting a bit of a rise out of him. So we turned our attention to other things. Education became the motto, and the gentler ways of pen and plodding pencil sought to demonstrate their superiority to the erstwhile pastimes of tummy-thrusts and throat-jabs. No doubt this latter-day Renaissance of learning served its purpose, for there was no ambiguity about the volume of keen interest it aroused amongst the men.

A cottage in Ponchaux served as the school, its thatched roof liberally punctured in the shell-storm which preceded the victorious advance of General Frizell's Brigade of the 25th Division. And here Potter and Sergeants Hodges and Whittaker, aided by anyone who could resuscitate any lingering remnants of the lessons of boyhood's days, sought to instruct the eager proselytes in reading, 'riting and 'rithmetic, and a haphazard medley of subjects such as Shorthand, Political Economy, Agriculture, Music, Steam Engines and Art.

We found one or two men who were completely illiterate, and they, at least, will be able to follow the racing news in the evening papers as a result of midnight oil at Ponchaux. The delight of one boy who told me that he had managed to write his first letter home to his mother had something touching about it.

It was very greatly a case of brick-making without straw. For the Armistice, like the War, caught England bending, and the hastily-worked-out scheme of Army education had little chance to come to bearing-time. We had instructions and admonitions on the subject months before any materials or books arrived, and one remembers the momentous day when the first educational material for the Brigade arrived—three 12-inch rulers for three thousand men! Yet more humorous was the arrival of *one* typewriter keyboard for the instruction of the Division in typing—10,000 men spread over 20 miles of countryside!

But though the educative efforts in general bore scanty fruit at the moment, one feels that somehow and somewhere the phenomenal burst of enthusiasm

x

First Row: Lts. Graham, Gage, 2/Lt. Potter, Rev. D. Randell, 2/Lt. Wilkinson, Capt. Knopp, 2/Lt. Holmes, 2/Lt. Southcott.
Middle Row: Capt. Ord, 2/Lt. Moore, Capt. Nunn, 2/Lts. Lord, Fog, Taylor, Lt. Moore, 2/Lts. Bostock, Bragg, Lts. Lebeup, Morris, Capt. Thompson, 2/Lts. Faulkner, Enoch, Evans, Jaggers, Lt. Hewkley, 2/Lt. Denham.
Sitting: Lts. Stitt, Nicol, Jordan, Capt. Skeat, Lt.-Col. Banks, Capts. Hardaker, Bland, Wemley, Byerley.

OFFICERS' GROUP, GENEVE, XMAS, 1918.

which they aroused in the ranks, inspiring the unlikeliest of men to work late into the evening voluntarily at their books, will not be lost. And if they but made it clear to a few that education is the key to better life and ampler opportunities, perhaps a generation following on the heels of Daddy's schoolroom labours in the Great War will reap a benefit from seeds thus laboriously scattered on the winds.

Christmas intervened while we were still in the wastes of Genève. But the aridity of the countryside did not prevent oases springing up in the Company messes, and these flowed liberally with milk and honey—with beer and rum and turkey and pork and good things galore.

One of the most notable features of this Xmastide was the distribution of surplus stocks to the isolated peasantry who had crept back here and there to their pitifully shattered homes. These were poor folk who had known the rigours of the German yoke. Their gratitude to the khaki Santa Claus was tremendous. They trudged for miles from all around with sacks and wheelbarrows to collect the small gifts of soap and tea and eatables which Quartermaster Jordan had put by for them. And many a story they told of the cruel times they had been through.

One little cluster of farms at Vaux-le-Prêtre had gruesome tales of the brutality of the invaders, for here had been located a British prisoners' camp, and tucked away from prying neutral eyes the commandants were not subject to any restraint. They told us how a British prisoner was beaten to death on the roadside, and a civilian worker who did not please his taskmasters suffered a similar fate.

An old lady—"la meilleure femme" in Montbrehain, they described her—who was ill in bed, died from shock after two Boche ruffians had invaded her room and pretended to slit her throat with their saw-edged bayonets.

Petty fines and annoyances were everyday occurrences under the yoke of the Prussian. He just seemed to delight in venting his spleen on these hapless people. At Beaurevoir all horses had to be paraded once a week, and the arrogant inspectors would keep the farmers waiting the whole day long merely in order to assert authority. One man related how the ticket with which each horse had to be identified was eaten by a neighbouring horse while he was not looking. That heinous offence was promptly visited with a fine of 20 marks.

And so on. The tales could be multiplied indefinitely.

But the pride of the French did not bow readily before their subduers. One frail Frenchwoman in March, 1918, to whom a boastful Boche officer was vaunting that in five days they would be into Amiens, in another ten they would have swept the Engländer into the sea, and in a month the German colours would be in Paris, asked him quietly : '

" And then, m'sieu, when is it that we shall have Alsace and Lorraine ?"

" Never, never, never !"

" And then, m'sieu, I tell you that never, never, never will you enter Paris, and, tout officier que vous êtes, your hide will bleach with thousands more upon the road that leads, you think, to Paris."

Ten days later she heard that he had been killed, and that Amiens still remained inviolate.

* * * * * *

Christmas left some heavy heads and sluggish livers, and a costumed football match for the officers was convened next day as an antidote, when the appearance of the Town Major of Le Cateau, arrayed in a white straw hat and a khaki uniform, reduced the spectators to a pulp of mirth.

The genius of invention was kept busy providing amusements throughout the January days in the wilderness. The Battalion, represented by Thompson, Byerley, Wilkinson, Howard and Banks, pulled off the Brigade Cross-Country Cup. Rejected made some money for the sporting fraternity in the Essex ranks at a Divisional race-meeting; but Maconochie, the grey mule (Piggott up) lost more than was won by charging helter-skelter into the crowd.

A snowball fight with the Royal Berks, raging through the day on January 27th, left both sides claiming the victory. But if the issue was doubtful there was no doubt about the results. And it was a battered battalion that turned out for parade next day, headed by a C.O. whose eyes were bunged with bruises!

Indoors, education proceeded apace. Captain Bland, who had assumed the genial role of Mayor of Ponchaux, developed a host of amenities in his municipality, and the innovation of a Debating Society, open to officers and men without discrimination, proved a tremendous draw once a week. Perhaps the greatest success of all was an Eisteddfod, in which a beauty competition amongst the well-known characters of the Battalion produced such tumult as had not been known in these parts since the British barrage had passed through the village.

Early in January the first envied drafts left for Blighty and the looked-for joys of a civvie suit. There was little regret amongst the men who went. But some of us had strange lumps in the throat to see them turn their backs on the unit which owed so much to their wondrous uncomplaining efforts.

In company together we had faced unimagined

hardships; in company we had learned to thresh the chaff from the grain, to face the grimmest things with a cheery laugh, to prize comradeship and manly worth above the trappings and the manifold delusions of life before the cataclysm.

And now the arts of peace were claiming the flower of the nation's manhood again. Would they sink or swim in the struggles of peace-time? Would the lessons of common effort for the common weal be lost? Would all that wealth of comradeship be dissipated like the smoke of last year's barrages?

So there was sadness in the final handshake as one passed down the ranks and wished each sterling fellow "Good luck." There was inadequacy in the simple words by which one strove to phrase the Nation's thanks. And when the band played them out on their homeward way with the Essex march and "Auld Lang Syne," the family circle seemed bereft; and we turned sadly back to billets with heart-felt hope that all would be well with them in the heritage of peace which they had earned so nobly.

The end of January saw the exile in the battle-wilds concluded, and the Battalion en route for Clary along the frozen slipperiness of the roads.

Clary is a village typical of the little agriculture-cum-factory townships of the region round Cambrai. The inhabitants combined the tilling of the fields with the shuttling of their looms, and lived in comfortable circumstances in substantially built houses—until the Boche came! Then in 1914 the battle of Le Cateau burst like a thunder-clap upon the quiet industrious routine of their lives. And flushed with visions of easy victory before the fall of the leaves, the Prussians hustled into the village one September night, and for two days terror reigned. The town hall was burnt down, and the glare of many other fires lit up the skies.

Fugitive parties of the retreating British Army were hunted down remorselessly through the gardens and the orchards of the town. Shots rang round the street corners. Cafés were sacked, and young girls shot or bayoneted in their homes. And up on the road, within a few hundred yards of the village, a company of the Dublin Fusiliers, surrounded in an old distillery, fought a long fight till half of them were killed and the remainder surrendered for lack of ammunition. No wonder the good folk of Clary spoke with shudders of those nightmare nights of 1914.

Then the wave of ferocity passed on, and the long years of German occupation succeeded. Hard years they were, and growing steadily harder as the pinch of famine became progressively severer.

But the courage of the French, one and all, was unwavering. The youngsters grew prematurely aged, one could see it in the lustreless look in their eyes; the old people carried on. Then when the British advance brought deliverance they seemed to say their " Nunc Dimittis " and passed peacefully away. It was astonishing to note the number of old folk who died in the winter of victory.

Thus was Clary when the Essex marched up its main street to the old Regimental tune :—

" The Essex boys they do love duff,
They do love duff, they do love duff.
But the poor little beggars can't get enough,
They can't get enough, they can't get enough."

It was a paradise after the desolation of Genève, and we revelled in the good billets and the open-handed hospitality. But we didn't neglect to give something in return. And I think that the children and the young maidens of Clary will not forget the Essex occupation when they are bent-backed greyheads.

Cinema performances free to the kiddies—to many of whom the movies were a novel wonder—woke an exuberant enthusiasm, and it was touching to hear their shrill voices singing the " Madelon " or the " Marseillaise " in the pitch of their ecstasy. Bun-fights and Xmas parties for their benefit made them even firmer worshippers of the man in khaki. And the dances organised for the men and maidens were red-letter events in the lives of soldiers and civilians alike. These brought down the fulminations of the curé upon our heads. But a counter-blast in the shape of a petition to M. le Colonel, signed by " les jeunes filles patriotes de Clary," begged for a continuance of the dancing. Here was a pretty problem in administration for the " competent military authority."

" ARTHUR."

M. le Maire was consulted, and shrugged his shoulders. " Que voulez-vous, m'sieu le Colonel." Curés were born like that. Young folk are young folk, whatever the Church of Rome may say. And as the French Constitution has a blind eye in things ecclesiastical, " alors, continuez, les danses, m'sieu." So the dancing continued with redoubled vigour.

In March a large party from the Battalion was detailed to join the 15th Essex at Calais. We were already dying by the steady attrition of demobilisation. This was in the nature of an amputation, and there would be little left of the invalid when it was completed. So the farewell called for signal observance. The whole village was invited to a soirée. The Battalion concert troupe, which the efforts of Byerley, Gage and Sergeant Patrick had created, gave a slashing performance, with an officers' jazz band at the end to bring the house down—Colonels, Majors and subalterns alike in the limelight. Then there was a feed for the four-year-famine-stricken. How they revelled in it!

Spoons for the custard ran short, but the young ladies, whom Arthur, with customary gallantry, " took in to supper," lapped it up all-standing from the plate without a shadow of embarassment! A raffle, in which the Maire got a pair of kippers and Mdlle. Emmeline a pair of braces, was a long roar of joy. And the noteworthy evening finished with dancing and " Auld Lang Syne."

The draft left for the 15th Essex next day, and as the train bore them away into the farthest distance waving to the little group of officers left behind, the world seemed to have grown suddenly colder. The substance of the 10th Essex had gone; the skeleton and memories alone remained.

This Special Order of the Day bade farewell to the draft and the glories that were past:—

> " On the occasion of the departure of the draft for the Army of Occupation and the reduction of the 10th Battalion the Essex

Regiment to cadre strength, the Commanding Officer wishes to thank all ranks for the magnificent way in which one and all have steadfastly maintained the reputation of British arms and have added lustre to the proud record of the Regiment.

"Whether fighting or training, and throughout the trying waiting period after the Armistice, the record of the Battalion has been unsullied, and its gallantry and devotion to duty of a markedly high standard.

"Its fighting record is long and illustrious, and includes most of the famous battles in France since 1916, in which the 10th Essex have played a conspicuously successful part.

"The spirit of comradeship between all ranks has been particularly fine and durable throughout.

"Now, as the Battalion breaks up, many are continuing to serve their country in other units, while some return to civil life.

"In bidding them farewell and good luck, the Commanding Officer is confident that, wherever the old members of the Battalion may be, the high record that they have helped to create will serve as an inspiration and will keep their heads high."

From March until the return of the cadre to England in June, 1919, it was merely a matter of marking time until railway facilities would permit the transport of the equipment which we brought back. The homeward journey was made *via* Havre and Southampton, and the last quiet rites of disbandment were performed at Fovant, on Salisbury Plain.

The London *Evening News* gave us our epitaph:

" Essex Battalion's Sombre Home-coming.

"Over the holiday season (Whitsun, 1919) there was quietly disbanded in a tucked away part of Wiltshire a gallant Battalion, the 10th Essex, which was born in the feverish days of the autumn of 1914, formed part of what was colloquially known as Kitchener's Second Hundred Thousand, and saw the war through on some of the bloodiest fields of France.

"No glitter, no electric cheering ceremony accompanied the disbandment. The colours were sent quietly to the depôt at Warley, and the men dispersed to their own homes.

* * *

"The official figures show the fighting qualities of the Battalion:—

" Passed through the Battalion (Officers) 227
"   ,,   ,,   ,,   (Men) ... 5274
" *Total killed or died of wounds*   ... 1103."

Sic Transit Gloria! Yet something still remains.

Within the individual experience there is something for which the memory of the 10th Essex stands, something of a fact and something of an ideal—something which might be termed the Greater Comrade-

THE LAST PARADE.
"*Good luck. Keep your heads high.*"

ship. Each man who served in the Battalion will treasure that memory throughout his life. And with the passing of the old unit into the mists of the things that were, there remains a heritage of achievement, of courage and self-sacrifice, of duty done, which belongs to the Regiment, the Nation and the Cause of Freedom in whose service the 10th Essex laboured and Made Good.

ROLL OF ACTIONS.

1915	Thiepval Wood	... ...	August, 1915.
	Mametz	... ...	September, 1915.
1916	La Boisselle	... ...	Sept., 1915—Feb., 1916.
	Maricourt	... ...	March—April, 1916.
	Carnoy	... ...	June, 1916.
	⚔Montauban Alley	... ...	July 1st, 1916.
	⚔Caterpillar Wood	...	July 3rd, 1916.
	Bernafay & Trones Wood	...	July 14th—17th, 1916.
	⚔Delville Wood	... ...	July 19th, 1916.
	⚔Thiepval	... ...	September 26th, 1916.
	⚔Regina Trench	... ...	October 21st, 1916.
	Regina Trench	... ...	Oct.—Nov., 1916.
1917	Ancre	... ...	Jan.—February, 1917.
	⚔Folly Trench	... ...	February 8th, 1917.
	Boom Ravine (Grandcourt)	...	February 17th, 1917.
	Miraumont	... ...	March, 1917.
	⚔Irles	... ...	March 10th, 1917.
	Arras	... ...	May 3rd, 1917.
	Cherisy & Fontaine	... ...	May—June, 1917.
	⚔Ypres-Menin Road (Glencorse Wood)	... ...	July 31st, 1917.
	Stirling Castle (Inverness Copse)		August, 1917.
	Poelcappelle	... ...	October, 1917.
	⚔Meunier House	... ...	October 22nd, 1917.
1918	Houthulst Forest	... ...	Nov., 1917—Jan., 1918.
	Moy	... ...	February—March, 1918.
	⚔Ly-Fontaine	... ...	March 21st, 1918.
	⚔Rouez	... ...	March 23rd, 1918.
	⚔Caillouel	... ...	March 24th, 1918.
	⚔Baboeuf	... ...	March 25th, 1918.
	Gentelles (Hangard Wood)	...	April, 1918.

⚔ Hangard Village	April 12th, 1918.
⚔ Hangard Wood (Villers-Bretonneux)	April 24th—26th, 1918.
Albert-Amiens Road	May, 1918.
Millencourt (Albert)	June—July, 1918.
⚔ Bray-Corbie Road	August 8th, 1918.
⚔ Tara Hill (Albert)	August 23rd, 1918.
⚔ Trones Wood	August 27th, 1918.
⚔ St. Pierre Vaast Wood	September 3rd, 1918.
⚔ Canal du Nord	September 5th, 1918.
⚔ Ronssoy	September 18th, 1918.
⚔ Tombois Farm	September 21st, 1918.
⚔ Egg Post	September 23rd, 1918.
St. Quentin Canal	September, 1918.
⚔ Richemont Brook (Le Cateau) ...	October 23rd, 1918.
⚔ Mont Carmel (Petit Planty) ...	October 26th, 1918.
⚔ Mormal Forest	November 4th, 1918.